DIVERSITY IN AMERICA

DIVERSITY IN AMERICA

4th Edition

Vincent N. Parrillo

Routledge
Taylor & Francis Group

LONDON AND NEW YORK

First published 2013 by Paradigm Publishers

Published 2016 by Routledge
2 Park Square, Milton Park, Abingdon, Oxon OX14 4RN
711 Third Avenue, New York, NY 10017, USA

Routledge is an imprint of the Taylor & Francis Group, an informa business

Library of Congress Cataloging-in-Publication Data for this book is available from
the Library of Congress.

Parrillo, Vincent N.
    Diversity in America / Vincent N. Parrillo.—4th ed.
    p. cm.
    Includes bibliographical references and index.
    ISBN 978-1-61205-253-3 (hc. : alk. paper)
    ISBN 978-1-61205-254-0 (pbk. : alk. paper)
    1. Cultural pluralism—United States—History. 2. United States—Race relations.
3. United States—Ethnic relations. I. Title.
    E184.A1P329 2013
    305.800973—dc23

                                                                    2012023863

Designed and Typeset by Straight Creek Bookmakers.

ISBN 13: 978-1-61205-253-3 (hbk)
ISBN 13: 978-1-61205-254-0 (pbk)

Contents

List of Art

FIGURES

TABLES

Preface

The fourth edition of this book comes at an important juncture for race and ethnicity in the United States and the interaction of gender relations within that context. Because of this special focus, my use of such terms as *diversity* and *multiculturalism* does not include sexual preference, the aged, or the physically challenged, as in other books on diversity with a wider perspective. Although this book examines the subject of multiculturalism, it is not a paean to anti-assimilationists or to anti-pluralists. Instead, it is a moderate approach to a volatile subject with the goal of demonstrating that multiculturalism is neither a new social phenomenon nor a threat to U.S. society.

All of us know something about diversity in this country. We probably learned a little about it in our past, continue to bear witness to it in our present, and may hold expectations about it for the future. Yet although many extol the legacy of our immigrant heritage and/or lament the injustices of our race-relations history, to many we seem to be on the brink of a societal unraveling. As in generations past, voices rise up against immigration, foreign language retention, "nonproductive" or "non-assimilating" racial/ethnic groups, and racial/ethnic leaders espousing separatist policies or actions. Similar concerns find expression in Australia, Canada, and Europe, where unprecedented migrations of diverse racial/cultural groups also have made an impact.

THE BACKSTORY TO WRITING THIS BOOK

These voices were the catalyst for my writing the first edition of this book. All of my discussions on the subjects of multiculturalism or diversity—with students and colleagues, government officials, the general public during my various lecture tours abroad for the U.S. Department of State's Information Agency (USIA) and its Bureau of International Information Programs (IIP), or listeners and viewers when I appeared on numerous Canadian or U.S. radio/TV call-in shows—played a role that impelled me to write this book. Between the arguments of voices advocating policies that challenge the dominant culture and those denouncing multiculturalism as a threat to society are, I believe, the ambivalent but concerned feelings of the vast majority.

As a sociologist aware of the patterns of dominant-minority relations, I wanted to dispel misconceptions about our past, misunderstandings about our present, and anxieties about our future that appear to be so prevalent. This book is written for the general reader, but is rooted in the sociological perspective. It is thus an effort to look at U.S. diversity objectively, not with a revisionist or a special advocacy position.

Both pluralism and assimilation have been dual realities throughout the often raucous history of intergroup relations in the United States. This book is an effort to show that, in many ways, what we witness today is a continuation of those dual processes, that the social dynamics we observe are not new, including the efforts of minority separatists and the outcries of alarmists. In fact, most Americans can find examples of the duality of pluralism and assimilation in their own family histories.

A PERSONAL EXAMPLE

To illustrate the last point, when my grandmother, Mary Kerr, came to the United States from Ireland, many native-born Americans still looked on the Irish with scorn and dismay. By then the large presence of Irish Catholics had been a reality for a couple of generations, but other Americans remained convinced that this "inferior" group tainted the "purity" of the American character. Undaunted, the Irish persevered, overcoming religious bigotry and flagrant discrimination, to become an integral part of American society.

Andrew Kohn, my maternal grandfather, typified the immigrant saga. The son of German immigrants who lived in Paterson, New Jersey, in the mid-19th century, he (like thousands of other first- and second-generation Americans) worked in the city's textile mills, but he also eventually opened his own business. He became a political leader and one of his greatest satisfactions as an American was personally escorting presidential candidate Woodrow Wilson to a major political rally in Paterson, New Jersey, in 1912.

Andrew and Mary Kerr Kohn had 14 children, several of whom died young, and they also adopted three newly orphaned kin. Betty, my mother, was their second-youngest child and, as a beautiful and personable woman, had many Irish American suitors. All of her older sisters married Irish Americans, each a successful middle-class businessman. But Betty, resisting family pressures to do likewise, broke the endogamy pattern when she married my father, Vince, a second-generation Italian American who was the second of three sons born to Nicola and Giovanna Infante Parrillo.

Like Betty's mother, Mary, Vince's mother died when he was a youth. Nicola had been a highly respected Italian community leader, entrepreneur, and publisher of an Italian weekly newspaper before his death, but Vince's family background hardly impressed Betty's family. They were aghast at her even dating Vince, let alone marrying him, convinced that he and his family—in fact, all Italians—were beneath them. Although restrictive immigration laws a decade earlier had drastically reduced the flow of new arrivals from southern, central, and eastern Europe, these groups—particularly Italians and Jews—remained stigmatized as personifying all that was wrong with America. They had replaced the Irish as the subculture deemed "unassimilable." Betty, however, was an independent and open-minded person who rejected such prejudices.

Her job as a school secretary in Paterson's North Ward brought her into daily contact with youngsters and parents from all backgrounds, so possibly this interaction helped break down some barriers. I think her acceptance of others was heavily augmented by a vacation in Cuba before she met my father. Her interest with Hispanic culture began there and was furthered by later visits with my father to the Caribbean, South America, and Spain.

The oldest of five children, I grew up exposed to more than just my mixed cultural heritage. We lived on the northern edge of Paterson in a neighborhood that straddled a tight-knit Dutch community on one side and a mixed second-generation German/Italian/Polish neighborhood on the other. Not surprisingly, my boyhood pals were of all four backgrounds, as were my first dates.

My family lived nine blocks from the Black neighborhood down the hill that, in my boyhood, I would often walk through, without incident, on my way to or from the movies downtown. When I reached Paterson Central High School—through classes, sports, and other extracurricular activities—my social world expanded to include many African American and Jewish students, along with many other second-generation White ethnic students.

As the years passed, this mixture of race and ethnicity among my closest companions continued and expanded as I moved through high school, college, graduate school, and into academia. On my wedding day, my closest friend, an African American, served as best man in my marriage to a Scots-English Presbyterian woman. Dennis remains one of my best friends among others who are Czech, English, German, Greek, Irish, Italian, and Saudi Arabian; their religions are Christian, Greek Orthodox, Islamic, or Jewish. What is important here is not just that I have such diversity within my social circle, but that each of these persons also has welcomed me into his or her social circle as well.

In my lifetime, I first witnessed the influx of African Americans and Puerto Ricans into nearby urban areas, then the arrival of Korean, Cuban, and Vietnamese refugees, and thereafter the immigration of millions of Asians, Latinos, and Middle Easterners. Their difficulties in acculturating, their determination to succeed, and their struggles to gain acceptance are in many ways similar to those on both sides of my family in years long past. So, too, are the criticisms, social ostracism, and discrimination that today's newcomers all too frequently encounter, although no one in my family suffered from the racism that many people of color still encounter today.

As an American of mixed ethnic heritage, my biography is far more representative than it is unique. Hundreds of millions of American biographies contain homogenizing/integrating elements across racial, religious, and ethnic lines. Often these did not come about quickly or easily, but, taken together, they form an interwoven tapestry that is forever a tribute to the American spirit. Despite the isolationists and separatists, despite the radicals and reactionaries, despite the skeptics and pessimists, assimilation continues as a powerful social force, keeping alive the country's motto of e pluribus unum ("from the many, one").

Witnessing the millions of Americans living in poverty, in cultural isolation, or out of the mainstream, one might reasonably argue that the preceding statement is too sweeping and ignores harsh reality. Yet the imperfections of U.S. society do not negate the social forces within it or the means its members have to accelerate the process. This book offers both a sociohistorical perspective and a sociological analysis to provide insights into U.S. diversity and into how the forces of pluralism are a necessary counterpart to the forces of assimilation.

WHAT'S NEW IN THIS EDITION

This revised edition contains a thorough updating of all data and information, and it includes the most recent and relevant studies not only in sociology, but in many other related fields as well. New to the fourth edition are as follows:

1. An extensive revision of what had been Chapter 10 on multiculturalism after 9/11 and its placement earlier as Chapter 8, allowing for greater coherence in the discussion of different eras before subsequent chapters giving a holistic analytical commentary;
2. An expanded discussion in Chapter 8 on how fears about terrorism and concerns about illegal immigration affect perceptions and responses to multiculturalism;
3. Integration of data retrieved from the 2010 Census into every chapter;
4. New population projections for 2050 as based on the most current demographic data;
5. Inclusion of the latest information on world events in the chapter sections, "The Larger Context," that place multiculturalism in a comparative perspective to other developed countries;
6. New graphs and tables to enhance visually the data presented;
7. New photographs to set chapter themes in a visual context.

ACKNOWLEDGMENTS

I thank Dean Birkenkamp, President and Publisher of Paradigm Publishers, for his strong support and encouragement for this new edition. Also, I am especially grateful for the valuable comments and critiques from reviewers of all previous editions, whose helpful comments were incorporated into this book.

Previous editions benefited from input by the following people. I thank them for their input.

Richard D. Alba
SUNY Albany

Kevin Delaney
Temple University

Raul Fernandez
University of California, Irvine

Charley Flint
William Paterson University

Lynn Hempel
Mississippi State University

Susan Hoerbelt
University of South Florida

Ronald Glassman
William Paterson University

Bao Ming Li
The Pennsylvania State University

John S. Mahoney, Jr.
Virginia Commonwealth University

Laura Martocci
Wagner College

Geoffrey Pope
William Paterson University

Luis Posas
Minnesota State University Mankato

Peter Rose
Smith College

Ellen Rosengarten
Sinclair Community College

Gonzalo Santos
California State Bakersfield

Peter J. Stein
University of North Carolina

Rita Takahashi
San Francisco State University

Maura Toro-Morn
Illinois State University

Leigh A. Willis
University of Georgia

I hope this book provides readers with a greater understanding of our multicultural past and present. If so, perhaps more of us can break down the barriers of social distance that separate us, becoming more aware that diversity is not the problem. Intolerance by anyone—assimilationist, multiculturalist, or undeclared—is the problem we must fight.

—Vincent N. Parrillo
parrillov@wpunj.edu

About the Author

Vincent N. Parrillo is an internationally recognized expert in the fields of immigration and multiculturalism. He has spoken on these subjects on numerous occasions throughout Asia, Canada, Europe, and the United States to government officials and to public and university audiences under the sponsorship of the Department of State's U.S. Information Agency (USIA) or its International Information Program (IIP).

A Fulbright scholar in 2000 in the Czech Republic, he was a visiting scholar at the University of Liege, Belgium, in 2010; at Roehampton University, England, in 2005; and at the University of Pisa in 1998 and 2006. Listed in the *International Who's Who in Education* and a past recipient of the *Outstanding Educator of America* award, he was the 2005–2006 Williams Distinguished Lecturer of the Eastern Sociological Society (ESS) as well as ESS Vice President in 2008–2009. Dr. Parrillo is professor of sociology at William Paterson University in Wayne, New Jersey, and was honored by his university with its Excellence in Scholarship Award.

His publications, some of them translated into nine languages, include the following books: *Strangers to These Shores* (10th ed.), *Cities and Urban Life* (6th ed.), *Contemporary Social Problems* (6th ed.), and *Rethinking Today's Minorities*. General Editor of the two-volume *Encyclopedia of Social Problems,* he also is author of an historical novel, *Guardians of the Gate,* and the writer and producer of the award-winning PBS documentary *Ellis Island: Gateway to America* and the Emmy-nominated *Smokestacks and Steeples: A Portrait of Paterson.*

1

Perception and Reality

The question is not what you look at, but what you see.
—*Henry David Thoreau*

People only see what they are prepared to see.
—*Ralph Waldo Emerson*

We don't see things as they are; we see things as we are.
—*Anaïs Nin*

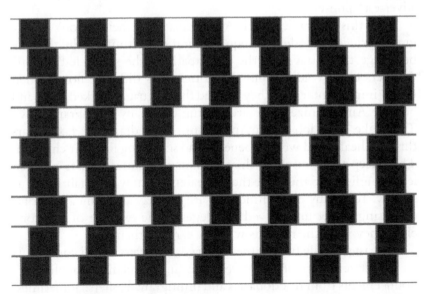

"*Café Wall Illusion*" *by Fibonacci (2007) depicts the difference between perception and reality. Things are not always as they appear to be. In this case, the horizontal lines are parallel to one another, even though they seem not to be, even after you know they are.*

Emblazoned in virtually every individual's mind is the knowledge that the United States is a nation of immigrants. That realization—taught in our schools and reinforced in political speeches, particularly on the Fourth of July—serves as a source of nationalistic pride for all Americans, even those who trace their ancestry back to 17th-century colonists. The American Dream—that promise of freedom of choice, education, economic opportunity, upward mobility, and a better quality of life—inspires many to come here. It also serves as the underpinning for basic value orientations that are the foundation of American beliefs, behaviors, definitions of social goals, and life expectations.

Today, immigrants continue to arrive in pursuit of that dream, just as others have done for hundreds of years. Yet these newcomers frequently trigger negative reactions among the native-born population despite Americans' pride in belonging to a nation of immigrants. In many parts of the United States, we often find expressions of fear, suspicion, anxiety, resentment, hostility, and even violence in response to the immigrant presence. Immigrants are not the only group triggering a backlash, however. African American and Native American assertiveness often provokes resistance. Challenges to the status quo by feminists and gay rights activists also regularly provoke adverse responses.

Why this contradiction? If Americans value their nation's immigrant heritage and ideals of equality and opportunity, why do they begrudge those traveling the same path to the same destination? Answers come readily from the critics. It is different now. When earlier immigrants came, they learned the language, worked hard, and became Americanized. We are getting too many immigrants now. They take away jobs from Americans. They drain our tax dollars through health and welfare benefits and schooling for their children. They keep to themselves, they do not want to assimilate or even learn English, and therefore they threaten to unravel the fabric of our society. Too many other minorities are just lazy and want a handout, expecting to get undeserved privileges at the expense of everyone else. They want the rewards without earning them.

At least partially fueling these everyday conversational complaints by the citizenry are provocative stories in the media or public pronouncements from reactionaries and immigrant-bashers. Sometimes, however, even respected scholars are in the forefront. For example, in the 1990s, noted historian Arthur M. Schlesinger, Jr. denounced "the cult of ethnicity" (an insistence on maintaining vibrant ethnic subcultures) as a forerunner to the imminent "balkanization" of U.S.

society.[1] His reference to then ongoing violence and "ethnic cleansing" among Bosnians, Croats, and Serbs in the Balkan Peninsula was a scary one. No one wanted U.S. society disintegrating into a collectivity of groups hostile to one another. Nor did they want the "snuffing out" or "shipwreck" of the American republic by new immigrants that Peter Brimelow—ironically himself an immigrant (from England)—warned us about with apocalyptic rhetoric in *Alien Nation* (1996).[2]

Minority actions also reinforce nativist perceptions. The rhetoric of leaders from the National Council of La Raza and from the League of United Latin American Citizens (LULAC) for the maintenance of Spanish language and culture, demonstrates to many native-born Americans an unwillingness to assimilate.[3] The insistence of some African American leaders for slavery reparation payments to all Blacks enrages many Whites as an unreasonable demand. The "clannish" retail shopping patterns of Asian Americans and their apparent non-involvement in local community activities annoy many local residents and merchants. News reports about militant actions, public mayhem, street crimes, and mob violence all trigger other negative reactions against minorities.

Once we talked about the United States as a melting pot. Now the prevailing concept is multiculturalism, which some Americans fear is undermining the cohesiveness of U.S. society.

What is happening? Are such instances illustrations of a different pattern emerging than in previous generations? Are we witnesses to a new social phenomenon? Are we being inundated with a flood of immigrants who do not wish to integrate? Are they and the people of color born in the United States pursuing separatist paths that will lead to the disuniting of our society? Is the land of *e pluribus unum* ("from the many, one") disintegrating into *e pluribus plures* ("from the many, many") right before our very eyes, as Diane Ravitch warned?[4]

WHAT THIS BOOK IS ALL ABOUT

These questions and issues reflect real concerns. They require responses that are more than subjective impressions of the current scene, for what people may think is happening is not necessarily what is actually occurring. This book is an attempt to provide those responses.

The famed Roman orator Cicero once remarked, "Not to know what happened before we were born is to remain perpetually a child." Just as children gaze with wonderment on new sights, so, too, can adults react to social phenomena as new and different unless they recognize these phenomena as variations of past patterns. It is my contention that the perception of many Americans is tainted because, first, they lack an accurate understanding of past U.S. diversity, and second, they fail to view contemporary events in a larger context.

As mentioned in the Preface, this book is about race and ethnicity in the United States and the interaction of gender relations within that context. As such, it does not include other aspects of diversity (age, disability, and sexual orientation) found in other books on the subject of diversity. The book's origins trace back to my replies to the many concerned (and similar) questions asked of me during a U.S. State Department–sponsored lecture tour in 1993 throughout Canada and Western Europe. Just as Alexis de Tocqueville attempted to explain our form of government in *Democracy in America* in the 1830s, I have sought to explain our diversity—past, present, and future—in this book, deliberately entitled *Diversity in America,* in homage to Tocqueville, although some may criticize my use of the term *America,* because others living in North or South America can also be considered "Americans." (In that context, consider the member nations in OAS, the Organization of American States.)

A central thesis of this book is that multiculturalism has always been part of the U.S. scene and is no more a threat to the cohesiveness of society today than at any time in the past. Rejecting claims that modern circumstances create a different situation than in the past, this book shows parallels, similarities, and continuities. It also shows instances in the past when U.S. society was actually more multicultural than today.

Another central tenet of the book is that assimilation and pluralism are not mutually exclusive entities, nor are they necessarily enemies of one another. They have always existed simultaneously among different groups at different levels. Whether they are persistent or multigenerational convergent subcultures, culturally distinct groups have always existed. Even when their numbers have been great, they never threatened the core culture. Assimilation remains a powerful force affecting most ethnic groups, although it has been less effective in enabling all racial minorities to achieve full integration. Proponents of one position may decry the other, but both pluralism and assimilation have always been dual realities within U.S. society.

The idea behind this book, then, is to place the current debate on immigration and multiculturalism in a proper sociohistorical perspective. Within a sociological context of social patterns and social change, the historical record of past and present cultural diversity in the United

States is presented. Included are factors such as economic conditions, elitism, nativism, racism, social class biases, and the struggle for power that militate against harmonious intergroup relations.

The first half of this book contains a brief portrait of U.S. diversity through five eras: Colonial, Early National, Expansion, Industrial, and Information Ages. These chapters outline how cultural diversity has always been a characteristic of U.S. society. They also show the continuity of various social patterns from one era to the next, down to the present.

Women, of course, have constantly been an integral part of the U.S. experience, although their efforts often received little public attention until recent decades. Partly to compensate for that neglect, the period portraits in the following chapters include information about women during these times. My intent is to emphasize more fully their gender experiences of status, power, and influence within a sociohistorical framework as a prelude to understanding today's feminism.

In these discussions of women, you will learn how women's experiences varied greatly depending on their locale, social class, and length of residency in the United States. Indicators of how they fared compared to men delineate gender diversity in terms of rights and power. Explanations about women's social activism also show a parallel to the militancy of other minority groups seeking equal treatment.

SEEING IS BELIEVING, BUT IS IT KNOWING?

Some people believe what they see, but appearances can be deceptive, as are optical illusions or mirages. Magicians are illusionists, and the good ones can stupefy us with their artful tricks on a grand scale. We know they tricked us, but we don't know how.

In everyday life, we think we know what we see, but here, too, we may be deceived. As Peter Berger once observed, "The first wisdom of sociology is this—things are not what they seem."[5] He was suggesting that social reality has many layers of meaning, and as you discover one layer, your perspective of the whole changes. So, perceptions about diversity or anything else can change with increased knowledge. Seeing is not enough. You need to know what it is that you are seeing.

To understand how people could mistakenly accept a reality as natural or obvious requires an understanding of social constructionism. The major focus of this perspective is that an individual's views form through social interaction, interpersonal communication, and cultural influences. What emerges is a perceived reality, one that societal members have created and institutionalized into a shared tradition and understanding. Like the actual reality replaced by the perceived reality presented to us by the illusionist, another social reality of the past or present may possibly exist "out there," independent of the cultural view that dominates people's interpretation and acceptance. However, the only reality of significance to societal members is the one on which they agree. This social construction of reality thus serves as the basis for their approval or criticism, acceptance or rejection of events and/or groups that complement or run counter to the "facts" as they see them.

Another dimension also exists that may affect whether what we believe we see is actually what we truly understand. Complementary to Berger's statement is the traditional saying, "You can't see the forest for the trees." Its message is clear. When you are too close to the situation, you can't see the entire picture. You can't get a sense of the whole because you are caught up in the small details. It is necessary to become more objective if you are to comprehend what you see. (Later in this chapter, we discuss the reverse problem of perception and reality, not only that seeing is believing, but also believing is seeing.)

We can find that needed objectivity in the sociological perspective, which provides, says Berger, "a special form of consciousness" (p. 23). It enables us to focus impartially on aspects of our social environment that may have previously escaped our notice, allowing us to interpret them in a different, meaningful way. If we add a historical frame of reference along with a sociological analysis to our study of diversity, we gain a valuable dimension to observe what continuities and changes are occurring.

THE CULTURAL HOMOGENEITY MYTH

Diversity has been an ongoing social reality in the United States, not just since its inception as a nation, but even in its primeval colonial cradle. This viewpoint is not the prevalent one. The prevailing belief, that this nation was essentially a culturally homogeneous launching pad for the new nation, is steeped in the historic myth that the 13 colonies were almost entirely populated by English immigrants and their descendants. Such was not quite the case. As we see shortly, this "historic reality"—this fallacy of cultural homogeneity—changes under careful sociohistorical analysis.

That we are a nation of immigrants is an undeniable fact, but often not connected to the current multicultural picture. Contemporary public views on multiculturalism often assume erroneously that what occurred in the past were fleeting moments of heterogeneity that yielded to fairly rapid assimilation. Today's cultural diversity is misperceived as different, more widespread, and resistant to assimilation—something to be celebrated, respected, and maintained, say its proponents—thus making it, in the eyes of alarmed others, not only a new construction, but somehow also a threat to the cohesiveness of society.

Only an objective analysis that peels away layers of myths, assumptions, presumptions, and misconceptions can provide an accurate assessment. To do so, we must take a sociohistorical perspective, moving beyond present-day realities and noting instead long-term patterns throughout the nation's history. In this way, we can put the current scene in a wider context and determine more precisely how unique our situation is or is not.

Before we can embark on this examination of our past and present, however, we must first address three areas that affect judgments about diversity in the United States. The first of these is the changing views about minority adaptation to U.S. society. The second is the melting pot concept and the limitations of its application. The last, but extremely important, area is the Dillingham Flaw, in which perceptions about immigrants can be misdirected through faulty comparisons.

THE RISE, FALL, AND RISE OF PLURALISM

Because the term is of recent vintage, many incorrectly conclude that multiculturalism is therefore a fairly new social phenomenon, the product of a changing world and of changing government policies. But as Nathan Glazer (1993) and Peter Rose (1993) correctly asserted, multiculturalism is actually a refashioning of an older concept of cultural pluralism.[6]

Early Advocates

In the early 20th century, educator John Dewey and social worker Jane Addams both spoke out against assimilation destroying the cultural values of immigrants. In 1915, Horace Kallen, an immigrant from Eastern Europe, advocated this ideology in an essay in the publication *Nation*; by citing the persistence of cultural identity among the

Irish in Massachusetts, Norwegians in Minnesota, and Germans in Wisconsin, he promoted a multicultural society, a confederation of national cultures.[7] As Peter Rose puts it,

> To Kallen ... the United States was not a fondue of amalgamation but a symphony of accommodation. Pushing his own metaphor, Kallen saw the orchestra—that is, the Society—as consisting of groups of instruments—nationalities—playing their separate parts while together making beautiful music resonant with harmony and good feeling.[8]

Kallen's ideas, expanded in his seminal work on cultural pluralism, *Culture and Democracy in the United States* (1924), contained only incidental references to racial groups.[9] Foreshadowing today's opponents to multiculturalism, part of Kallen's focus was on public concern that the recent arrivals of his time might not integrate fully into society.

Assimilationists Prevail

Despite the pluralist advocates, a chain of events encouraged assimilation over ethnic persistence. Patriotic hysteria following U.S. entrance into World War I effectively ended the German subculture. Restrictive immigration laws in the 1920s, a world depression in the 1930s, and World War II in the 1940s dramatically reduced immigration. With little new blood to keep everyday ethnicity viable, with the second generation growing up as Americans, and with the housing and education entitlements offered to GIs, White ethnics by midcentury had moved closer to the center, loosening their ethnic ties as they did.

As the old idea of America as a melting pot seemed to reaffirm itself, major books by sociologists Robert E. Park[10] and Milton M. Gordon[11] influenced social scientists to think more about assimilation than pluralism.

In *Race and Culture* (1964), Park offered a universal cycle theory suggesting that all groups go through a progressive, irreversible process of contact, competition, accommodation, and eventual assimilation. Park acknowledged that the process might take centuries, possibly even including a semipermanent racial caste system, but ultimately even racially subordinate groups would assimilate.

Gordon delineated, in *Assimilation in American Life* (1964), seven processes of group adaptation to the host society. Most important was his distinction between cultural and structural assimilation, showing how a group can change its cultural patterns but not yet mainstream into primary relationships in the cliques and associations of the society.

The Reassertion of Pluralism

Just as a series of social changes enabled assimilationists to prevail over the pluralists, a new set of circumstances reversed the situation. The civil rights movement of the 1960s and the White ethnic revival of the 1970s were precipitating factors. However, a major element was the third wave of immigration that began after the 1965 immigration law removed national quota restrictions, opening the door to millions of developing-world immigrants.

Pluralism had previously flourished at a time of peak immigration to the United States and ebbed when immigration declined. With a new influx of culturally distinct immigrants, it flowered again. Renamed multiculturalism, its advocacy of the preservation and appreciation of ethnic cultures and identities, as well as peaceful coexistence among groups, echoed the sentiments of Kallen, Addams, Dewey, and other cultural pluralists.

This time, however, the movement included people of color, not just White ethnics. Some arrived with a strong background that empowered them economically, allowing them to organize more effectively and assert themselves more so than past immigrants. Their ranks included educated, articulate spokespersons who used TV and computerized direct mailings to reach millions of potential members whom their predecessors could not.

Yet even as pluralism gained new advocates, another influential sociological voice reaffirmed assimilationist patterns. In *The Ethnic Myth* (2001), Stephen Steinberg argued that pluralism only appeals to groups that benefit from maintaining ethnic boundaries.[12] Disadvantaged groups, he maintained, willingly compromise their ethnicity to gain economic security and social acceptance. Moreover, he claimed, the United States was closer than ever before to welding a national identity out of its mélange of ethnic groups.

The Multiculturalist Challenge

Nevertheless, with minority group assertiveness, massive immigration, and bilingual/pluralist government policies, the change in popular usage from cultural pluralism to multiculturalism helped suggest to some that a new era for social consciousness of diversity had arrived.

To others, it signaled that the disuniting of America through "ethnic tribalism" was upon us. The battle was joined and still continues.

Multiculturalism is especially strong on college campuses, where the ranks of multiculturalists include many college professors whose advocacy in their teaching and publications has spread the doctrine far and wide to millions of others. They have challenged the once-prevailing idea of the United States as a melting pot, a concept many social scientists now regard as an idealized myth.

THE MELTING POT

In an often-quoted passage in *Letters from an American Farmer* (1782), Michel Guillaume Jean de Crèvecoeur, an immigrant to the United States from France, defined an American and popularized the concept of America as a melting pot:

> What is an American? He is either a European, or the descendant of a European; hence that strange mixture of blood which you will find in no other country. I could point out to you a man whose grandfather was an Englishman, whose wife was Dutch, whose son married a French woman, and whose present four sons have now four wives of different nations.... Here individuals of all nations are melted into a new race of men, whose labors and posterity will one day cause great changes in the world.[13]

Overstating Ethnic Intermarriages

Even if Crèvecoeur actually knew of such an exogamous family and did not invent it to illustrate his idealized concept of a melting pot, he was not accurately portraying the reality of his times. His example would have been an atypical family in the late 18th century, because most White ethnics then did not intermarry. In-group solidarity—based on nationality, clustering, geographic separatism, and most especially religion—lessened the probability of personal social interaction among the distinct groups, let alone intermarriage.

When Crèvecoeur spoke of those English, Dutch, and French intermarriages, he was covering three generations, a considerable span of the 18th century, and most likely including several religious faiths in a time when religious ecumenicism was practically unknown. Religious tolerance may have slowly evolved out of a period of bigotry, close-mindedness, and intolerance just a few generations before, but that hardly meant that the ethnocentric barriers had vanished and amalgamation was flourishing.

No Racial Minorities

The greatest problem with Crèvecoeur's melting pot model is his omission of African and Native Americans.[14] Was this omission a reflection of his ethnocentrism or a deliberate choice to augment his concept? Surely he was aware of their presence in significant numbers throughout the colonies. Perhaps he thought they were not relevant to the destiny of a nation struggling to be born.

Many shared this attitude. The framers of the Constitution, in Article I, Section 2, excluded "Indians" and counted each slave as three fifths of a person to determine a state's representatives. In 1790, the First Congress passed the Naturalization Law, which limited citizenship only to free White aliens. Until passage of the Fourteenth Amendment in 1868, people of color born in the United States were not citizens.

Crèvecoeur's melting pot model thus was not accurate for several reasons. By restricting its application only to those with political power (Whites), it excluded a sizable segment of the population (people of color). It clearly did not describe a society that had "melted." Moreover, even in its narrow focus on Whites, the model ignored the existing cultural diversity and social distance existing among the diverse White groups.

Emerson's Vision

Crèvecoeur influenced others who helped popularize the image of the United States as a melting pot. Ralph Waldo Emerson, for example, struck a similar theme in 1845:

Well, as in the old burning of the Temple at Corinth, by the melting and intermixture of silver and gold and other metals, a new compound more precious than any, called Corinthian brass, was formed; so in this continent—asylum of all nations—the energy of Irish, Swedes, Poles, and Cossacks, and all the European tribes—of the Africans, and of the Polynesians, will construct a new race, a new religion, a new state, a new literature, which will be as vigorous as the new Europe which came out of the smelting-pot of the Dark Ages, or that which earlier emerged from Pelasgic and Etruscan barbarism.[15]

Emerson's private journal entry is interesting for several reasons. He "hated" the "narrowness" of nativist reactions against immigrants as "precisely the opposite of true wisdom." Significantly, he included people of color (but not Native Americans) in his vision of an amalgamated society, and it was a vision of the future, not a pretense about his times or of Crèvecoeur's time 63 years earlier. For Emerson, America as a melting or smelting pot was a tomorrow to come, not a reality that was.

Turner's Frontier

In contrast, Frederick Jackson Turner saw the American frontier as the catalyst that had already fused the immigrants into a composite new national stock. His frontier thesis of 1893 followed the 1890 declaration of the Census Bureau that the "unsettled area has been so broken into ... that there can hardly be said to be a frontier line."[16] Unlike Emerson's private musings known only to a few, Turner's update of Crèvecoeur's melting pot greatly influenced historical scholarship for more than 40 years.

> Thus, the Middle West was teaching the lesson of national cross-fertilization instead of national enmities, the possibility of a newer and richer civilization, not by preserving unmodified or isolating the old component elements, but by breaking down the line fences, by merging the individual life in the common product—a new product that held the promise of world brotherhood.[17]

The previous quotation is taken from Turner's 1920 book, *The Frontier in American History,* where he expanded on his 1893 essay. He argued that, because pioneers confronted many problems and harsh conditions, their adaptation necessitated innovative solutions that they shared with others. Out of this mutual assistance evolved a new and distinct culture, a blend of shared cultural contributions, but noticeably different from any of their source cultures.

Turner's argument popularized further the romanticized notion of a melting pot, but it also did not accurately reflect frontier reality any more than Crèvecoeur had depicted his times. The pioneers did adapt to their new environment, but the culture remained Anglo-American in form and content. Furthermore, in many areas of the Middle West that Turner speaks about, culturally homogeneous settlements of Germans or Scandinavians, for example, often maintained distinct ethnic subcultures for generations.

Zangwill's White Fusion

Another voice raised in support of the melting pot was Israel Zangwill in a 1909 play appropriately called *The Melting Pot*. Some of its oft-quoted lines are these:

America is God's Crucible, the Great Melting Pot where all the races of Europe are melting and reforming!

... Germans and Frenchmen, Irishmen and English, Jews and Russians, into the Crucible with you all! God is making the American!

... the Real American has not yet arrived.... He will be the fusion of all races, perhaps the coming superman.

... what is the glory of Rome and Jerusalem where all nations and races come to worship and look back, compared with the glory of America, where all nations and races come to labor and look forward![18]

The term *race* once referred more loosely to either racial or ethnic groups. So, Zangwill appears to mean only White ethnic groups in the melting or fusion of all races when he speaks of the "races of Europe" and excludes any specific example of people of color. Although he curiously includes Syrians as Europeans, Zangwill's words nonetheless echo those of Crèvecoeur in describing the melting pot as a White ethnic phenomenon, thereby implying that an American is a White person.

In this book, we use the contemporary applications of race and ethnicity. A racial group, therefore, is one in which its members share visible biological characteristics and regard themselves or are regarded by others as a single group on that basis. An ethnic group is one in which its members share a common culture, language, nationality, and/or religion. Of course, members of a racial group are also members of an ethnic group, and vice versa. What clouds this distinction, however, is that members of the same racial group can be members of different ethnic groups (e.g., Black Americans, Haitians, Jamaicans, and Nigerians), and members of one ethnic group can be members of different racial groups (i.e., Hispanic Blacks, Whites, and mulattos).

Recent Studies on Intermarriage

The White ethnic intermarriage that Crèvecoeur prematurely asserted as evidence of his melting pot has been a reality for more than a generation. In 1991, for example, Richard Alba reported that only half as many third-generation Italians of unmixed ancestry born after 1949 had spouses of unmixed Italian ancestry, compared with third-generation Italian males born before 1920.[19] Three years earlier, Stanley Lieberson and Mary Waters had found significant declines in endogamous marriages among virtually all White groups.[20] That pattern continues today, not just among third-generation White ethnics, but also among their Hispanic counterparts.[21] Another recent study found that about half of all immigrants marry within their national-origin group and only one-fourth of their children do so.[22] The least endogamous are western European groups, followed by eastern European groups, Central and South American groups, and Asians, in that order. Nearly two-thirds of Americans today claim a single ancestry.[23]

Although such intermarriage patterns provide support for melting pot proponents, they do not necessarily indicate assimilation. Cultural determinants (early-marriage patterns, religion, language, cultural globalization) and structural determinants (group size, sex ratio, education, size of the third generation) can impact group distinctiveness and social distance between an ethnic group and the mainstream society.[24] Furthermore, within-group marriages are still fairly common among people of unmixed ethnic ancestry.

When race and culture are similar, marital assimilation is more likely. If the past patterns of 19th- and 20th-century White Americans are an indicator, however, this process may require three or more generations to blend together the post-1965 ethnic groups. Another emerging pattern, explored later in this book, is the Black/non-Black divide, in which Asians, Hispanics, and Whites are intermarrying and thereby creating the isolation of Blacks in the marriage market.[25]

THE DILLINGHAM FLAW

The continuing debate between assimilationists and pluralists revolves around the issue of cultural homogeneity. Part of those polemics often contain what I identify as the Dillingham Flaw, an erroneous way of comparing people from one time period with people living in the present. As a consequence, one group usually suffers in the comparison and is judged negatively.

The Dillingham Commission

Senator William P. Dillingham of Vermont chaired the House-Senate Commission on Immigration (1907–1911), which listened to the testimony of civic leaders, educators, social scientists, and social workers. It even made on-site visits to Ellis Island and New York's Lower East Side, where hundreds of thousands of impoverished immigrants lived. After completing its investigation, the Commission issued a 41-volume report, partly based on social science research and statistics.

Unfortunately, the report was flawed in its application and interpretation of the data. It was more than the fact that the Commission members, however well intentioned they may have been, reflected the perceptions and biases of their times. The Dillingham Commission committed several errors of judgment that led them to conclude that the immigration from southern, central, and eastern Europe was detrimental to U.S. society. Their conclusion led them to recommend the enactment of immigration restrictions.

The Commission erred in its use of simplistic categories and unfair comparisons of the "old" and "new" immigrants, thus ignoring differences of technological evolution in their countries of origin. It also erred in overlooking the longer time interval that immigrants from northern and western Europe had to adjust, as well as the changed structural conditions wrought by industrialization and urbanization.

No doubt influencing the Commission members were the highly reported intelligence test findings. By 1908, Alfred Binet and Thomas Simon had developed the intelligence quotient (IQ) measurement scale. Using an alpha test (for those literate in English) and a beta test (for those illiterate or non-English-speaking), the low scores of newly arriving southern, central, and eastern Europeans, in contrast to higher scores by native-born Black and White Americans, seemingly gave "scientific evidence" that mentally deficient ethnic groups were entering the United States.

Although many social scientists today recognize that cultural biases affected those outcomes, controversy continues about whether "intelligence" tests reveal genetic or environmental differences. (This "nature versus nurture" issue boiled over in the 1990s with the publication of *The Bell Curve* by Richard Herrnstein and Charles Murray.[26] These writers argued that genetic differences existed between Black and White Americans, a point fiercely contested by many others.)

Back in 1911, however, these test results were unquestioned and were just one more factor to convince Commission members about the rightness of their views. The social conditions in 1911 help explain the unquestioned acceptance of such flawed conclusions. President Theodore Roosevelt had called for the Commission to address the "immigrant problem," thereby creating a mind-set about the situation in the first place. Both he and the Commission reflected the biases and perceptions of most native-born Americans witnessing the unprecedented mass influx of immigrants who were culturally, and often physically, different. The Commission's findings reinforced public opinion and were therefore readily accepted.

The Concept of the Dillingham Flaw

In our society, similar errors of thinking also influence people's perceptions of outgroup members. An *outgroup* is any group with which an individual does not identify or belong. In our discussion, we are referring to the foreign born as the outgroup to native-born Americans of different backgrounds.

Because some of today's negative judgments flow from the same faulty logic as that of the Dillingham Commission, I call this weakness the *Dillingham Flaw.* Quite simply, this term refers to inaccurate comparisons based on simplistic categorizations and anachronistic observations. We make these comparisons when we apply modern classifications or sensibilities to a time when they did not exist, or, if they did, they had a different form or meaning. To avoid the Dillingham Flaw, we must avoid the use of modern perceptions to explain a past that its contemporaries viewed quite differently.

One example of an inappropriate modern classification would be the term *British* to describe colonial Americans from the British Isles. Today, this word refers collectively to the people of Great Britain (the English, Welsh, Scots, and Scots-Irish). However, in the 18th century, *British* had the much narrower meaning of only the English and for good reason. The English, Scots, and Scots-Irish may have been English-speaking, but significant cultural and religious differences existed among them. Moreover, the geographic segregation, social distance, and even hostility that existed between English Anglicans and Scots-Irish Presbyterians created a wide cultural gulf between them. They did not view each other as similar. Among the English, divergent religious beliefs created various subcultures whose shared sense of identity, social insulation, and endogamy resulted in limited social interaction. *Ecumenicism,* the tendency toward greater Christian unity that is occurring in our times, is a far cry from the antipathy among the Protestant sects of colonial America.

Religion, a meaningful component of everyday life in the 18th century, was cause for outgroup prejudice and avoidance, and we must not overlook its significant impact on intergroup relations. It would be a mistake to presume that the English were a single, cohesive entity.

It also is misleading to speak broadly of either African slaves or Native Americans as single entities. In a period of White dominance and racial exploitation, ethnocentric generalizations such as these failed to pay heed to the fact that these groups consisted of diverse peoples with distinctive cultures. Similarly, European immigrants were not alike despite their collective grouping by mainstream society. Instead, all of these groups—African American, Native American, and immigrant—were diverse peoples with linguistic and cultural distinctions that set them apart from one another.

The Dillingham Flaw Chain Reaction

Once someone falls victim to the Dillingham Flaw, other misconceptions usually follow about one's own time. This phenomenon is to be expected. Such victims falsely believe that they understand their nation's past and so confidently assess their own world in what they presume is a wider context. Certain that they have a knowledgeable, objective frame of reference, they tend to be highly critical of the present scene because they perceive it as different from the past.

However, because their observations and reactions are predicated on a reference point rendered inaccurate by the Dillingham Flaw, they are more likely to reach incorrect conclusions. Like that old congressional commission, they are susceptible to mistaken impressions about a threat posed by recent immigrants whose presence and behavior they view as different from past immigrants.

For instance, some people suggest that today's steadily increasing ranks of Asians, Hispanics, and Muslims present an unprecedented challenge to an integrative society. The undercurrent of this thinking includes the continuing large numbers of new arrivals, their racial group membership and/or non-Judeo-Christian background, and their alleged non-assimilationist patterns.

Such concerns and fears are echoes of those raised about earlier groups, such as the racist responses to the physical appearance of southern Europeans or the anti-Semitic reactions to eastern European Jews. Or, consider the nativist reaction to a petition to Congress by 19th-century Germans in the Northwest Territory to create a German state with German as the official language; it easily matches the fear of some nativists today that the Southwest may become "America's Quebec."[27]

BELIEVING IS SEEING

In writing about the improper use of biology as ideology to justify the naturalness of gendered behavior and social statuses, Judith Lorber (2007) informed us that the way we think about a particular social phenomenon affects what we actually see or at least what we think we see.[28] The actions of the Dillingham Commission and the politics of those times are another illustration of this concept. When we feel most threatened by outsiders who are different because of their religion, skin color, or social class, we may see different things in the current immigration (they are a threat because there are too many of them and/or they "fail" to assimilate) rather than see other things (ourselves, our ancestors, past generations of immigrants, new workers, new consumers, new taxpayers, human capital to fuel our economic growth).

In other words, the two major themes of this book are interconnected. The political controversies swirling around the assimilation/pluralism debates affect how people think about and react to diversity in society at any given time. Thus, the influence of beliefs on perceptions and reactions is an important element in understanding why some groups or issues become problematic and others do not.

THE BOUNDARY FLAW

With the oldest democratic constitution among all nations and its centuries-old experience of accepting tens of millions of immigrants from all parts of this planet, the United States certainly offers a rich reservoir of history, social change, and patterns of intergroup relations. Furthermore, it was the first to offer the promise of freedom and opportunity to one and all, while showing the rest of the world its willingness to accept and include foreigners within its societal mainstream. Yet, however special many of these elements may have been, they did not occur in a global vacuum. A second flaw we must thus avoid is the boundary flaw, the assumption that we can explain everything solely in the context of internal social dynamics unique to U.S. culture.[29]

Virtually nothing has ever occurred in the United States that was self-contained or universal within its borders. In the early stages of its sociocultural evolution, when it was a minor player on the world stage and there was no such entity yet as a global community, regional—even local—cultural differences abounded. In the sociocultural epochs described in the next six chapters, the United States went through changing positions in the world order even as it was buffeted by external social forces that affected its citizens' sense of self and perceptions of demographic and technological changes.

This interplay of regional, national, and global forces often generated tensions as sociocultural changes occurred and new migration patterns emerged. Part of the explanation for the dualities of, and conflicts between, assimilation and pluralism trends lies in recognizing this process.

In each of the following chapters, then, we attempt to identify the place of the United States in the world system as a key referent to understanding more fully the developing themes of this book.

UNDERSTANDING TODAY BY KNOWING ABOUT YESTERDAY

Understanding the past sociohistorical reality of U.S. diversity allows for a more accurate comparison with today's multicultural society without falling victim to either the Dillingham Flaw or the Boundary Flaw.

In this way, we can avoid those flaws and debunk the cultural homogeneity myth. It is essential to know truly what we were if we are to comprehend what we are now and what we are becoming.

Telecommunications today enable each of us to bear witness to many aspects of our multicultural society, but our knowledge about our nation's past comes to us chiefly through the words of others whose ethnocentric perceptions often hid from us what truly was that reality. Although rarely presented in the comprehensive form found in this book, enough data exist to peel away the layers of nationalist myth-building to get at the sociocultural actualities about our multicultural past.

What follows is not an exercise in revisionist thought, but a sociohistorical analysis of the past and present. Hopefully, this book provides you with the insight that diversity is the nation's strength, not its weakness.

NOTES

1. Arthur M. Schlesinger, Jr., *The Disuniting of America: Reflections on a Multicultural Society,* rev. ed. (New York: W. W. Norton, 1998).

2. Peter Brimelow, *Alien Nation: Common Sense about America's Immigration Disaster* (New York: Harper Perennial, 1996).

3. Hispanic leaders' views on language maintenance appear in Linda Chavez, "Hispanics vs. Their Leaders," *Commentary* (October 1991): 47–9.

4. Diane Ravitch's much-discussed views appeared in her article "Multiculturalism: E Pluribus Plures," *American Scholar,* 59 (1990): 337–54.

5. Peter Berger's thoughts are expressed in his wonderful sociological primer, *Invitation to Sociology* (Garden City, NY: Doubleday, 1963), p. 23. Another classic on perception and reality is Peter L. Berger and Thomas Luckmann, *The Social Construction of Reality* (New York: Doubleday, 1966).

6. The comparison of multiculturalism and cultural pluralism by Nathan Glazer and Peter Rose appeared in the special issue edited by Peter I. Rose, "Interminority Affairs in the U.S.: Pluralism at the Crossroads," *The Annals of the American Academy of Political and Social Science,* 530 (1993). The two articles are Nathan Glazer, "Is Assimilation Dead?" 122–36; Peter I. Rose, "Of Every Hue and Caste," 187–202.

7. Horace Kallen, "Democracy versus the Melting Pot," *Nation,* February 18, 1915, pp. 190–4, and February 25, 1915, pp. 217–20.

8. Rose, "Of Every Hue and Caste."

9. Horace Kallen, *Culture and Democracy in the United States* (New Brunswick, NJ: Transaction Publishers, 1997; originally published in 1924).

10. The posthumous publication of Robert E. Park's writings is *Race and Culture: Essays in the Sociology of Contemporary Man* (New York: The Free Press, 1964).

11. Milton Gordon's seminal work on assimilation is *Assimilation in American Life* (New York: Oxford University Press, 1964).

12. Stephen Steinberg, *The Ethnic Myth,* 3d ed. (Boston: Beacon Press, 2001).

13. Crèvecoeur's famous statement appears in *Letters from an American Farmer* (1782; reprint, Mineola, NY: Dover Publications, 2005), p. 26.

14. Observations about Crèvecoeur's omission of racial minorities first appeared in Vincent N. Parrillo, *Strangers to These Shores* (Boston: Houghton Mifflin, 1980), p. 98, and then in all subsequent editions; Nathan Glazer expressed a similar view in "Is Assimilation Dead?" p. 124.

15. Emerson's recorded thoughts appear in *Selected Writings of Ralph Waldo Emerson,* reprint ed. Edited by William H. Gilman (New York: Signet Classics, 2011), p. 111.

16. William L. O'Neill, "The Cycle of Reform," *Humanities, Social Sciences and Law,* 27 (1990): 63.

17. Frederick Jackson Turner, *The Frontier in American History* (North Charleston, SC: CreateSpace, 2011; originally published 1920), chap. xiii.

18. Israel Zangwill, *The Melting Pot: Drama in Four Acts* (Charleston, SC: Nabu Press, 2010; originally published in 1909), pp. 33, 34, 184.

19. The intermarriage findings of Richard D. Alba are reported in "The Twilight of Ethnicity among Americans of European Ancestry: The Case of the Italians," *Rethinking Today's Minorities.* Edited by Vincent N. Parrillo (Westport, CT: Greenwood Press, 1991), pp. 29–62.

20. The study by Stanley Lieberson and Mary C. Waters is *From Many Strands* (New York: Russell Sage Foundation, 1988).

21. Daniel T. Lichter, Julie H. Carmalt, and Zhenchao Qian, "Immigration and Intermarriage among Hispanics: Crossing Racial and Generational Boundaries," *Sociological Forum*, 26 (2011): 241–64.

22. Matthijs Kalmijn and Frank van Tubergen, "A Comparative Perspective on Intermarriage: Explaining Differences among National-Origin Groups in the United States," *Demography*, 47 (2010): 459–79.

23. U.S. Census Bureau, *2006–2010 American Community Survey 5-Year Estimates*, Tables B04004 and B04006.

24. Kalmijn and van Tubergen, "A Comparative Perspective on Intermarriage."

25. Miri Song, "Is Intermarriage a Good Indicator of Integration?" *Journal of Ethnic and Migration Studies*, 35 (2009): 331–48; Vincent Kang Fu, "How Many Melting Pots? Intermarriage, Pan Ethnicity, and the Black/Non-Black Divide in the United States," *Journal of Comparative Family Studies*, 38 (2007): 215–37.

26. Richard J. Herrnstein and Charles Murray, *The Bell Curve* (New York: Free Press, 1996).

27. See Samuel P. Huntington, *Who Are We? The Challenges to America's National Identity* (New York: Simon and Schuster, 2004), pp. 222–30.

28. Judith Lorber, *Understanding Inequality* (Lanham, MD: Rowman and Littlefield, 2007), pp. 153–60.

29. I am indebted to Gonzalo Santos for suggesting this concept.

2

Diversity in
Aboriginal America

That those tribes cannot exist surrounded by our settlements and in continual contact with our citizens is certain. They have neither the intelligence, the industry, the moral habits, nor the desire of improvement, which are essential to any favorable change in their condition. Established in the midst of another and a superior race, and without appreciating the causes of their inferiority or seeking to control them, they must necessarily yield to the force of circumstances and ere long disappear.

—*President Andrew Jackson*

"Amerikanska Folk" from either the first edition (1904) or second edition (1926) of the Nordisk familjebok, a Swedish encyclopedia (1876–1957), depicts 33 representatives of indigenous peoples from 29 different tribal groups throughout North and South America.

Multiculturalism flourished in the land for centuries before Europeans ever set foot on its soil. Although students enrolled in an anthropology course on Native Americans learn that fact quickly, most Americans typically fall victim to the Dillingham Flaw when thinking about these diverse people. For many, the image of Native Americans is a stereotypical generalization of tipis, buffalo, warriors on horseback, war paint, feathers, moccasins, and either brutish savages, as depicted in countless Westerns, or romanticized noble primitives, as portrayed in the film *Dances with Wolves* (1990). Such Hollywood Westerns easily lent themselves to good visuals and action sequences; the more common lifestyles among the different tribes were less dramatic and so stereotypical films of the Plains warriors became the norm.

Even before the movie industry came into existence, simplistic misconceptions were commonplace. Those early explorers, missionaries, traders, soldiers, colonial officials, and settlers were untrained observers who generalized about the various tribes as if they were a single entity. Reflecting both ethnocentric judgments and racial prejudice, most Whites saw little value in learning about the cultural differences among the tribes. Their concerns rested primarily on conquest, expansion, profit, survival and their own welfare. Whites tended to view "Indians" more as an obstacle to their own goals than as a people of equal importance and worthy of understanding instead of exploitation.

As a result, a social construction of "Indians" evolved, beginning with Columbus's mistaken impression that he had reached the Indies (which Europeans then called Asia) and thus bestowing on the natives an incorrect, but indelible, name. Thereafter, in virtually all the interactions between the indigenous peoples and Whites—whether explorers, colonial or frontier settlers, or soldiers—the Europeans and their descendants developed and shared what became the institutionalized, traditional view that the natives were "uncivilized." They were savages who must get out of the way, yield to the superior Whites, or be eliminated. This multigenerational stereotype—besides overlooking their cultural complexities, even their humanity—provided a generalized, one-size-fits-all interpretation that served as the basis for continuing exploitation.

In modern times, most films also have offered simplistic portrayals, stamping in the average moviegoer's mind a picture of the nomadic Plains Indians on horseback as representative of all tribes. However, the indigenous peoples have always been far more diversified than these simplistic portrayals. Cultural pluralism was the ongoing reality before the Europeans arrived, although those who became members of other tribes—usually through capture by raiding parties—typically assimilated into the culture of their new tribe.

To offer a detailed account of the many aspects of Native American diversity would require an entire book much larger than this one.[1] In the pages that follow, then, is only a brief overview to provide the reader with at least some sense of the multiculturalism present in pre-colonial America.[2]

THE LARGER CONTEXT

Although the many tribes experienced differentiated local socio-cultural evolutions for centuries before European contact, they also encountered certain outside influences through contact with other aboriginal societies. Migrations and trade led to a gradual cultural diffusion that altered certain ways of life, most significantly through domestication of the plant, but also in adaptation of other values and practices that intrigued the tribes. Thus, even as local and regional cultures retained unique characteristics because of their relative isolation and adaptation to their environment, they were not immune to certain hegemonic trends on the continent.

In addition, it is also possible that Asian cultures may have influenced some indigenous cultures. Most anthropologists insist that the Native Americans did not have any contact with transoceanic voyagers before Columbus. However, a few maverick anthropologists argue that unearthed artifacts suggest some pre-Columbian contact between the Chinese and Japanese cultures and the indigenous peoples of the Western Hemisphere.

Although almost all of these controversial claims involve Central and South America, one intriguing claim concerns the Zuni people of New Mexico, whose culture, language, physical appearance, and religion are significantly different from other Native Americans.

Anthropologist Nancy Yaw Davis maintains that these differences are the result of the migration of some Japanese around 1300 CE and their integrating with the tribe. Supporting her theory are blood studies that show 10 percent of Zunis have type B blood; virtually no Native Americans have type B blood, but 20 to 40 percent of East Asians do. Moreover, unlike other Native Americans, the Zuni suffer a high rate of kidney failure from a health condition common among Japanese but rare among other Native Americans. She also points out that ancient Japan's belief in yin and yang (itself a cultural diffusion originating in China) and the Zuni religion both contain complicated, yet similar, ideas. Although others disagree with her interpretation, she identifies 20 Zuni religious words as having apparent roots in Japanese.[3]

Although that world context remains contested, another does not. As early as the 17th century, Europeans established significant trade relations with the Native Americans that immediately brought them into the world economy. In great demand in Europe were tobacco, furs, and hides, particularly beaver pelts for hat making. In exchange, the natives received awls, axe heads, cloths of all types and colors, fish hooks, glass beads, jewelry, kettles, knives, linen shirts, woolen blankets, and, unfortunately, brandy, rum, and whiskey.

DIVERSITY IN LANGUAGE

Before European colonization, between 2 and possibly 10 million aboriginals—divided into about 200 or more distinct societies—spoke approximately 200 mutually unintelligible languages, along with hundreds of dialects. The reasons these languages were so incomprehensible among the tribes were the many variances in phonetics, speech sounds, and grammatical structure.

In their expedition to chart the northern section of the Louisiana Territory (1804–1806), Capt. Meriwether Lewis and Lt. William Clark repeatedly commented in their journals about the phonetic differences among the languages of the various Native American people they met. As the explorers traveled from tribe to tribe across the North American continent, they observed how some of the tongues sounded harsh and guttural, whereas others were liquid and melodious.[4]

The Interdependence of Language and Culture

The significance of these many Native American languages is the mutual interdependence of language and culture. Although a culture's language expresses how that society perceives and understands the world, the language influences that society's perceptions and understandings. This concept was effectively argued three generations ago by Edward Sapir and Benjamin Whorf, pioneers in American linguistics. They contended that human beings live in a social reality that is at the mercy of their language.

The so-called real world is, to a large extent, subconsciously built up on the group's language habits. Because no two languages are ever sufficiently similar to represent the same social reality, they reasoned, the worlds in which different societies live are distinct worlds and not merely the same world with different labels attached.

For example, in 1929, Sapir explained that the Hopi in the Southwest use verbs that have no tense—no past, present, or future.[5] Instead, their verbs differ depending on such factors as the relative length of time an event lasts, its completion or expected occurrence, and its regularity or predictability of occurrence. The Hopi focus on the recurring cycles of life, rather than view their reality as a segmented series of events locked into a time frame.

Another example was the now-extinct Yana people of California, who used both masculine and feminine forms of most words, the former used only in all-male conversations and the latter in male-female or all-female conversations. The language of another tribe, the Navajo, does not distinguish among such third-person pronouns as his, her, its, or their and instead uses a compound word of adjectives and nouns, such as one-wife-of-one-man to indicate his wife.

These examples are just small indicators of the significant differences in grammatical structures among Native American languages. The many languages of the indigenous people are not a single entity with 200 minor variations. Their differences are far too complex and reflect the different worlds of the many diverse tribes.

Language and Social Reality

The prevalence of 200 distinct languages is one dimension of the multicultural reality of pre-Columbian America. Just as we view White ethnic groups speaking different languages as distinct from one another, so, too, must we look upon the many Native American tribes as diverse entities.

Speaking in different tongues, they constituted a mosaic of separate worlds, each aware of neighboring tribes, but nonetheless dissimilar in language. We begin to overcome any Dillingham Flaw simplistic judgments by recognizing further that the interdependent relationship of language with culture results in a social reality for tribal members that sets them culturally apart from another tribe that is linguistically different. Although it may take a skilled linguist to understand the diversity among these 200-plus languages, social observers can distinguish other cultural attributes more easily, as we now discuss.

DIVERSITY IN GENDER ROLES

One good example of the lack of uniformity among Native Americans was in role expectations and behavior for men and women. These varied by region, by social structure, and by tribal means of survival.

In matrilineal and matrilocal societies, women had considerable power because property (housing, land, and tools) belonged to them. Because property usually passed from mother to daughter and the husband joined his wife's family, he was more the stranger and yielded authority to his wife's eldest brother. As a result, the husband was unlikely to become an authoritative, domineering figure. Moreover, among such peoples as the Cherokee, Iroquois, Pueblo, and Navajo, a disgruntled wife, secure in her possessions, could simply divorce her husband by tossing his belongings out of their residence.

Women's role in tribal governance was often influential in matrilineal societies, as among the Iroquois, where the principal civil and religious offices were kept within maternal lineages. The tribal matriarch or a group of tribal matrons nominated each delegate, briefed him before each session, monitored his legislative record, and removed him from office if his conduct displeased the women. Despite the feminine checks and balances, however, the actual business of government was a masculine affair.

Division of Labor

In the Northeastern Woodlands and on the Plains, where hunting and warfare demanded strenuous activity away from home, the men often returned exhausted and required a few days to recover. Wearied by both these arduous actions and their usual accompanying religious fasting, the men relaxed in the village while the women went about their many daily tasks.

Seeing only female busyness in these native encampments, White observers misinterpreted what they saw and wrote inaccurate stereotypical portrayals of lazy braves and industrious squaws. Such was not the case. Moreover, in the Southeast and Southwest, men and women performed their daily labors with observable equality because the men did not go out on grueling expeditions as did the men in the Northeast and Plains. In California, the Great Basin, and the Northwest Coast, the sexual division of labor existed somewhere between these two variations.

Women had certain common tasks in each of the U.S. culture areas: cleaning and maintaining the living quarters, tending to children, gathering edible plants, pounding corn into meal, extracting oil from acorns and nuts, cooking, sewing, packing, and unpacking. Certain crafts also were usually their responsibility: weaving such items as cloth, baskets, and mats; brewing dyes; and making pottery. In the Southwest, however, men sometimes made baskets and pottery, and even wove cloth.

In regions where hunting provided the main food supply, the women also were responsible for house building, processing carcasses of game, preparing hides or furs, and whatever food gathering or farming that could be done. In the mostly agricultural societies in the East, the women primarily worked in the fields and the men built the frame houses, as both shared duties for preparing hides or furs. Similarly, in the fishing communities of the Northwest, the men built the plank houses and helped with the processing of animal skins. In California and the Great Basin, most aspects of labor, except the defined female tasks of weaving and basket and pottery making, were fairly evenly shared. In the Southwest, the men did most of the field work, house building, weaving, cloth manufacture, and animal skin processing.

Status and Influence

Female prestige among the Iroquois grew greater after the Revolutionary War, as male prestige ebbed as a result of continual defeats and the men's inability to do much hunting because of scarcity of game. By the 19th century, mothers played a greater role in approving marriage partners for their children and more consistently got custody of their children in a divorce, unlike the uncertainty of custody in earlier times.

Among many southeastern tribes, the women were influential in tribal councils, and, in some places, they cast the deciding vote for war or peace. The Cherokee designated one female as "Beloved Woman," through whom they believed the Great Spirit spoke. Consequently, her words were always heard, but not necessarily heeded. However, she headed the influential Woman's Council, made up of a representative from each clan, and sat as a voting member of the Council of Chiefs, where she exercised considerable influence. She also held absolute authority over prisoners, and when she died, a successor would be chosen.

The Cheyenne also held women in particularly high regard. They played an influential role in determining warfare and sometimes even fought alongside the men. A woman's display of grief over a slain son was an effective arousal for a punitive expedition. On a war party's successful return, the women danced about while waving the scalps, exhibited their men's shields and weapons, and derived honors from their husbands' deeds.

The statuses and roles for men and women thus varied considerably among Native Americans depending on each tribe's cultural orientations. Property possession, inheritance, power, and influence rested on whether a tribe's structure was matrilineal or patrilineal. Although a few universal female-designated work tasks existed (cleaning, nurturing, edible plant gathering, food preparation, cooking, packing, and unpacking), others varied by region, means of food production, and social organization. Such variances in gender roles further exemplify the diversity that existed among Native Americans.

DIVERSITY IN CLOTHING

Choice of clothing was in large measure dependent on the geographical environment and the materials available from which to make them. Although all tribes fashioned clothing from hides and fur, these were less available to tribes primarily dependent on agriculture or seafood products, so they tended to make more clothing from plant materials, unlike the tribes who mainly hunted. Yet even among tribes using similar materials, a wide variety of styles could be found.

Generally speaking, the men plucked their facial and body hair, typically using shells as tweezers. Both women and men wore necklaces and earrings made of shells, claws, teeth, beads, or precious stones. Otherwise, great variance in clothing and bodily adornment could be found.

Northwestern Native Americans

Because cedar trees abound along the Pacific Northwest coast, tribes twisted strips of inner bark into string and wove this string into clothing. In summer, the men usually went naked, but sometimes wore tunics; in winter and on ceremonial occasions, they wore a knee-length robe made of animal skins (especially otter) or woven plant fiber. If traveling to the interior, they wore leggings and moccasins.

Women were always clothed, usually with a plant fiber skirt and a woven robe over both shoulders covering the upper body. Frequent rainy weather occasioned the wearing of conical hats of woven plant fiber and waterproof ponchos of the same material. Both men and women wore tattooed family crests and other designs on their face, chest, back of arms, or front of legs. On festive occasions, both sexes applied red, white, and black paints to their bodies.

Southwestern Native Americans

The Pueblo of Arizona and New Mexico and their Anasazi ancestors were unique in wearing mostly cotton garments. Women's dresses were rectangular cloths worn under the left arm and tied above the right shoulder, the open right side of the dress kept fastened by a belt of the same material. Buckskin leggings were wrapped around lower legs, and the buckskin moccasins had buffalo hide soles.

Men wore a cotton loincloth, its ends held in place by a belt. Over this cloth, they wore a kilt that came to mid-thigh, set off by a sash of braided cotton cords around the top of the kilt and hanging down one side. Sometimes they wore shirts tied at the sides, with flaps for sleeves. Moccasins also had the stiff buffalo hide for soles sewn to buckskin that covered the ankle or else went halfway to the knee. Cold weather prompted the wearing of woven rabbit fur blankets or a cape of feathers fastened to a netted base.

Interestingly, the men wore more jewelry than the women. Both sexes styled their hair the same: bangs just above the eyes, below the ears on the sides, and full length in back.

Northern Plains Native Americans

As elsewhere, the women of the Northern Plains wore more clothing than the men. Their dresses, mid-calf in length and fringed at the bottom, were made of two deer or elk hides sewn together. Below-knee leggings and moccasins completed their outfit. The men often wore only moccasins and a breechcloth, adding leggings tied to a belt when they traveled. A buckskin shirt with sleeve flaps was worn only on special occasions or in cold weather, as was a buffalo robe. Women sometimes wore such robes also, and they could be pulled over the head in bitter weather. Otherwise a fur cap might be worn.

Plains natives often made their clothing more elaborate by ornamenting the material with quills and/or beads. Both sexes seldom tattooed their bodies. They wore their hair in two braids hanging in front, and the men typically wore one or more feathers in their hair depending on tribal custom.

Southeastern Native Americans

In the Southeast, both sexes covered the upper part of their bodies only in cold weather or on special occasions, at which time they wore robes made of animal hide or feathers thatched on a netted base.

Otherwise, the men wore a buckskin breechcloth and the women a wrap-around skirt from the waist to the knees. These skirts could be made of buckskin or woven from such materials as grass, inner bark, or bison hair. When traveling, the men wore moccasins and full-length leggings fastened at the belt, and women seldom wore moccasins and only half-length leggings, fastened with a garter just below the knee.

Both sexes had tattoos of elaborate design on their faces, trunks, arms, and legs. Women grew their hair full length, sometimes wearing it upswept and other times parted and braided. Men grew a scalp lock from the crown of their heads; the remainder of the scalp was either completely shaved or else partially shaved except for a crew cut-style border running from front to back around the scalp lock.[6]

Northeastern Native Americans

Native Americans living in the Northeast woodlands wore little clothing in the summer. Children were usually naked, whereas the men wore only deerskin breechcloths and the women knee-length skirts and wampum headbands. In southern New England, both men and women might wear light capes or shawls of woven textiles. Colder weather throughout the Northeast required robes of fur or woven downy, water-proof turkey feathers, along with leather leggings and moccasins made of moose or deer skin.

Boys' hair was kept short until they turned 16, whereas girls and women wore full-length hair. Hair styles—some elaborate and decorated with porcupine quills—varied from tribe to tribe. Males from the Lenni Lenape and several Algonquian tribes would pluck their hair with mussel-shell tweezers except for a central cock's crest, but other tribes did not follow this practice. Among all Northeastern tribes, ornamental jewelry included necklaces of beads or pearls with copper tubing; jeweled earrings; and bracelets, pendants, and belts of brightly colored or shining stones, shells, and beads.[7]

Clothing and body adornment, varying so greatly both among and within the 10 culture areas (see Map 2.1), were cultural attributes that further attested to Native American diversity. As the tribes made cultural contact with one another, style fashions spread from one to the other. European contact also brought changes in materials and styles as trade brought in more furs, hides, and needles to sew better garments, often in imitation of European full-length sleeves and trouser legs. When game became scarce, use of the Whites' clothing fabrics and styles became more common among Native Americans.[8]

MAP 2.1 Cultural Areas and Tribal Locations in North America

Source: Alvin M. Josephy, Jr., *The Indian Heritage of America* (New York: Knopf, 1968).

DIVERSITY IN HOUSING

Climate, terrain, and available building materials all influence housing construction, of course, but so, too, does the culture of a people. Because extensive cultural diversity existed among Native Americans, their housing styles varied significantly.

John White's exquisite 16th-century watercolor of a typical Algonquian village of the Secotan tribe in North Carolina depicts the layout of one type of permanent Native American settlement. In his rendering, along a thoroughfare stands a series of barrel-roofed, multifamily houses made of arched saplings covered with bark and woven mats that are easily removable to let in light. Nearby are newly planted and ripening corn fields, an open ceremonial center with a circle of elaborately carved posts, a place of solemn prayer, and a tomb for departed chiefs.

Large Communal Structures

Although all tribes lived within a tribal enclave, some did so within larger communal structures. Perhaps the greatest of these was in Chaco Canyon, New Mexico. There, the ruins of Pueblo Bonito reveal a gigantic, crescent-shaped, single-structure housing project covering more than three acres. It rose to a height of four or five stories around its outer rim and was enclosed along the front by a long wall. In the central plaza, around which the Pueblo Bonito arched, were two great kivas or enormous subterranean ceremonial chambers, each able to accommodate hundreds of people for the sacred rites performed there.

This edifice housed 1,000 people and thrived for 400 years until a sustained drought ended its existence in the late 13th century. At its peak, this monolithic dwelling place contained 660 rooms, with the adjoining units interconnected by doorways and built on a series of graduated terraces that served as streets. Built of stone set in mud mortar, the ceilings were supported by wooden beams and made of sticks, grass, and several inches of mud.

In New York State, the five nations of the Iroquois Confederation—the Cayuga, Mohawk, Oneida, Onondaga, and Seneca (later, a sixth nation, the remnants of the Tuscarora, were admitted in 1722)—lived in rectangular-shaped longhouses. These ranged in size from 50 to 150 feet in length and 18 to 25 feet in width depending on the number of families living inside.

A barrel-shaped roof, made from seasoned elm bark sewn in overlapped layers, hung like shingles over a framework of wooden poles from elm trees lashed together. Smaller versions existed among many eastern tribes. A similar multifamily concept could be found in the rectangular plank houses in the Pacific Northwest. Built of wide planks including the floor, they measured anywhere from 30 by 45 feet to 50 by 60 feet. Roofs were two-pitched with a gable end facing the sea. Inside, families each had their own allocated sleeping quarters that, like those of the Iroquois, had drop screens for privacy. These areas were typically on platforms, or else the center of the house was excavated to achieve the same effect. Fire smoke went out through an opening in the roof with a sliding panel that was closed during inclement weather. Outside the house, a totem pole—native only to the Northwest people and bearing accumulated family crests and honors—indicated a clan's history and rank.

The Pueblo lived in rectangular, flat-roofed rooms directly adjoining one another in multistoried complexes that are comparable to modern low-rise apartment buildings. The Hopi and Navajo lived in mud-and-stone dwellings with heavy wooden roof beams, the scarcity of wood in the Southwest prompting them to salvage beams from old housing for any new construction.

The Mojave-type multifamily structure of the Colorado River Yumans was almost square-shaped, its side dimensions about 20 or 25 feet and covered outside on three sides by sand. The dwelling had a low, four-pitched roof without a smoke hole, requiring the fire to be placed near the door.

Single-Family Dwellings

Elsewhere, most housing units held single families, although extended family units within the tribal village usually clustered in adjacent dwellings. Southeastern tribes lived in small houses almost square-shaped, the mud plastered over wooden-pole walls about 15 feet long on each side, covered by a 6-foot-high, two-pitched, thatched roof. In contrast, the Seminole in Florida lived in an open-sided, thatched-roof dwelling called a *chickee*.

The Lenni Lenape mostly lived in round, domed bark wigwams, whereas the same style of housing among the tribes around the western Great Lakes was made of other materials. The Menominee typically covered theirs with mats of reeds and cattails, whereas other tribes used pieces of bark and hide, in addition to woven or sewn mats. Nearby, the Kickapoo tribe lived in picturesque reed-woven lodges.

Among the nomadic tribes of the Plains, their pursuit of the roaming buffalo led to portable housing: well-constructed conical tipis made of long wooden poles covered with tailored buffalo hides. These tipis often stood 10 to 12 feet high and were 12 to 15 feet in diameter. As in most Native American structures, the fire was in the center and the beds were around the sides. In the Southwest, the Apache resided in a *wickiup,* a small domed hut made of slender poles, brush, and grass that stood about 6 feet high. In the same region, the impoverished Ute lived in primitive lean-tos.

These differences in housing style were much more than architectural variations. They were another cultural mark that reflected the diversity among the tribes. Their differing value orientations about family life, communal living, social hierarchy, and tribal welfare affected their housing designs.

DIVERSITY IN SOCIAL ORGANIZATION

Most Native American tribes maintained a more democratic structure than that found among the indigenous people in Africa and Oceania. In America, they usually had a tribal structure of equal clans, although some societies were organized into small bands. These bands could be a loosely organized number of extended families with no central tribal government, such as the Apache, or they could be like the Plains natives, who remained in separate groups most of the year, but came together as a composite tribe for the annual summer encampment.

Social Status Variations

Among the tribes in the Great Basin culture area (Nevada, Utah, parts of California, Oregon, Idaho, Wyoming, and Colorado), differences in social class, status, and rank, other than those based on age and sex, were minimal. This arid region—home to the Paiute, Shoshoni, and Ute—offered only a meager, harsh livelihood to the sparse native population. Leadership was not hereditary, but rested in the most competent man in skills and judgment until he proved otherwise and was then replaced by someone better.

Other indigenous peoples had some ranking system to determine social standing, usually determined by an office held, wealth, or war deeds. After introduction of the horse and trade with the Whites, Plains culture changed. Accumulation of wealth—such as medicine bundles, horses, guns, and kitchenware—became important, and a class structure based on wealth arose out of previously egalitarian societies.

Northwestern Slavery

A notable exception to the democratic structure was the people of the Northwest Coast, where two distinct social classes—free men and slaves—existed. Usually obtained as prisoners in raids, slaves could thereafter be bought or sold in an institutionalized slave trade. Normally, they could marry one another, but their children then typically became slaves also. Captive slaves could be ransomed by relatives, but the stigma of a slave status was so great that some refused to do so.

Slaves could be freed on such occasions as the death of the slave's owner, or when the owner's child had ears pierced for earrings, or at a potlatch to demonstrate the owner's wealth in giving up such property. However, "freed" often meant killing slaves on these occasions and was, in fact, mandatory as foundation sacrifices when building a new home. At this time, the slaves' bodies were thrown into the holes dug by the front door to hold the carved totems. In their lifetimes, slaves performed only menial tasks and served primarily as prestige items, offering visible evidence of their owners' wealth and high rank.

Southeastern Caste Systems

A caste system apparently existed among the Chitimacha in Louisiana, where endogamous marriages maintained a dichotomy between nobles and commoners. However, the most stratified social order existed among the Natchez people of Mississippi, headed by a chief known as the Great Sun, who claimed descent from the sun. Natchez society consisted of three levels of nobility, Suns, Nobles, and Honored People, and a single group of commoners called Stinkards. The Great Sun held unlimited power over his subjects, but a council of elders limited his authority on matters of general concern to the entire society. Curiously, the three upper ranks could only marry Stinkards, although the latter group also could marry within their own social group. The potential depletion of the Stinkards through their upward mobility marriages was offset through replenishment by people from nearby conquered tribes.

Both the Chitimacha and Natchez are thought to be remnants of a Mississippian culture that peaked from about 1200 to 1500 CE. From Ohio to Louisiana, from Arkansas to Tennessee, these mound builders constructed pyramidal or conical mounds as foundations for temples or chiefs' houses. These earthworks, still standing today, were built by tens of thousands of people who, without benefit of wheeled vehicles or beasts of burden, carried all the dirt in baskets to the sites. Most impressive is Monk's Mound at Cahokia, Illinois, across the Mississippi River from St. Louis. It is a massive earthwork 1,000 feet long, 700 feet wide, and 100 feet high, upon which stood either a temple or the residence of Cahokia's ruler.

Iroquois Consensus-Building

The Iroquois confederacy, or League of the Five Nations, was an alliance apparently formed to end warfare among the Cayuga, Mohawk, Oneida, Onondaga, and Seneca. It permitted each tribe to govern itself, with larger issues such as relations with other tribes decided at the annual meeting of the Great Council. At this meeting, the 49 councilors, with representation apportioned among the five tribes, acted on an issue only after reaching unanimous agreement.[9]

Oratorical skills were important in persuading other members and the process resulted in some historians identifying this primitive democracy form as a prototype for such provisions of the U.S. Constitution as reconciliation of differing House-Senate legislation, impeachment, and territorial expansion. Just as the Iroquois admitted the Tuscarora in 1722 as a Sixth Nation, so did the new U.S. government admit new states.

The Iroquois model of a collective political institution more broadly resembled the form of authority within almost all North American tribes. The chief held an honorary status and primarily played ceremonial and religious roles. Real authority rested not in an individual, but in a group, the tribal council.

Variances in Tribal Organization

In this section, we discussed social structures that ranged from the southeastern caste system and northwestern slave system to mostly democratic structures elsewhere. Leadership could be hereditary or not, and social class could be nonexistent (Great Basin) or significant (Plains). There could be loose bands with no central tribal government (Apache), tribes who merged once a year (Sioux), or a formal confederacy (Iroquois). The plurality of tribal organizations offers us yet another instance of Native American diversity and further ammunition against the Dillingham Flaw of simplistic categorizations of the past based on present-day sensibilities.[10]

DIVERSITY IN VALUES

Among the many tribes throughout the land, value orientations about wealth varied. The Hupa, Karok, and Yurok of northern California were obsessed by personal wealth; it was to be accumulated, ostentatiously displayed, guarded, and bestowed intact on one's children. In contrast, the people of the Northwest Coast accumulated quality possessions only to have enough to give away at a potlatch. They did so to gain honor among their people, humiliate enemies, or legitimize hereditary claims. In contrast, the Shoshoni measured wealth by the kin upon whose aid one could depend, and the Zuni considered wealth as determined by the time and resources one had to participate in religious ceremonies and host the ceremonial dancers.

Religious values and beliefs permeated every aspect of Native American life in thought, word, and deed, but once again differences existed among the tribes. Their religiosity ranged from the simple social organization of the Iroquois, who believed in the Great Spirit as a supreme being, to the complexity of interrelated religious groupings among the Zuni, who were possibly the most religious indigenous people on the continent. The Pueblo acknowledged numerous spiritual entities as equally ranked gods, and the people of the Plateau and Great Basin culture areas also believed in large numbers of spirits.

Full-time priests existed within the Mississippian culture and the derivative cultures such as the Natchez, whereas part-time priests, who also earned their livelihood in some other economic activity, functioned among the Pueblo. Shamans operated only in the Plateau and Great Basin regions, but religious leaders in most of the East and Southwest, on the Plains and Prairies, in California, and on the Northwest Coast displayed attributes of both priests and shamans. For example, Northwest Coast shamans typically came from families specializing in shamanism, virtually creating a permanent priesthood. They performed ceremonial rites that also had strong social functions, unlike the Sanpoil in the Plateau area of eastern Washington. The Sanpoil had no standardized rituals and drew their shamans—who held little distinction from others—from anyone in the tribe whose vision quests resulted in unusual good fortune. Perhaps the most important aspect of Native American cultural values was the ubiquitous idea that humans were "embedded" in nature. This concept was different from the Europeans' view of nature as something meant to serve them. These contrasting values would generate controversies with Whites virtually from first contact to the present.

THE NEXT HORIZON

As culturally distinct as the hundreds of tribes were from one another, the arrival of Whites would have a single effect on all of them: catastrophe. All the tribes would find their self-reliant way of life changed forever by disease, conquest, and loss of their ancestral lands.

Far more deadly than all warfare would be European diseases, against which the Native Americans had no immunity because they had been isolated from that continent's sicknesses for thousands of years. Carried by European explorers, fishermen, and fur traders, these diseases would spread like wildfire among the indigenous tribes. Smallpox, measles, typhus, tuberculosis, chicken pox, influenza, cholera, and diphtheria would weaken and kill them by the thousands, wiping out whole villages and even decimating entire tribes.

Tribal disintegration would further result from other causes. In return for axes, blankets, cloth, kettles, knives, and rum, many tribes would deplete their environment of beaver and deer to meet European demand for their hides or else raid neighboring communities to procure slaves for local colonists or slave traders. Westward expansion would lead to continual land thefts, warfare, further decimation, subjugation, segregation on reservations, and dependency.

The rich, vibrant multiculturalism that predated European contact would yield to this relentless onslaught of settlement and expansion. Any violent resistance would reaffirm the European and Euro-American stereotype of Native Americans as "cruel, bloodthirsty savages." They would lose their lands and independence and become a colonized, exploited people.

Although their conquerors would continue to view them as a single entity, the Native Americans were never that. Some tribes would internalize others' views of themselves and try to act "White." Other tribes would attempt to negotiate a path of marginality, taking what they considered to be the best of both worlds. Many others would struggle, as best they could, to preserve both their culture and their identity.

NOTES

1. An excellent, highly readable overview of Native American civilizations is Peter Farb, *Man's Rise to Civilization as Shown by the Indians of North America from Primeval Times to the Coming of the Industrial State* (New York: Penguin, 1991).

2. Much of the material about Native American cultural attributes is drawn from Carl Waldman, *Encyclopedia of Native American Tribes*, 3d ed. (New York: Checkmark Books, 2006); Michael Johnson and Richard Hook, *Encyclopedia of Native Tribes of North America*, 3d ed. (Richmond Hill, Ontario: Firefly Books, 2007).

3. Nancy Yaw Davis, *The Zuni Enigma* (New York: W. W. Norton and Company, 2000).

4. Two good sources for information about Whites' perceptions of Native Americans are Philip J. Deloria, *Playing Indian* (New Haven, CT: Yale University Press, 1999; Robert F. Berkhofer, Jr., *The White Man's Indian: Images of the American Indian from Columbus to the Present* (New York: Knopf, 1979).

5. The original source of Edward Sapir's observations is "The Status of Linguistics as a Science," *Language*, 5 (1929): 207–14. Other references include Edward Sapir, *Selected Writings in Language, Culture and Personality* (Memphis, TN: General Books, 2010); and J. B. Carroll, *Language, Thought, and Reality: Selected Readings of Benjamin Lee Whorf* (Cambridge: MIT Press, 1964).

6. Helpful information about Southeastern Native Americans can be found in Robbie Ethridge and Charles Hudson, eds., *The Transformation of the Southeastern Indians, 1540–1760* (Jackson: University Press of Mississippi, 2008); Gregory A. Waselkov and Kathryn E. Holland Braund, eds., *William Bartram on the Southeastern Indians* (Lincoln: University of Nebraska Press, 2002); James Adair, *The History of the American Indians* (Tuscaloosa: University of Alabama Press, 2009).

7. A good source for further information about Northeastern Native Americans is David Murray, *Indian Giving: Economies of Power in Indian-White Exchanges* (Amherst: University of Massachusetts Press, 2000).

8. Native American response to culture contact is detailed in Colin G. Calloway, *After King Philip's War: Presence and Persistence in New England* (Hanover, NJ: University Press of New England, 1997).

9. The Iroquois political consensus model is fully examined in Bruce Johansen, *Debating Democracy: The Iroquois Legacy of Freedom* (Santa Fe, NM: Clear Light Books, 1997).

10. You can read succinct insights into Native American tribes and their social structures in Mark Q. Sutton, *Introduction to Native North America*, 4th ed. (Upper Saddle River, NJ: Prentice Hall, 2011).

3

Diversity in Colonial Times

All of our people all over the country—except the pure-blooded Indians—are immigrants or descendants of immigrants, including those who came over on the Mayflower.

—*President Franklin D. Roosevelt, 1944*

U.S. colonial cities were bustling ports of commerce, even though they only contained about 5 percent of the total population. This 1830s view of Broadway in New York City illustrates its expansion as an export center after the Revolutionary War.

What most people remember about early U.S. history is that the 13 English colonies fought for their independence from the "Mother Country" of England. Because the English held cultural and political preeminence in the colonial and early national periods, this myth of cultural homogeneity arose. The actions and/or writings of contemporary English American leaders, historians, and literary figures enhanced the myth, and their dominance and influence cast a long shadow across subsequent generations.

THE LARGER CONTEXT

Colonial America existed on the periphery of the "civilized world." Although England was dominant in its cultural, economic, and political influence, Europe also exerted a profound impact. For example, the Age of Enlightenment—an 18th-century philosophical movement that embraced rationalism, emphasized learning, and encouraged a spirit of skepticism and practicality in social and political thought—guided the Founding Fathers in their thinking and eventual formulation of a new nation. Before the new republic became a reality, however, what occurred in colonial thoughts, words, and actions reflected, for the most part, the dominance of European culture, both abstract (values, ideas) and material (fashions, manufactured goods).

Beginning mostly as commercial enterprises or feudal proprietorships thanks to royal land grants, the colonies eventually became royal colonies. However, England was too absorbed in its civil war (1642–1649) and Oliver Cromwell's Puritan rule to engage in any effective colonial policy. Even after restoration of the Stuart dynasty with Charles II becoming king, England still did not pursue any centralized administrative policy.

Yet 18th-century colonial politics closely resembled those of England. Colonial legislatures, like the English Parliament, held powers to initiate legislation and to vote on taxes and expenditures, often bringing them into clashes with the royal governors who sought to impose their own will. This battle of wills and evolving notion of self-government set the stage for the rebellion that would follow in the latter part of the century.

Colonial cultural norms reflected European patriarchal values, which became embedded in English law. For example, a woman's marriage automatically transferred the legal ownership of the bride's personal property—money, land, household goods, and clothing—to her husband. If he died, the property went to the children, not her, with male heirs receiving larger inheritances than their sisters. Even children could become the wards of the father's male relatives and not of his widow. In the rare instance of a divorce, the father indisputably retained custody of the children.

CULTURAL PLURALISM

As to the composition of the colonial population under English rule, the presence of non-English colonial Americans at first was not a significant factor. In commenting about the population composition of the 17th century, historian Mildred Campbell remarked,

> For despite the Dutch on the Hudson, and small groups of Swiss, Swedes, Finns, and French Huguenots pocketed along the coast, the small vessels which set out on the American voyage were chiefly English built and English manned. Their cargoes, moreover, consisted largely of Englishmen and, later and in smaller numbers, Englishwomen. Even the Scots and Irish, who in the next century would crowd the harbors of the New World, were a minority in the first century.[1]

By the early 18th century, however, an important change in immigration dramatically altered the population mix. As Stephen Steinberg observed,

> The simple truth is that [the] English were not coming in sufficient numbers to populate the colonies.... If there were no compelling "pull" factors luring Englishmen to America, neither were there potent "push" factors. In fact, after 1718 labor shortages at home induced the British government to place restrictions on emigration, especially of skilled artisans and other laborers needed in Britain's nascent industries. It was this scarcity of emigrants from Britain that induced colonial authorities to permit the immigration of non-English nationalities.[2]

Historians Bruce Catton and William B. Catton described the new colonial immigration as continually increasing:

> Homogeneity was altered in a different way by the increasing infusion of non-English elements into the colonial bloodstream. This did not become noticeable until late in the seventeenth

century and assumed its largest proportions in the eighteenth, when the seaboard colonies entered upon their great period of sustained growth. Of greatest significance was the large-scale influx of men and women of African descent. Next in importance were those from the Rhine Valley and the north of Ireland. (p. 165)[3]

The Cattons also provide some insight into differences among the so-called British immigrants, a theme introduced earlier in the first chapter with reference to the Dillingham Flaw, which I will develop further in this chapter:

> The Scotch-Irish added something special to the colonial brew. They tended to be hard cases politically—unyielding Presbyterians, schooled and scarred by generations of turmoil in Ireland, caught in the middle between oppressed Irish Catholics and the Anglican establishment, hated from both sides, returning the hatred at compound interest. (p. 166)

One of their other observations relates to the social distance the ethnic groups deliberately set between themselves:

> These people did not all want the same things, beyond the elemental notions of escape and a fresh start. If, for a determined handful, this meant social engineering and creating communities, for untold larger numbers it meant simply a vague but compelling desire to go where they could be left alone. "Get off my back" is a piece of twentieth-century slang, distinctively American, which well summarized the prime motivation and prevailing mood among immigrants to Britain's mainland colonies. (p. 168)

Some social scientists, while admitting the continued presence of cultural pluralism up to the Revolutionary War, suggest that it was minimal and that assimilation was virtually complete, even among non-English-speaking ethnic groups. Lawrence Fuchs, for example, asserted that

> ... by the time of the Revolution, most of the children and grandchildren of Dutch, French, German, and Swedish immigrants in the colonies spoke English and were otherwise indistinguishable from the children and grandchildren of English

settlers, although in Albany, where the Dutch predominated, it was difficult to assemble an English-speaking jury, and several counties in Pennsylvania were overwhelmingly German-speaking. Hostility toward speakers of Dutch and German and toward the English-speaking Scotch-Irish, the newest large immigrant group, was widespread. (p. 12)[4]

Fuchs's claim of indistinguishable characteristics among these four groups is questionable for reasons beyond his own inclusion of contradictory examples, illustrating both cultural pluralism and intergroup tensions. Many Dutch, French, and Germans continued to live in social, sometimes even geographic, isolation within culturally distinct ethnic communities apart from English American society. Moreover, Fuchs cites *To Seek America* (1988) by Maxine Seller as the source of his Dutch and German "exceptions." Yet in the chapter on which Fuchs draws, Seller argues that, although by the outbreak of the Revolution, "The Swedes ... had become indistinguishable in language and lifestyle from the dominant English ... [o]thers—including some Jews, some French Huguenots, many Dutch, and many more Germans, had not."[5]

This minimization of ethnic diversity that overstresses English American cultural and political hegemony illustrates the Dillingham Flaw. So, too, do claims that English numerical superiority reflects cultural homogeneity. Stephen Steinberg, for example, presets this view by stating, "Three-fourths of the white population in 1790 had their origins in the English-speaking states of the British Isles." (This statement ignores the different cultures, religions, and Gaelic and Scottish languages.) Then, after saying the other immigrants were mostly from northern or western Europe with "important cultural affinities to the English majority" (a claim many Scandinavians, Germans, and French might question), he adds,

At its inception, the United States had a population that was remarkably homogeneous in terms of both ethnicity and religion [Protestant]. Devoid of its invidious implications, the claim that the nation was founded by white Anglo-Saxon Protestants is reasonably accurate.

To be sure, there was some ethnic differentiation in terms of both population and patterns of settlement. New York still reflected its Dutch origins, and had a far greater ethnic mix than did New England. Pennsylvania had sizable concentrations of Germans and Scotch-Irish, and the Southern states, which a

century later would become the last bastion of "ethnic purity,"
were characterized by a high degree of ethnic heterogeneity, at
least in comparison to New England. But it would be a mistake
to construe this as evidence of a rudimentary pluralism, at least
in a political sense. Not only were the English predominant
numerically, but they enjoyed a political and cultural hegemony
over the life of the fledgling nation.

Non-English colonials were typically regarded as aliens who
were obliged to adapt to English rule in terms of both politics
and culture.[6]

Steinberg is correct in saying that political pluralism did not exist.
However, cultural pluralism did exist in a real sense. Non-English
colonials, often clustered in their own ethnic communities, did not
necessarily feel any compulsion to forego their language and culture,
nor did officials force them to do so. Furthermore, the English were
not as cohesive a group as one might think, as the following pages
illustrate.

The colonies were not a culturally homogeneous launching pad
for the new nation, which only later received several waves of "different" immigrants. Colonial America was a rich mixture of racial
and ethnic heterogeneity right up to the Revolutionary War. As Gary
B. Nash states, "Any attempt to portray the colonies as unified and
homogeneous would be misguided."[7]

COLONIAL BEGINNINGS

Coming in the 17th century to a land already populated by indigenous
people of many cultures was a steady stream of adventurers, debtors,
opportunists, social outcasts, and desperate people, all risking a peril-
ous 3-month journey across an often-stormy ocean to forge a better
life for themselves in the New World. Sickness, disease, and death
were common traveling companions on those voyages, and many
never completed their journey, their lives ending with burial at sea.

A Patchwork Quilt of Ethnic Settlements

Those who successfully completed their journey came from many
parts of the European continent, speaking different tongues and
varying in their religious beliefs, customs, skills, and talents. When
they settled in this new land, they sometimes intermingled, but

more often they clustered together with their own kind, creating a mosaic of subcultural enclaves, at first on or near the coast and later inland.

The names given to areas by early settlers reflected this ethnic mix by colony (New Belgium, New England, New France, New Netherland, New Spain, and New Sweden). Settlement names were either new versions of their homeland—New Amsterdam (Holland), New Orleans (France), and New Smyrna, Florida (Greece)—or simply the same as in their native land—Cambridge (England/Massachusetts), Guttenberg (Germany/New Jersey), Haarlem (Holland/New York), Hamburg (Germany/New Jersey), and Plymouth (England/Massachusetts). At first fairly self-contained and separate from one another, most were culturally homogeneous within their boundaries, but together they constituted a patchwork quilt of ethnic diversity. Two early settlements, however, attracted a variety of people almost from their inception.

Diversity in the Early Settlements

Philadelphia and its adjoining area offered one example of cultural pluralism. Still a small village in 1700, its population was mostly English and Welsh, but this area also included Danes, Dutch, Finns, French, Germans, Irish, Scots, and Swedes. Even within these individual groups, further diversity could be found.[8] The 300 or so Germans, for example, were a mixture of Lutherans, Mennonites, and Quakers, each group remaining separate from the others.

The greatest concentration of cultural diversity, however, was in New Amsterdam, where 18 languages were spoken on Manhattan Island as early as 1646. The Dutch, Flemish, Walloons, French, Danes, Norwegians, Swedes, English, Scots, Irish, Germans, Poles, Bohemians, Portuguese, and Italians were among the settlement's early inhabitants. After the English takeover in 1664, New York's slave population became the largest north of the Chesapeake region. In 1720, the city's Black population numbered 20,000, one-third of the total; by 1741, slaves were still a substantial proportion, one-sixth of the population.

Elsewhere in the colonies, some European ethnic mix could be found in most small cities. For the most part, however, the various groups clustered together, at first on the outskirts of the municipality and then more and more to the west along the edge of the frontier. By the late 17th century, the English dominated all 13 colonies. By 1689, the population of colonial America had reached an estimated 210,000

Europeans, about 80 percent of them "transplanted Englishmen." After that, however, the proportion of English Americans declined. Between 1689 and 1775, the population increased twelvefold to about 2.6 million, with only a small portion due to natural increase. Rather, the rapid growth of African slavery and the influx of hundreds of thousands of non-English immigrants in the mid-18th century significantly changed the character of the colonial population.

GEOGRAPHIC VARIANCES IN DIVERSITY

Three geographic regions developed distinct population mixtures and cultures. The following data are based on information from the U.S. Bureau of the Census, as well as 1790 census data extrapolations and anthropological estimates about the Native American population at that time.[9]

The New England Colonies

The greatest degree of cultural homogeneity was in the New England colonies, with English Americans representing about 70 percent of all inhabitants (see Figure 3.1). In Massachusetts, home to two of every five New Englanders, lived the greatest concentration of English Americans of all 13 colonies, with 82 percent of the more than 250,000 people being English. The lowest proportion of English was in Maine, with 60 percent, but its population was only about 31,000. Scots accounted for about 4 percent and the Scots-Irish for about 3 percent. Interestingly, the 16,000 Africans in New England represented slightly more than 2 percent of the total, which was more than the combined numbers of Irish, Dutch, and Germans also living in New England at that time.

By 1775, this region contained a greater share of fifth- and sixth-generation Americans than the Middle or Southern Colonies. Most of these New England inhabitants had coalesced into reasonably unified communities, shaped in part by their consensus-driven town meetings that allowed widespread public participation in the discussion of local issues.

The Middle Colonies

The Middle Colonies were the most diverse of the three regions (see Figure 3.2). Here, the English, totaling almost 41 percent, did not

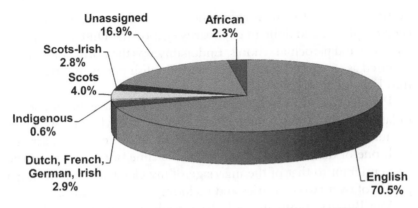

FIGURE 3.1   New England Colonies, Approximate Population in 1776

Source: U.S. Census Bureau, *Historical Statistics of the United States, Part II,* Series Z-20-132 (Washington, DC: U.S. Government Printing Office, 1976).

constitute a numerical majority. About 15 percent were German, and more than 12 percent were African. The Dutch, Scots, and Scots–Irish were each slightly more than 6 percent of the total. Notably, ethnic clannishness prevented any cohesive cultural evolution as occurred in New England.

Throughout the New York–New Jersey region, the Dutch remained socially insulated and maintained ethnic solidarity up through the Revolutionary period. Buoyed by their numbers (one in six residents in New York and New Jersey was Dutch), their culture

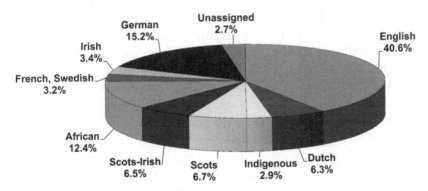

FIGURE 3.2   Middle Colonies, Approximate Population in 1776

Source: U.S. Census Bureau, *Historical Statistics of the United States, Part II,* Series Z-20-132 (Washington, DC: U.S. Government Printing Office, 1976).

flourished. Amid the steep-roofed houses—with double doors, blue-tiled fireplaces, and built-in cupboards—stood the Dutch Reformed churches and parochial schools. Endogamy was the norm, and Dutch endured as an everyday language, with English not even introduced into Dutch schools until 1774.

President Martin Van Buren illustrated Dutch endogamy and social isolation during the colonial and federal periods when he wrote in his autobiography that his family was "without a single intermarriage with one of different extraction from the time of the arrival of the first emigrant to that of the marriage of my eldest son, embracing a period of over two centuries and including six generations."[10]

Van Buren's comment could have applied to most of the Dutch families and other ethnics of his time. Fluent in Dutch, Van Buren was chided, rather unfairly, by critics such as John Randolph for his inability to "speak, or write, the English language correctly," a complaint often made today about newcomers.[11]

It was in Pennsylvania, the most heavily populated of the Middle Colonies with almost 300,000 residents, where the most ethnic and religious diversity existed on the eve of the Revolution. With its Quaker-inspired religious tolerance and liberal land policies serving as important lures, Pennsylvania superseded all other colonies in attracting a mixed group of non-English immigrants. In 1766, Benjamin Franklin reported to the House of Commons that the Germans and Scots-Irish each comprised one-third of Pennsylvania's population.

The Germans were splintered into numerous religious groupings. They were Lutherans, Reformed, or pietists: Quakers, Moravians, Mennonites, and Dunkers (Baptists). Like the Dutch, the different German groups lived in community clusters, persevering as vibrant, distinct subcultures. Countering German pacifist sentiments were Scots-Irish Presbyterians, whose fierce anti-Anglican feelings and swift alignment with the rebel cause were key elements in tipping the Pennsylvania colony into a revolutionary posture.

Although some, like the French Huguenots and Welsh, were quickly absorbed into the dominant Anglo-American mainstream, others, such as the Germans and Scots-Irish, created separate and distinct communities for themselves where they maintained cultural cohesiveness, despite their close proximity to other ethnic groups. United by their strong ethnic ties, they practiced a voluntary allegiance to their own distinct social groups. The Scots-Irish would eventually assimilate more quickly than the Germans, who remained clustered within a persistent subculture for several more generations.

In Delaware, the least populated colony with slightly more than 41,000, the Swedes were the second largest ethnic group, with about 9 percent of the total. Delaware was where the short-lived colony of New Sweden (1638–1655) existed before Dutch takeover. The English were clearly dominant, however, with 60 percent of the total, and the Scots were a close third at 8 percent.

The Southern Colonies

In the Southern Colonies, the English, at 37 percent of the total, also were in the numerical minority, but, as in the Middle Colonies, they were the largest single group. From a sociological viewpoint, they were the dominant group in terms of power and control in both regions.

Slavery made the Africans the largest group, at 39 percent (see Figure 3.3). Virginia, the most populated colony with more than a half-million inhabitants, had about two-fifths of all slaves in the region, but in South Carolina, the Africans outnumbered the Europeans. If we include the approximately 40,000 Native Americans estimated to be living in the Southern Colonies at the time, this figure makes the Southern Colonies the most racially diverse of the three regions. Here, the non-White population was about 42 percent, or two of five inhabitants. The remaining 21 percent of the inhabitants were non-English Whites. Numbering more than 300,000, they were mostly Scots, Scots-Irish, Germans, Irish, and French Huguenots.

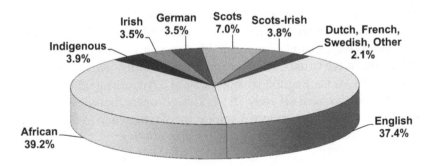

FIGURE 3.3 Southern Colonies, Approximate Population in 1776

Source: U.S. Census Bureau, *Historical Statistics of the United States, Part II,* Series Z-20-132 (Washington, DC: U.S. Government Printing Office, 1976).

African Diversity on the Plantations

Cultural diversity also existed among the African slaves, who came from different tribal backgrounds in western Africa—particularly Angola, the Gold Coast, Nigeria, and Senegambia. Because of this cultural mixing, no tribe or language group predominated, with the newly transported slaves speaking about 100 languages or dialects. The colonists, however, did not look on the Africans as a diverse group, instead viewing them as a single racial collectivity as well as less than human.

It was not simply the slave system that caused the colonists to ignore African diversity and generalize, because they did the same thing with Native Americans. Nor was it simply a racist response or a pre-modern lack of sophistication. Ingroup members typically generalize about outgroups, failing to note their diversity. Other examples of unnoticed diversity are when Americans a few generations ago viewed the many diverse people from central, southern, and Eastern Europe as a single entity or today generalize about all Asians or Hispanics.

In colonial times, the Africans adapted to their harsh new reality and, interacting with one another, soon overcame their tribal barriers through the process of ethnogenesis.[12] The Africans became bilingual, even trilingual, conversing in their native tongue to members of their tribe or language group and in broken English to their owners. To converse with other slaves in the Carolinas, the Africans created Gullah, a dialect amalgamating some English and many African words into an African grammatical structure.[13]

By the 1730s, an African American culture began to evolve that became more cohesive after the end of the legal slave trade in 1808. In a harsh, arbitrary world separated along racial lines, enslaved Blacks developed a peasant-like culture. Like European peasants, they, too, formed close-knit communities based on family and kinship, with religion as an important center of their lives. Although Gullah gradually faded away, many elements of African origin remained in music, dance, marriage rituals, and housing floor plans (front-to-back rooms instead of two rooms side by side in front). Africans held onto their incest taboo as well. Rarely did marriage occur between cousins, unlike such common practice among the slave owners, who usually did so to maintain inherited property and power.

Three Regional Cultures

By 1725, regional differences in the New England, Middle, and Southern Colonies led to distinct cultures evolving in each of these areas.[14] New England, with its unified farming societies, maintained a strong religious orientation. Its high educational standards, even in rural areas, resulted in a literacy rate of about 90 percent for men and 50 percent for women in 1790. Here, a more integrated society functioned and it shared, for the most part, a common ancestry.

In the Southern Colonies, a different culture emerged. Most adult White women and more than one-third of the White men could not read or write, not even their own names. Illiteracy occurred because a large number of White people, mostly tenant and small, independent farmers, lived in poverty and had little or no formal schooling. A small aristocratic elite ruled over this socially stratified and racially divided region, with its ethnically distinct backcountry inhabitants, for whom education was a low priority.

Within the Middle Colonies, the ethnic clannishness of the diverse groups prevented any cohesive regional culture from developing. Thus, 18th-century colonial America was literally a multicultural place, a fact frequently commented upon by European visitors and congressional representatives in the 1790s, who noted the significant cultural differences among the three regions.

Throughout the three regions, regional residence and social class greatly affected the quality of women's lives. Most spun thread and made clothing, candles, and soap, but rural women had to be even more self-sufficient in a variety of productive tasks. These tasks might include milking goats or cows, churning butter, working in the fields, or other farm chores.[15]

Women in affluent families had servants to do menial tasks while they devoted their free time to such activities as playing a musical instrument, creating fine embroidery, or perhaps reading good books, particularly Scripture. Working-class women more likely produced goods for sale (cheese, cloth, shoes, yarn) or rendered services (working as cooks, domestics, or possibly servers at inns, restaurants, or taverns).

Ethnic background was another important variable in determining women's place in the social order. Those of English descent were most likely to be found indoors, either engaged in duties in and about the house or, if working class, in such public establishments as those mentioned previously. Those ethnic groups living even just a short distance away from these English-dominated settlements—the Germans, Scots-Irish, and French-Canadians especially—would normally have their women performing a variety of agricultural tasks, as they worked in the barns, fields, meadows, and stables, wherever they were needed.[16]

RELIGIOUS DIVERSITY

Religious diversity was another significant component of cultural pluralism throughout colonial America. Religion played a major role in colonial life, from its importance as a force for initial settlement by many different Christian groups to its influence on the everyday lives of the settlers. Clergy were highly honored members of the community, and their advice extended beyond spiritual matters to include economic and political concerns, as well as gender relations.

Religious values—echoing such teachings as Paul's assertion that "wives should submit to their husbands in everything" (Ephesians 5:24)—greatly influenced social norms in colonial communities. When Anne Hutchinson, a middle-aged midwife and wife of a merchant, challenged both her subordinate status and the traditional teachings of Puritan clergymen by holding weekly prayer meetings in her house, she was banished in 1637 for heresy. Ann Hopkins, wife of the colonial governor of Connecticut, had been a voracious reader and written many books, but died deranged, causing Massachusetts Governor John Winthrop to declare,

> For if she had attended her household affairs and such things as belong to women, and not gone out of her way and calling to meddle in such things as are proper for men, whose minds are stronger, etc., she had kept her wits and might have improved them usefully and honorably in the place God had set her.[17]

Most women were the socialized products of their times and did not challenge the pervasive male authority promulgated by the clergy. Illustrative is *The Well-Ordered Family* (1712), in which its author, Reverend Benjamin Wadsworth, counsels his female readers,

> Though possibly thou hast greater abilities of mind than he has, want of some high birth, and he has a more Mean Extract; or didst bring more estate at Marriage than he did; yet since he is thy Husband, God has made him the head and set him over thee.[18]

What a woman could only do, he admonished, was to fulfill her "duty to love and reverence him."

Religious Intolerance

Seventeenth-century religion was an all-encompassing force that helped people to endure the hardships and sacrifices of daily life in settlements. Moreover, colonial religiosity instilled a narrow, intolerant view of other faiths. The expulsion of Roger Williams and Anne Hutchinson from the Massachusetts colony as religious dissidents is well known. Less known is the fact that many colonies at this time enacted discriminatory legislation against Catholics and Jews, usually by banning their immigration or right to vote.

Seventeenth-century English settlers were mostly Puritan in New England, Anglican in the South, and a variety of religious sects in the Middle Colonies, reflecting the population diversity and liberal stance of the governments, particularly in Pennsylvania. The American beginnings of the Baptist Church commenced in 1639 in Rhode Island with Roger Williams. After that time, Baptists became the most persecuted sect in New England for the rest of the century. Fines, beatings, and whippings were not uncommon. Not until 1708 could Baptists legally have a house of worship in Connecticut. In contrast, Baptists thrived in the more tolerant Middle Colonies, establishing in Philadelphia by 1700 the strongest Baptist center in the colonies. When the 1691 Massachusetts charter extended "liberty of conscience" to all Christians, including Baptists, it specifically excluded "Papists" (Catholics).

Dislike of Catholics was one common ground on which all the Protestants could agree. The Presbyterians, Baptists, Quakers, German Reformed, and Lutherans along the "frontier" were intolerant of one another, yet often shared a strong dislike of Anglicans. The Anglicans, strongest in Virginia but prevalent throughout the South, disdainfully looked down on the New England Puritans, while the New Englanders reciprocated and jealously guarded their communities against the Anglicans achieving any inroads.

By the 18th century, secular forces lessened the force of religion, although it remained an important social influence. A lessening of religious devotion and church attendance, together with the advance of humanitarianism and rationalism in this Age of Enlightenment, combined to make this so. As a consequence, religious tolerance increased, but only slightly. There were still conflicts to come.

The Great Awakening

A momentous, far-reaching religious revival movement in the 1740s, known as the Great Awakening, brought even more conflict and diversity onto the American religious scene.[19] It was initiated by Massachusetts preacher Jonathan Edwards (1703–1758), who proclaimed that an individual's "born again" spiritual awakening was strong evidence of a predestined life of heavenly bliss. Other clergy picked up this theme, but the most influential was George Whitefield (1714–1770), an eloquent English evangelist who tirelessly and effectively spread this message of revivalism from Maine to Georgia.

The new movement generated much bitterness between "Old Light" traditionalists and the "New Light" evangelists. The emotional preaching and theme of individual salvation through the Bible appealed to many and challenged the formal services and conservatism of the churches dominated by the elite. The movement spread rapidly, with memberships increasing dramatically among the evangelical sects. Baptists benefited the most from these gains, often at the expense of Anglicans and Congregationalists. The Great Awakening also caused schisms in the Congregationalist, Dutch Reformed, and Presbyterian churches, further increasing the bitterness of the established churches against the dissenting sects.

Significantly, the Great Awakening brought democratization to religion as the general public gained a larger voice in the church. In doing so, it strengthened the trend toward liberty of conscience as it raised fundamental questions about the nature of God and human behavior, about moral and political authority, and about economic comportment. Another interesting consequence was that revivalists boldly went into any hospitable church regardless of creed. Thus, they helped break down provincial barriers to create a more unified evangelical Protestantism that became part of the American character. Furthermore, the Great Awakening reinforced strong community values held by Americans outside the coastal towns and cities.

During this tumultuous religious period, every major Christian sect, concerned about preserving its faith and transmitting its values and beliefs to future generations, took steps to ensure its survival. Each established its own college to educate new clergy and, as historian Daniel J. Boorstin stated, "to save more Americans from the untruths of its competitors."[20]

The Legacy of Religious Pluralism

No single religion dominated, and the proliferation of sects and the growth of religious enthusiasm in 18th-century America produced an unplanned and often undesired religious tolerance. Religious pluralism slowly, sometimes painfully, led to tolerance because no one group was powerful enough to coerce the others. One example is the early creation of interdenominational boards of trustees at the previously mentioned denominational colleges, partially in response to the reality that no single sect could supply its entire student body from the limited population base in its area.

United by their nationalism after winning their war for independence, the colonists put aside their prejudices by institutionalizing that tolerance and establishing a bedrock principle of U.S. culture: separation of church and state. Freedom of religion was more an act of practical necessity than of democratic ideals. It is one legacy from America's multicultural past.

A KALEIDOSCOPE SOCIETY

Some historians have found colorful expressions to describe the diversity of colonial America on the eve of the Revolution (see Map 3.1). Michael Kammen called it an "invertebrate" society composed of disconnected religious, ethnic, and racial groups lacking a "figurative spinal column."[21] James Stuart Olson described the colonies in 1776 as "a cultural kaleidoscope of three races and dozens of ethnic and religious groups."[22]

English Americans may have held political power in the 13 colonies, but they constituted less than half the total population. In the Middle and Southern Colonies, they were decisively outnumbered by the combined racial and ethnic groups and in South Carolina by African slaves alone. However, the Anglo-Americans were the dominant group: They held political and economic power and were backed by the English military. Their language and culture constituted the mainstream, but the English did not force other White ethnics to assimilate, allowing them instead to retain their own schools to teach their children in their native languages.

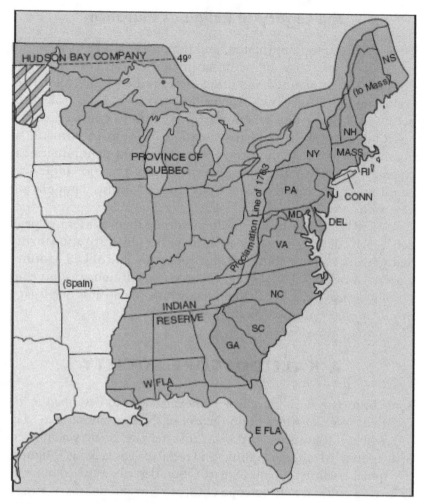

MAP 3.1 United States in 1775

Minority Separatism

Ethnic colonials thus lived under this tolerant English rule, typically residing apart in culturally distinct ethnic communities. If geographically isolated, they also remained culturally insulated. If living within the English American cities, they adapted as urban ethnics always have, but also retained many vestiges of their ethnicity and maintained an ingroup solidarity among their own kind.

Native Americans also desired to live among their own kind and maintain their way of life, but, unlike White ethnics, they were not left alone to do so. African Americans, mostly enslaved, had no voice in their own welfare, but, within the slave communities, they developed their own subculture. Although relegated to a subjugated existence, racial diversity remained a reality in colonial America.

The separate White groups gave at least grudging tolerance to one another, united as they were in their fear and defense against the native peoples and the French. Later, with the threat from England, they put aside their differences to fight for their freedom and to maintain their rights through local politics.

The Multicultural Revolutionary Army

The success of Washington's troops in defeating the English lies partly in the multicultural elite, who played key roles in military training, strategy, and leadership. Baron Friedrich Wilhelm von Steuben (Prussia), Gen. Casimer Pulaski and Gen. Thaddeus Kosciuszko (Poland), and Marquis de Lafayette and Baron de Kalb (France) were the most prominent volunteers from Europe who were of great value to the American cause, although de Kalb's death in 1780 at the Battle of Camden, South Carolina, was a major blow to American efforts to recapture the South at the time.

Just as the military leadership consisted of non-English individuals, so, too, did the ranks of fighting men. More than 5,000 Blacks served in the colonial forces, fighting in every major battle from Lexington in 1775 to Yorktown in 1781. Some distinguished themselves in combat, such as Peter Salem and Salem Poore at the Battle of Bunker Hill and Lemuel Haynes at the Battle of Fort Ticonderoga. James Lafayette, a Virginia slave, was so effective in gaining strategic intelligence about the English for Lafayette's troops that the Virginia Assembly purchased his freedom as a reward.

Patriotic groups formed within ethnic communities, often cooperating or even merging with similar non-ethnic groups out of necessity. Numerous ethnic communities recruited their own companies or regiments, staffed with their own officers. Soon they mixed with other ethnic groups or those of English ancestry as they united against a common enemy. Then the cultural barriers and suspicions between groups faded as they shared common dangers, common hardships, and, ultimately, common victories.

THE NEXT HORIZON

The American Revolution would have both obvious and subtle consequences. Most obvious would be the birth of a nation, but one of the subtle outcomes would be the gradual acculturation of the ethnic minorities of that time. Scots-Irish and French Huguenots, both Calvinists who adapted easily to the individualistic, success-oriented society developing in the English colonies, would assimilate quickly. They did not maintain the ethnic isolation of the Dutch and Germans, whose cultural pluralism endured, but even for these ethnics, the cultural barriers and social distance would be reduced.

A process of cultural homogenization among the Whites would begin, bolstered by the attempt to build a national identity, but that widespread homogenization would be short-lived. The catalyst then, however, was the new nation's audacious declaration that leaders ruled only by the consent of the governed and that all men were created equal and entitled to life, liberty, and the pursuit of happiness.

Those rights and privileges were not yet to be fully extended to women and racial minorities, but the promise of freedom and opportunity would soon attract thousands of hopeful others. Ethnic communities would be revitalized and new ones would form, rejuvenating diversity in a land where it had always flourished.

NOTES

1. Mildred Campbell, "Social Origins of Some Early Americans," in *Seventeenth-Century America,* ed. James M. Smith (Chapel Hill: University of North Carolina Press, 1959), p. 63.

2. Stephen Steinberg, *The Ethnic Myth,* 3d ed. (Boston: Beacon Press, 2001), p. 10.

3. Bruce Catton and William B. Catton, *The Bold and Magnificent Dream: America's Founding Years, 1492–1815* (New York: Gramercy, 1999), pp. 165, 166, 168.

4. Lawrence H. Fuchs, *The American Kaleidoscope: Race, Ethnicity, and the Civic Culture* (Hanover, NH: Wesleyan University Press of New England, 1990), p. 12.

5. Maxine S. Seller, *To Seek America: A History of Ethnic Life in the United States* (Englewood, NJ: Jerome S. Ozer, 1988), p. 37.

6. Steinberg, *The Ethnic Myth,* p. 8.

7. Gary B. Nash, ed., *Class and Society in Early America* (Englewood Cliffs, NJ: Prentice-Hall, 1970), p. 19.

8. Gary B. Nash, *The Urban Crucible: The Northern Seaports and the Origins of the American Revolution* (Cambridge, MA: Harvard University Press, 1987).

9. U.S. Census Bureau, *Historical Statistics of the United States, Part II* (Washington, DC: U.S. Government Printing Office, 1976), pp. 1168–72.

10. Ted Widmer, *Martin Van Buren* (New York: Henry Holt and Company, 2005), p. 22.

11. See John C. Fitzpatrick, ed., *The Autobiography of Martin Van Buren* (New York: DaCapo, 1973), p. 9.

12. See Richard D. Alba, "Models for Viewing American Catholicism," chap. 1 in *Italian Americans: Into the Twilight of Ethnicity* (Englewood Cliffs, NJ: Prentice Hall, 1985), pp. 9–12.

13. See Carl Bridenbaugh, *Myths and Realities: Societies of the Colonial South,* reprint ed. (Westport, CT: Greenwood Press, 1981).

14. Lawrence H. Fuchs, "True Americanism: The Foundations of the Civic Culture," chap. 1 in Fuchs, *The American Kaleidoscope.*

15. See Merril D. Smith, *Women's Roles in Seventeenth-Century America* (Westport, CT: Greenwood Press, 2008).

16. Nash, *Class and Society in Early America.*

17. Perry Miller and Thomas H. Johnson, eds., *The Puritans: A Sourcebook of Their Writings* (Toronto: General Publishing Company, 2001), p. 140.

18. Quoted in Oliver Steinert-Lieschied, *Margaret Fuller's Concept of "Gender" in the Context of Her Time* (Munich: GRIN Publishing, 2007) p. 29.

19. Thomas S. Kidd, *The Great Awakening: The Roots of Evangelical Christianity in Colonial America* (New Haven, CT: Yale University Press, 2007).

20. Daniel J. Boorstin, *The Americans: The Colonial Experience* (New York: Vintage, 1964), p. 179.

21. Michael Kammen, *People of Paradox: An Inquiry Concerning the Origins of American Civilization* (Ithaca, NY: Cornell University Press, 1990), p. 57.

22. James Stuart Olson, *The Ethnic Dimension in American History* (New York: St. Martin's Press, 1994), p. 51.

4

Diversity in the Early National Period

One great object of the Constitution was to restrain majorities from oppressing minorities or encroaching upon their just rights.

—*President James K. Polk*

"Scene at the Signing of the Constitution of the United States" by Howard Chandler Christy (1940) depicts that moment at the Constitution Convention in Independence Hall in Philadelphia in 1787. It is one of the most famous paintings about that era.

C ultural differences were put aside in the fight for independence, bringing previously isolated groups together in the common cause, reducing the social distance between groups, and lessening cultural barriers. Another effect was disruption in the traditional division of labor and status between the sexes. Military service caused the absence of husbands, older brothers, or fathers, thereby requiring thousands of women to assume major responsibility for managing the shops or farms. Thrust into such unexpected roles, women grew in decision-making skills and self-confidence in their leadership ability.

Traditional gender role expectations returned after the war, but the brief emancipation of women did not fade completely. Although their social and political subjugation continued during the early national period, the struggle for independence had sown seeds in women's minds. Many women, for example, freely discussed political issues in letters and social conversations, much to the dismay of the men. Complaining that the men thought women had no business talking about politics, Eliza Wilkinson wrote in 1783, "I won't have it thought that because we are the weaker sex as to bodily strength we are capable of nothing more than domestic concerns. They won't even allow us liberty of thought, and that is all I want."[1]

Although gender relations did not advance much, another social process was evolving. Cultural homogenization, begun with the intermingling of ethnic soldiers and support groups during the American Revolution, continued at a rapid pace between 1783 and 1820. These years were crucial in the development of the American political tradition and a common culture. American leaders made strong efforts on many fronts to establish a civic culture and socialize the population into following common tenets.

THE LARGER CONTEXT

The United States' place in the world system at this time went from that of a colonial periphery to that of a semi-peripheral republic. The first U.S. consul outside the Western Hemisphere was Samuel Shaw, assigned to Canton in 1794. In fact, China played a role in early U.S. history, as New England merchants sought a monopoly on the lucrative China trade, an issue that became important in the struggle for American independence. Chinese sailors served on U.S. ships in the early 1800s, and a short-lived Chinese colony was established at Nootka Sound in 1792.[2]

Even as it attempted to forge what would become a distinct culture, and even though the dynamics of open land and upward mobility opportunities would shape an anything-is-possible mind-set among many, global events still affected the new society. Turmoil in France created political turmoil in the United States, as Federalists and Jeffersonians engaged in fierce rhetoric about the excesses of the French Revolution. A few years later, as France and England declared embargoes on one another, the United States was drawn into the conflict. After the British navy captured more than 400 U.S. merchant ships and forcibly impressed more than 10,000 U.S. seamen into its own navy, a new political faction—the War Hawks, led by Henry Clay—demanded a declaration of war against England.

Aiding their cause was the brutal violence in the Ohio River Valley, where Indian tribes that had backed the British during the Revolutionary War now attacked and killed many American settlers. Tacitly supported by the British seeking dominance in the lucrative fur trade, the Indians—uniting under the leadership of Tecumseh—fought for an independent Indian nation. Anger at England's actions on the high seas and in supporting the Indians led to the War of 1812; France and the United States were again allies in fighting the British. Eventually, the war ended in a stalemate, with the only losers those killed and the Indians, whose dream of an independent nation was dashed in military defeat.

A minority group's armed conflict and the actions of two European powers were just a few of the forces affecting U.S. society. Others included advances in ship design, making travel faster, and the further spread of the Industrial Revolution; both would affect migration, trade, and the economy.

BUILDING A NATIONAL IDENTITY

Throughout the new nation, a surge of patriotic pride prompted the severing of Old World ties in ways other than political. For example, in such areas as arts and letters, language usage, and religious authority, a distinctly American form emerged. National myth-building, glorification of revolutionary heroes, and shaping of the public mind into a shared value orientation became part of building the nation.

Arts and Letters

The first American play was a 1787 comedy dealing with American life. In *The Contrast,* playwright Royall Tyler's contrast was between

American worth and the affectation of foreign manners. His character "Jonathan"—the shrewd, yet uncultivated New England farmer—evolved into the "Stage Yankee" and served as a model for many editorial cartoonists for depicting the "real" American for about 200 years.[3]

Songs, poems, and essays mostly appeared in the early federal years, but Washington Irving wrote one of the first pieces of imaginative prose in 1809. Interestingly, it was about an ethnic group, the Dutch. Called *A History of New York,* by Diedrich Knickerbocker, it is a delightful parody, now a classic of American humor and an early example of creative writing distinctly American in form and content. Painters, sculptors, and other writers lionized the new national heroes and practically deified George Washington. Books about U.S. history, not English, and other books containing American essays began to appear. The Fourth of July became a national holiday as a cause for celebration and part of the concerted effort to build a national identity.

In Jefferson's inaugural address on March 1, 1801, he asserted that common identity when he stated, "We are all republicans—we are all federalists." As the first political opponent in world history to replace a rival power as a national leader through a peaceful election process, Jefferson affirmed the new reality.[4]

Linguistic Independence

In 1783, a native-born Connecticut Yankee, Noah Webster, gave American English a dignity and vitality of its own when he published the *American Spelling Book,* which became commonly known as the "Blue-Backed Speller." The book legitimized American English and provided Webster with most of his income for the rest of his life. The book, never out of print, had total sales exceeding 100 million copies.

Webster followed with a grammar book (1784) and a reader (1785) with mostly American writings about democratic ideals and dutiful moral and political conduct. In 1828, he published the two-volume *An American Dictionary of the English Language,* and all 2,500 American copies sold out within a year. Advocating the superiority of language usage by the American commoner over the so-called artificiality of London, Webster successfully worked to have American language declare its independence from England.[5]

Religious Independence

Another manifestation of evolution into a distinctly American culture was in religion. One by one, the ethnic Protestant churches created local governing bodies to replace previous overseas authorities. Anglican churches, for example, renouncing allegiance to the Church of England, reorganized as the Protestant Episcopalian Church of America. Even conservative churches took this path. Dutch Reformed churches insisted on approving ministers ordained in Europe before they could preach from American pulpits. The German Lutheran Ministerium of Pennsylvania—a region previously mentioned as home of the largest German population—required a 3-year probationary period for European-trained ministers before they could be accredited for permanent assignment.[6]

In colonial times, there had been only about 25,000 Catholics, most of them living in Maryland, ostracized and out of the mainstream. After independence, Catholics established a special U.S. liaison to the Vatican, headed by Bishop John Carroll in Baltimore. He pioneered in exploring positive relations between Catholics and their Protestant fellow citizens, seeking to overcome the exclusion of Catholics, then so common in many colonies, especially where Congregational or Episcopal churches were supported by law. The actions of various Protestant denominations to sever Old World ties and of Catholics to seek a dialogue with Protestants contributed toward a further lessening of religious separatism. It would be short-lived, however. Beginning in 1820, the first wave of immigration to the new nation would revive the ebbing ethnoreligious differences. The influx of millions of Catholic immigrants would launch the Protestant Crusade, as nativist suspicion and hostility effectively countered these early ecumenical efforts.

SOCIAL STRUCTURE AND SOCIAL CLASS

The wealth and social status of 18th-century Americans varied according to where they lived: the frontier, small farm communities, commercial farm communities, or urban societies. Only a few individuals of considerable means might be found in the frontier or small farm communities, but the commercial farm communities contained larger concentrations of wealthy people in possession of large properties. Cities, whether small or major centers, typically contained a larger and richer wealthy class, in control of a greater proportion of the property, than in the other three communities.

On average, about one-third of the White population living in the North in the Revolutionary era was poor. Large property owners comprised about 30 percent, and small property owners almost as much. The wealthy elite comprised about 10 percent, a large proportion of them merchants benefiting from the growth and commercialization of port towns and their investments in city real estate.[7]

Lines of economic division and marks of social status, already evident prior to the Revolution, crystallized further afterward. As Gary B. Nash observed,

> This social transformation is statistically measurable, though we can never obtain mathematical precision in these matters, given the selective survival of documents. In the inventories of estate and tax lists lies the silent record of the redefinition of class categories. Most notable is the parallel emergence of the fabulously wealthy and the desperately poor.[8]

Within the cities, this growing void between the elite and the laboring class became more evident with the increase in urban mansions and four-wheeled carriages. Cities were less the repositories of ethnic Americans than they were of an economically stratified order of English Americans. Cultural pluralism was to be found in distinct sub-communities outside the cities, more often in rural and frontier communities.

Among the working-class, rural, and frontier families, the women continued working at many tasks that the genteel ladies of the mercantile and upper classes did not. However, almost all women shared one commonality, regardless of social class or residence. They married at a young age, had many children, and were usually grandmothers by the time they were 40. By 1820, the number of children under age 5 per 1,000 women between the ages of 20 and 44 was 1,295, about triple what it is today. Childrearing, keeping of home and hearth, and working in the fields if you were a farmer's wife were the areas of responsibility for most women. Only 6 percent of the women were in paid employment outside the home. For most women, the house— perhaps the farm—was their world, their reality, and their fate.[9]

RELIGION, POWER, AND GROUP CONSCIOUSNESS

In time, increased diversity and a political system allowing for freedom of choice prompted many changes involving religion. As more non-English Americans gained political power, they only supported dominant-group politicians promoting religious equality and sought to punish those who did not.

Religion and Politics

In the previous chapter, I mentioned that the doctrine of separation of church and state was a consequence of religious diversity. In all of New England except Rhode Island, however, the Congregational Church maintained its privileged position and public support from tax revenues. This close church–state relationship, made possible because of the predominance of English Americans in that region, remained until the 1830s.

Complete separation of church and state was not exactly the case in most other states either, at least when it came to qualifications to run for office. Full political rights were bestowed only on Protestant Christians. Some states were even more specific. Delaware required belief in the Trinity; North Carolina and Pennsylvania stipulated belief in the divine inspiration of both Testaments; New Jersey allowed only Protestants conforming to certain religious beliefs; and New York mandated elected office could be held only by Christians who renounced all foreign rulers, whether civil or ecclesiastical, thereby eliminating Catholics and Jews.

The Virginia planter elite, as members of the Anglican/Episcopalian Church, had long dominated the political scene despite frequent conflicts with Baptists and Presbyterians. So when Virginians Thomas Jefferson and James Madison led the successful struggle to secure separation of church and state, their efforts brought these men the enduring support of ethnic Americans throughout their political careers.

In a second Virginia action with national consequences, the state legislature rejected a bill supported by George Washington and Patrick Henry for a "general assessment" tax to provide funds for all religious groups. Jefferson then successfully sponsored a state bill in 1786 that endorsed the principle of individual liberty of conscience in religious matters, made all churches equal before the law, and stipulated no direct financial support to any religion. Jefferson considered passage of this religious liberty statute (a precursor of the national principle) as one of his three major achievements and had it so inscribed on his tombstone.

In Pennsylvania, that old critic of the Germans, Benjamin Franklin, joined with Robert Morris and Dr. Benjamin Rush to rally German support for the new constitution by endorsing the establishment of a German-sponsored college. Appreciative Germans named the institution Franklin College. Franklin further endeared himself to the various German denominations when he successfully led the opposition in overturning the "Test Act," which required several religious oaths as a prerequisite to holding any office.

In contrast, Rufus King, the American minister to London, was one of the more vocal opponents of Irish Catholic immigration to the United States. His protests that the country wanted no more "hordes of wild Irishmen" because they would "disfigure our true national character" were printed in the Irish American press.[10] Offended ethnics can have long memories. When King ran for the presidency against James Monroe in 1816, the Irish voted against him en masse and reveled in his defeat.

Parallel Religious Institutions

In the late 18th century, two groups of northern African Americans illustrated the conflict view of a rising group consciousness promoting social change from their previously accepted subordinate status. No doubt the new national doctrine of equality and the assertiveness of American churches against European dominance influenced two religious Black groups, who were fed up by subtle and overt forms of racism within the integrated churches they attended, to split from these churches.

In 1787, a group of African Americans withdrew from St. George's Methodist Episcopal Church in Philadelphia and formed their own congregation. They built their own church (Bethel) in Philadelphia, had their first ordained minister by 1799, and formally organized as the African Methodist Episcopalian (A.M.E.) Church in 1816. Today, their membership exceeds 2.5 million members.[11]

The origins of the African Methodist Episcopal Zion Church, a different entity, trace back to 1796, when the African American members of the John Street Methodist Church in New York City terminated their membership. They, too, formed their own congregation, built their first church (Zion) in 1800, and formally organized in 1821. Today, their church membership exceeds 1.4 million members.[12]

The creation of these separate churches was by no means the first or the last instance of minority groups establishing parallel social institutions. Because racial discrimination is more likely than ethnic discrimination to be a multigenerational reality, these Black churches became part of a larger pattern of racial segregation and isolation that would continue for generations, unlike ethnic churches that often ceased to exist after a few generations. Both Black churches, as their memberships attest, remain viable today.

THE NATION'S FIRST CENSUS

The 1790 census, with the exceptions of the survey of England conducted in 1086 during the reign of William the Conqueror and the registering of people in Sweden in 1749, was the first national counting of a population in a Western country.[13] That first U.S. census revealed a decidedly rural society. Only 3 percent lived in cities of 8,000 or more residents, and only 5 percent lived in towns of 2,500 or more. Most Americans lived in much smaller communities, sometimes in ethnic enclaves where Old World languages and customs still prevailed.

If we rely only on the commonly reported census data of 1790 (see Figure 4.1), we can fall into the trap of the cultural homogeneity myth. These data emphasize that the English, Scots, and Scots-Irish comprised 75.2 percent of the White ethnic population. This grouping makes some sense because, by then, these previously distinct cultural groups had begun to coalesce into a White-Anglo-Saxon-Protestant (WASP) collectivity. Moreover, as the culturally dominant group, they became the essence of the new national identity and remain to this day the reference group for comparison with subsequent demographic changes.

This Eurocentric view is misleading, however, because it ignores the actual diversity that prevailed, thus creating the origins for the Dillingham Flaw. It is one thing to speak of the culturally dominant group, but quite another to generalize about the entire population to argue for cultural homogeneity.

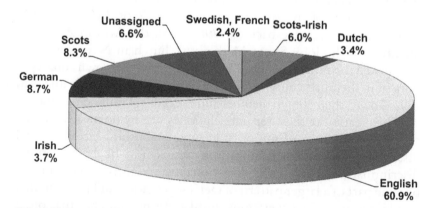

FIGURE 4.1 White Population Distribution in 1790

Source: U.S. Census Bureau, *Historical Statistics of the United States, Part II,* Series Z-20-132 (Washington, DC: U.S. Government Printing Office, 1976).

The Other Side of the Coin

If 75 percent of the White population was WASP, then 25 percent was not. This percentage of one in four individuals constituted approximately 793,000 people of the 3.1 million total population. Who were these non-Anglo-Saxon 25 percent? They were Dutch, French, German, Irish, and Swedish mostly, and they remained distinguishable in language and/or lifestyle from Anglo-Americans. In smaller numbers, they also were Belgian, Danish, Flemish, Italian, Norwegian, Polish, and Swiss, plus scatterings from many other countries. Together, they were the ethnically diverse population segment that did not fit into the WASP category and so contradict the false portrait of a new nation peopled almost entirely by Anglo-Americans.

With so many Americans from ethnoreligious and linguistically diverse groups living outside the mainstream, any discussion of late 18th- and early 19th-century Americans as alike becomes an application of the Dillingham Flaw. Too much cultural heterogeneity within socially isolated subcultural groups prevailed at this time. Too many differences in economic and political power, in social status and stratification, and in lifestyle and outlook comprising this period contradict erroneous generalizations about cultural consistency within a supposedly homogeneous population.

Yet it is not just that too many people forget about the many White ethnic Americans living in this era. These commonly reported data distort the past even more because they do not include racial minorities.

Eurocentric Use of Census Data

When we move past the Eurocentric presentation of the 1790 census data to include non-Whites, we acquire a more complete understanding of the extensive diversity in America at that time.[14] By doing so, we not only find a smaller proportion in society of dominant Anglo-Saxon groups, but also we can further dispel mistaken assumptions about our past that enable the Dillingham Flaw to affect past–present comparisons.

Census tabulations in 1790 counted 757,208 African Americans, including about 60,000 non-slaves, living primarily in the North. This figure increases the total population to 3.9 million, of whom 1.5 million are not WASPs. Thus, instead of the 25 percent of American society previously identified as not fitting the mold of an Anglo-Saxon populace, the figure becomes 38 percent.

We can go higher if we include Native Americans. They may not have been included in the census, nor protected by the Constitution, nor even then considered part of American society, but they were nonetheless part of the total population. Most may have lived apart from the Whites, but they still lived within the states' boundaries and were a factor in trade, land disputes, and warfare.

Exact numbers on Native Americans in 1790 are not available. According to many anthropologists, a conservative estimate of those living east of the Mississippi River at this time is about 70,000. Adding that number to our previous numbers, we reach a total U.S. population of approximately 4 million people.

Until the 1870 tabulations, we learn nothing from the U.S. Census Bureau about the Asian presence because it does not enumerate them until then. However, we learn from immigration records that their numbers were few until the 1850s, totaling just 89 between 1820 and 1840, about two-thirds of them from India and the rest from China.[15] As a result, the Asian population was not yet a major factor during the early national period.

Still, if we include all the people living in what was the United States in 1790—African, Asian, European, and Native American— we find that about 40 percent were not Anglo-Americans (Figure 4.2). This scenario is hardly the picture many Americans have today about that time period. In 1790, two of five Americans were out-group members whose race and/or culture set them apart from the dominant group of Anglo-American Protestants.

What makes the above information even more astounding is its comparison to the Census 2010 data. This 40 percent statistic far exceeds the 12 percent foreign-born population in 2010 and an additional 11 percent of the native-born population with at least

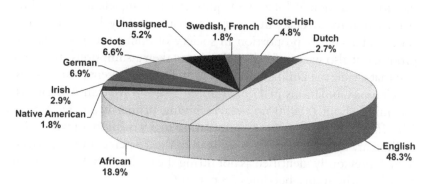

FIGURE 4.2 Total Population Distribution in 1790

Source: Interpolated from U.S. Census Bureau, *Historical Statistics of the United States, Part II,* Series Z-20-132 (Washington, DC: U.S. Government Printing Office, 1976).

one foreign-born parent. It also exceeds the 2010 combined total population of Asians (5 percent), Blacks (14 percent), Hispanics (16 percent), and Native Americans (1 percent). Clearly, our multiracial and multicultural present is a continuation of widespread diversity also found in 1790.

EXPANDING TERRITORY AND DIVERSITY

Between 1783 and 1820, the United States doubled its size. Each expanse, the result of diplomatic treaties, brought even greater cultural diversity within the nation's changing borders. Tens of thousands of farmers moved into the Northwest Territory (later Ohio, Indiana, Illinois, Michigan, and Wisconsin), where 57 percent of the White population in 1790 was French, reflecting that nation's prior control of this region. Only 30 percent were English, the smallest proportion anywhere in land claimed by the United States. Germans and Scots each accounted for about 4 percent, the Scots-Irish for 3 percent, and the Irish for about 2 percent. Clearly, this region possessed significant White ethnic diversity.

This westward migration—into lands inhabited by the Shawnee, Chippewa, Ottawa, and Potawatomi—brought frequent conflict into the Northwest Territory. The warfare ended with federal troops led by General "Mad Anthony" Wayne defeating the Western Indian Confederacy at the Battle of Fallen Timber in 1794. Another effort by a new confederacy leader, Tecumseh, to stop White encroachment of Native American lands was stopped at the Battle of Tippecanoe Creek in 1811, thereby sealing the fate of Native Americans with eviction from their ancestral lands.

In 1803, Jefferson's purchase of the Louisiana Territory (865,000 square miles of dazzling country) resulted in the incorporation of towns and settlements with a mostly French-speaking population into the United States (see Map 4.1). French influence in architecture, language, and culture, including Catholicism, remained vibrant in the Mississippi Delta, and its presence is still felt today. Also absorbed were many new Native American tribes, many of them encountered by Meriwether Lewis and William Clark in their expedition to chart the new U.S. region.

Another acquisition—the forced ceding of Florida to the United States in 1819—brought the Seminole and some Spanish inhabitants under U.S. authority. By 1820, the United States differed greatly from its 1783 beginnings. Twice as large as before, its newest territories

MAP 4.1 United States in 1810

Source: U.S. Census Bureau, *Historical Statistics of the United States, Part II*, Series Z-20-132 (Washington, DC: Government Printing Office, 1976).

contained mostly French, Spanish, and Native Americans. In fact, some of the new regions had no Anglo-American presence at all.

THE DROP IN IMMIGRATION

About 250,000 new immigrants came to the United States between 1790 and 1820. Because no detailed records were kept, we can assume that these newcomers were in reasonable proportion to the nationalities of those already living in the United States, thus suggesting that about three-fourths of the new arrivals were British. Two other nationalities also came in significant numbers. About 25,000 were French-speaking immigrants, not refugees from the French Revolution, but mostly from the French islands in the Caribbean, where slave uprisings caused an exodus of almost the entire White population. Thousands of others were Irish revolutionaries fleeing the failure of a major rebellion begun in 1798 against English rule.

Despite the arrival of political refugees, U.S. immigration was low at this time, averaging only 8,300 annually. One factor related to the drop in immigration was an English law passed in 1788, prohibiting the emigration of skilled artisans from Ireland and England. Then in 1803, England drastically lowered the maximum number of passengers permitted on a ship, thereby reducing the profit margin for shipping companies. The resulting higher fares lessened the demand for indentured servants because increased costs were passed on to purchasers of the indentured contracts.

Consequently, this form of migration decreased. Other European countries also tried to restrict the emigration of skilled artisans, as well as men of military age. Furthermore, the French Revolution and Napoleonic Wars (1802–1815), which eventually embroiled the United States in the War of 1812, disrupted European travel. Uncertainties and political turmoil in the United States between Federalists and Republicans also reduced the attraction of emigration.

THE SIGNIFICANCE OF NATURAL POPULATION GROWTH

Although immigration lessened between 1790 and 1820, the nation's population increased significantly from 3.9 million to 9.6 million in that same period. Only a small fraction was due to the territorial expansion because population growth primarily occurred in the older territories and states. Natural increase from high birth rates and the tendency to have large families were the main reasons for this rise in population. This growth spurt of mostly "American stock," itself a composite of many ethnic groups, enabled cultural homogeneity to evolve to a degree never before attained and never again realized after 1820. Without a significant influx of new ethnics to reinvigorate the ethnic communities, a new generation emerged with a new identity. Reared by parents who lived through the Revolution, taught in schools where all things American were emphasized, and attending churches where clergy preached about God's blessings upon America, these children were the first to be socialized into the newly developing U.S. culture.

EMERGENCE OF A COMMON CULTURE

Two other factors helped break down the walls of ethnic isolationism. First, fewer new arrivals meant no renewal of ethnic subcultures, thereby allowing acculturation of ethnic Americans to proceed unimpeded. Second, as western expansion continued, helped in part by lands given to Revolutionary soldiers in lieu of cash, many ethnic enclaves broke up as individuals and families left their old communities for the frontier.

The emerging American culture contained three major beliefs or value orientations. *Political democracy* had been at the core of the nation's founding, and it was indelibly reaffirmed with the peaceful transfer of power from Federalists to Republicans after the presidential election of 1800. *Individual enterprise* was the second hallmark and became an inspiration for both immigrant and native-born, as well as the basis for countless private economic initiatives. Third was the *institutionalization of a Protestant culture,* quite understandable in a society comprised almost entirely of Whites sharing that religious orientation, along with some converted African and Native Americans. Soon the influx of millions of Catholic immigrants would challenge this cultural attribute.

Even as a common culture emerged, French influence was evident in cooking, fashions, and manners. French ads in American newspapers advertised "restaurateurs" who had previously been conventional American cooks and bakers. French chefs and recipes were popular. Inns and taverns renamed themselves "hotels." Americans became eager to learn from French dancing and fencing masters or have their children become ladies and gentlemen by learning French manners and grace. French books, customs, dress, and music were all fashionable in the early 19th century.

As Americans sought to establish their own national identity, the prevalence of French influence on the public served to alarm some, particularly the Federalists. "Medusa's snakes are not more venomous," declared one Federalist writer, "than the wretches who are seeking to bend us to the views of France."[16]

Decline of Foreign Languages

Foreign language usage usually retains its vitality only under certain conditions. A continual inflow of compatriots will preserve the vitality of the alien language. Geographic isolation will prevent the typical pattern of children learning the host country's language. Social isolation may allow a persistent subculture to retain its language as part of outgroup norms. In the United States in the early national period, none of these conditions prevailed to any large degree. On the frontier, pockets of ethnic isolation still existed, and in those regions, foreign language remained vigorous, everyday realities.

Elsewhere, however, without an influx of new arrivals to sustain their resiliency, foreign languages went into decline. A good example is the Germans, who comprised the largest non-British population segment. Prior to the Revolution, Baltimore, New York, and Philadelphia each had two or three German-language newspapers, but by 1815 none was left. Other languages declined in use as well because, by now, the Dutch schools, the Scandinavian schools, and others had introduced English into the classrooms.

This is not to say that the old languages died out completely, because that was not the case. Many of the older adults, who were unable to master the English language to any appreciable degree, held on to their native tongues. Some churches held duplicate services in both languages, enabling worshippers to have a choice.

Antiforeign Responses

Although immigration was lighter than in earlier years and the populace was coalescing into a common culture, a visible foreign segment remained. It was comprised mostly of the French and Irish, whose numbers and buoyant ethnicity gave cause for alarm to some of the native-born.

The excesses of the French Revolution and the growing support for the Jeffersonians among the Irish and French foreign-born alarmed the Federalists, who sensed a weakening of their power. In fiery speeches and newspaper editorials, they argued that these immigrants would "contaminate the purity and simplicity of the American character." One Federalist wrote, "Generally speaking, none but the most vile and worthless, none but the idle and discontented, the disorderly and the wicked, have inundated upon us from Europe." Noah Webster admitted that some immigrants were industrious, peaceable, and even voted the Federalist ticket, but, he warned, "For one such 'good' European, we receive three or four discontented, factious men—the convicts, fugitives of justice, hirelings of France, and disaffected off-scourings of other nations."[17]

Controlling the three branches of the federal government, the Federalists used their power to eliminate what they viewed as a threat to American society and to their own privileged position. Their actions were the first of several instances in the nation's history when the dominant group would successfully legislate against an "undesirable" foreign-born element. In 1798, President John Adams signed three bills passed by Congress. The Naturalization Act extended the residency requirement for citizenship from 5 to 14 years, in the hope of curtailing this new voter base of the Democratic-Republicans. The Alien Act gave the president the power to arrest and report undesirable aliens at his discretion. The Sedition Act prescribed fines and imprisonment for anyone criticizing the government.

Although Adams never used the Alien Act, his administration did implement the Sedition Act—a serious invasion of individual rights and liberties—when it arrested several foreign-born newspaper editors for seditious writings. Despite this law's blatant violation of the First Amendment provision for freedom of the press, a principle originating with the celebrated court victory of Peter Zenger in 1734, Federalists enforced it. The Alien and Sedition Acts expired after 2 years and faded away forever. As president, Jefferson succeeded in revising the Naturalization Act back to its 5-year residency requirement, where it remains today.

THE FALSE HORIZON

No one living in it really knows when an era is drawing to a close. Only when it is past can we look back and mark the moment when the change occurred. So it was in 1820. That year saw Jefferson's friend and colleague, James Monroe, re-elected, surely one sign of continuity. However, it was the first presidential election in which the Federalists did not field a candidate because they had virtually disappeared as a political force by then. New, still unfelt, political winds were blowing. Although the Democratic-Republican Party seemed invincible, before the decade ended, it, too, would be gone.

A whole generation had grown up knowing nothing but independence. Older adults could look back on the far-reaching changes since their youth. Three states had been added to the first 13 by the turn of the century, and by 1820, that number had grown to 23 (see Map 4.2).

Commerce was flourishing in the Northeast, agriculture under an entrenched slave system was prospering in the South, and westward expansion at the expense of Native Americans was continuing unabated. Canals, railroads, highways, and steamboats—plus such inventions as the reaper, the cotton gin, and the telegraph—were helping create an enormous economic empire rich in natural resources.

Many White Americans probably envisioned a tomorrow that would be better and essentially a continuation of what they knew. This vision would not be realized, however. In 1820, a yet-unrealized new era was dawning, some of it to be influenced by babies born that year, such as Florence Nightingale, William Tecumseh Sherman, and the daughter of Massachusetts Quakers Daniel and Lucy Anthony, whom they named Susan.

Thanks to low immigration and high natural population growth, together with the pervasive acculturation process, society had become more culturally homogeneous. Assimilation and societal cohesiveness were far more prevalent than White ethnic pluralism. Because religious intolerance and conflict between the different Protestant denominations had virtually ended, many Americans may have deceived themselves into thinking that their society had evolved into its final synthesis.

This notion also was an illusion. Beyond the horizon was about to come the first great wave of immigrants since the nation began. The sheer numbers of these culturally distinct newcomers would pose enormous challenges to U.S. institutions, embroil many in violent conflict, and change forever the America that these Americans of 1820 knew.

MAP 4.2 U.S. Territories and States, 1820

NOTES

1. James A. Henretta, David Brody, and Lynn Dumenil, *America: A Concise History* (New York: St. Martin's Press, 2002), p. 192.

2. Clarence Bagley, *History of Seattle from the Earliest Settlement to the Present Time* (Memphis, TN: General Books, 2010), p. 6.

3. Jeffrey H. Richards, *Early American Drama* (New York: Penguin Classics, 1997), pp. 1–59.

4. Stanley Elkins and Eric McKitrick, *The Age of Federalism* (New York: Oxford University Press, 1995), p. 190.

5. Joshua Kendall, *The Forgotten Founding Father: Noah Webster's Obsession and the Creation of an American Culture* (New York: Putnam, 2011).

6. Sidney A. Ahlstrom, *A Religious History of the American People,* 2d ed. (New Haven, CT: Yale University Press, 2004).

7. Gloria L. Main and Jackson T. Main, "Economic Growth and the Standard of Living in Southern New England, 1640–1774," *The Journal of Economic History,* 48 (1988): 27–46.

8. Gary B. Nash, *The Urban Crucible: The Northern Seaports and the Origins of the American Revolution* (Cambridge, MA: Harvard University Press, 1987), p. 257.

9. U.S. Census Bureau, *Historical Statistics of the United States,* Part II, Series Z 20–132 (Washington, DC: U.S. Government Printing Office, 1976).

10. Vincent N. Parrillo, *Strangers to These Shores,* 10th ed. (Boston: Allyn and Bacon, 2011), p. 149.

11. National Council of Churches, *2010 Yearbook of American and Canadian Churches,* reported in U.S. Census Bureau, *Statistical Abstract of the United States: 2011,* Table 76, p. 62.

12. Ibid.

13. U.S. Census Bureau, *Historical Statistics of the United States,* Part II, p. 1168.

14. Gary B. Nash, *Red, White, and Black: The Peoples of Early America,* 6th ed. (Upper Saddle River, NJ: Prentice Hall, 2009).

15. U.S. Department of Homeland Security, *2010 Yearbook of Immigration Statistics* (Washington, DC: U.S. Government Printing Office, 2011), Table 2.

16. John C. Miller, *Crisis in Freedom* (Mattituck, NY: Amereon, 2003), pp. 41–2.

17. Ibid., pp. 51–2.

5

Diversity in the Age of Expansion

America was indebted to immigration for her settlement and pros-
perity. That part of America which had encouraged them most had
advanced most rapidly in population, agriculture and the arts.

—*President James Madison*

*"American Progress" by John Gast (1872) depicts the symbolic Miss Columbia
guiding settlers westward as they drive out the buffalo and Indians, aided by
railroad and telegraph technological advances, in their pursuit of the nation's
"Manifest Destiny."*

At first glance, the 8,385 immigrants entering the United States in 1820 may have seemed just a continuation of similar numbers for the preceding 30 years. Few paid much attention then, judging by the lack of printed commentary. Perhaps some commented to friends that they detected a few more Irish, but if they did, they probably attributed it to the 3,000-strong Irish labor crew building the Erie Canal.

We now know it was more than just a case of a few more Irish arriving. In 1820, 47 percent of the emigrants from Europe were Irish Catholics. That proportion, almost one out of two, was significantly larger than the fairly small Irish presence of about 4 percent among the population at that time.

In hindsight, we recognize that this ratio in 1820 was a clear signal of something new happening. That Irish group of newcomers became the vanguard of almost 2 million Irish who followed in the next 40 years, part of a then-record influx of more than 5 million immigrants entering the country between 1820 and 1860. From 9.6 million inhabitants in 1820, the nation grew to 31.4 million by 1860. In the 1820s, immigration totals represented less than 2 percent of the total population, but by the 1850s, that decade's immigration total constituted more than 11 percent of the total population.

THE LARGER CONTEXT

A young core power on the world stage, its vast resources and opportunities attracting farmers, factory workers, and mine workers, the United States continued to experience the effects of social forces exerting pressure elsewhere in the world. Newcomers mostly arrived from Ireland—driven out by famine, poverty, and oppression—and from Germany, where economic conditions and civil unrest prompted many to leave. It was not yet a dominant force in the international community, but the United States clearly was a magnet for the disaffected of the world. Then, as now, migration patterns resulted as much from the "push" factors in the world as they did from the "pull" factors of freedom and opportunity in the United States.

Political forces within the United States, notably Jacksonian Democrats in the mid-1840s, advocated the territorial expansion of the United States to the Pacific Ocean. Using the term *Manifest Destiny,* coined in 1845 by journalist John L. Sullivan in urging annexation of Texas from Mexico and challenging Great Britain's claim to the Oregon Territory, its advocates insisted that westward expansion was a preordained right of the United States. The Mexican War (1846–1848) and the Oregon Treaty (1846) brought the western region under U.S. political control (see Map 5.1). These acquisitions set in motion the disruption of life for hundreds of indigenous tribes and for thousands of Spanish-speaking inhabitants, which included more than 6,000 Mexican residents in California.[1] Discovery of gold in 1848 in Northern California at Sutter's Mill triggered the gold rush that drew fortune seekers not only west across the Great Plains and Rocky Mountains, but also east across the Pacific Ocean. California, becoming the 31st state in 1850, would be one of the nation's most multiracial, multicultural states by 1860—about 85 percent White, 9 percent Asian, 5 percent Native American, 1 percent Black, and perhaps 2 percent Hispanic.[2]

As usual, dual patterns of assimilation and pluralism flourished throughout the land. For the new arrivals in eastern and midwestern cities and in the self-contained rural communities elsewhere, ethnicity was an everyday reality. The persistence over generations of Chinese, Dutch, French, German, Norwegian, and Spanish languages remained a normal fact of life in 19th-century America.[3] It is also true that, with some exceptions, a language shift to English is usually a two- to three-generation phenomenon.[4]

TRAVELERS DISCOVER THE ETHNIC MOSAIC

Intrigued by the dynamics of a new nation and the diversity of its people and landscape, Europeans came to visit and record their impressions, often offering comments on the many displays of ethnicity that they found.

Tocqueville's Dismay at Racial Suffering

After a nine-month visit in 1831–1832, Alexis de Tocqueville produced *Democracy in America* (1835), a masterpiece in political sociology for its analysis of the vitality, excesses, and potential future of American democracy. His observations about American associational life, collective pressures, individualism, competition, and materialism remain the bedrock for modern analyses of the American character.

Witnessing a band of Choctaw crossing the Mississippi at Memphis as part of the government's Indian removal policy, and also seeing the

MAP 5.1 U.S. Historic Territory Acquisitions, 1783–1853

effects of slavery, Tocqueville observed, "I saw with my own eyes many ... miseries ... and was the witness of sufferings that I have not the power to portray." He envisioned a bleak American future with Native Americans perishing in isolation and African Americans, if freed from the slavery he condemned, continuing to experience racial prejudice. As Tocqueville explained,

> The prejudice of race appears to be stronger in the states that have abolished slavery than in those states where servitude has never been known.
> ...Thus it is in the United States that the prejudice which repels the Negroes seems to increase in proportion as they are emancipated, and inequality is sanctioned by the manners while it is effaced from the laws of the country.[5]

Martineau's Defense of Immigrants

Harriet Martineau was a remarkable Englishwoman who wrote fine analyses on social, economic, historical, philosophical, and religious topics. After her visit to the United States (1834–1836) in her early thirties, she wrote *Society in America* (1837), in which she offered many of her observations about the American people, including the immigrants. To those critics of the immigrants, she countered,

> It would certainly be better if the immigrants should be well-clothed, educated, respectable people (except that, in that case, they would probably never arrive). But the blame of their bad condition rests elsewhere, while their arrival is, generally speaking, a pure benefit.

She went on to illustrate the value of immigrants to America:

> Every American can acknowledge that few or no canals or railroads would be in existence now in the United States, but for the Irish labor by which they have been completed; and the best cultivation that is to be seen in the land is owing to the Dutch and Germans it contains.[6]

Another European visitor, Frederika Bremer, offered a warm and astute commentary about the ethnicity in midwestern cities in *The Homes of the New World* (1853). One city that appealed to her was St. Louis, Missouri, with its "interesting mixture" of French, German,

Irish, and Spanish characteristics, as illustrated in the diversity of books and magazines sold, the variety of retail stores, and the many languages spoken on the street.[7]

Olmsted's Reaction to Isolated Ethnic Communities

Frederick Law Olmsted—later to become the famed landscape architect of many city parks, including New York City's Central Park—surprised himself by unexpectedly stumbling upon isolated ethnic communities in his travels. He described in *A Journey through Texas* (1860) his seeing a farming community of Silesian Poles, as well as numerous German farming settlements throughout west Texas, where their homes, work, and leisure activities reflected their native origins.[8] He was especially impressed with New Braunfels, a German town named after Braunfels, Germany, located to the southeast of Bonn. He also chanced upon the village of Castroville, Texas, founded in 1844 by Alsatian French. Its population of 600 still spoke French, read French newspapers, and maintained two churches with worship services conducted in—what else?—French.

THE FRENCH

French cultural influence, so popular among the public in the early national period, diminished by the 1820s, but retained its vitality in the many areas where the French were concentrated. In the Mississippi Valley region, for example, elements of French influence from colonial times continued throughout the 19th century. Many rivers and towns bore names indicating their French origin, as did the names of the largest cities: Detroit, New Orleans, and St. Louis.

America's "Flanders"

Flanders extends along the North Sea in northern France and western Belgium and still retains its medieval appearance. When Charles Dickens visited St. Louis in 1842, he went into the older section of the city long ago built by French settlers. He would write in *American Notes* that it reminded him of Flanders.

> The thoroughfares are narrow and crooked, and some of the houses are quaint and picturesque, being built of wood, with tumble-down galleries before the windows, approachable by

stairs, or rather ladders, from the street. There are queer little barbers' shops and drinking-houses, too, in this quarter, and an abundance of crazy old tenements with blinking casements, such as may be seen in Flanders. Some of these ancient habitations, with high garret gable windows perking into the roofs, have a kind of French shrug about them; being lop-sided with age, they appear to hold their heads askew besides as if they were grimacing in astonishment at the American improvements.[9]

The large presence of French Catholics in St. Louis prompted the Vatican to create a new diocese there in 1823. Here, as in many other American cities, French priests dominated the American Catholic hierarchy until midcentury, when massive Irish immigration ended their power.

America's "Little Paris"

New Orleans remains foremost in its preservation of French architecture, language, and culture. A picturesque reminder of Old World cities, it did not yield to Sunday "blue laws," as Boston, New York, and Philadelphia did in the early 19th century. On Sundays, New Orleans stores remained open, street musicians continued to play and sing, the markets were busy, and the theatrical performances drew large audiences.[10] The richness of French culture partly revealed itself through the abundance of productivity, as seen in the New Orleans Theatre St. Pierre, which offered 70 operas in 1806–1811. Also, French historians, novelists, and poets created a vast outpouring of distinguished French literature between 1820 and 1860.

French Immigration

The French subculture remained resilient in part because of the steady arrival of new immigrants. More than 316,000 immigrants from France came from 1820 to 1880, almost half of them arriving from 1840 to 1860. Much of this latter immigration resulted from the political disturbances preceding the Second Republic in 1848 and the dictatorship of Louis Napoleon, who became emperor in 1852. The previous year, 1851, was the single greatest year of French immigration to the United States, when more than 20,000 arrived.

Typically, the French preferred city life, and so most settled in many American cities. Sizable French populations in pre–Civil War cities also could be found in Charleston, South Carolina; Chicago,

Cincinnati, New York, and Philadelphia. French newspapers and social organizations were commonplace. With the outbreak of the Civil War, French military battalions formed in many cities to join in the cause on both sides.

THE IRISH

The Irish dominated U.S. immigration statistics from 1820 to 1860, when almost 2 million came, with 1.2 million of them concentrated in the years between 1847 and 1854.

America's First Ghetto People

Although they were mostly tenant farmers in their homeland, the Irish were ill equipped for U.S. agriculture. Potato farming in Ireland required only rudimentary skills and equipment because it was all manual labor on fairly small plots of land. American farms required capital investment in larger tracts of land, as well as axes, saws, seed, horses, mules or oxen to pull the plow, and a means to survive until the harvest. Impoverished, the Irish had neither money nor credit. Moreover, the low population density of rural America was quite different from home, where they lived in tight clusters in their villages, about 300 per square mile.

With no capital to become farmers and industrial America offering numerous jobs in the cities, others settled in what became known as "Dublin Districts," living in overcrowded tenements, dirt-floor cellars, converted warehouses, or shanties made of wooden crates and tar paper. Conditions were deplorable. Poor ventilation, heating, and lighting were common, and so were the open sewers in the streets and poor sanitation systems that contaminated drinking wells. Epidemics of cholera, typhoid, diphtheria, smallpox, and tuberculosis caused thousands of deaths among the immigrants. In 1849, for example, 5,000 people, mostly Irish immigrants, died from cholera in New York City. In 1860, the mortality rate in Boston, New York, and Philadelphia was 34 deaths per 1,000, more than twice that in rural regions.[11]

Labor, Religion, and Politics

Some Irish males worked as farmers, miners, or businessmen, but most worked at manual labor jobs in or near cities. These jobs were in all types of construction: paving roads; laying down railroad track; digging out canals; and building dikes, houses, or ships. They loaded or unloaded freight on trains and ships; cleaned streets and other people's houses, laundry, and chimneys; and labored in the factories and mills.

Many Irish were single women taking jobs as domestics or nannies for the native-born urban elite. In 1800, there was one domestic servant for every 20 families, but by 1840, the ratio had dropped to one servant for every 10 families. Unmarried Irish (and Scandinavian) young women often came first to work in families' homes. Their typical workload was a 16-hour, 6-day week of cooking, cleaning, child care, and nursing the sick. The loss of husbands through accident, desertion, or sickness left many women without means to support large families except, perhaps, by taking in boarders or hiring out to do others' laundry or sewing at home. Among the Irish, female-headed households reached 18 percent by 1855. Although dropping to 16 percent by 1875, this proportion remained significantly higher than the national average.[12]

It was the Irish, more than the French and Spanish, who brought Catholicism to Protestant America on a large scale. Bringing along their priests and nuns and building churches, convents, and parochial schools, they established a church hierarchy that would dominate American Catholicism for generations, which would later create some occasional interethnic resentment by Catholic immigrants of other nationalities.

Andrew Jackson's election in 1828 opened the political door to the common man, and the Irish hastened through. Using their political organizational skills, they forged a powerful voting bloc, city political machines, and a spoils system second to none. Graft and corruption may have been an integral part of machine politics, but so, too, was the proactive aid to the poor with food, fuel, and jobs.

THE GERMANS

By 1820, German Americans were assimilating so rapidly that the Lutheran and Reformed churches were not only offering regular worship services in English, but also had opened their memberships to those of English, Scottish, Welsh, and Scots-Irish descent. As the wave of German immigration rose to tidal proportions in the 19th century, however, German culture quickly revived and flourished. Driven by hunger, political discontent, and a series of wars, 1.5 million Germans entered the United States between 1820 and 1860, followed by another 1.5 million in the next 20 years. Some came for political reasons, but economic reasons motivated most. By the 1850s, newly arriving German immigrants outnumbered Irish arrivals, a lead they would sustain for the next 60 years.

Massive German immigration and widespread settlement patterns made the German presence felt almost everywhere. They entered through almost every eastern or southern port city, some to put down roots in those areas and others to move inland by train or boat along the Erie Canal or the Ohio and Mississippi rivers. The Midwest—particularly Ohio, Indiana, Illinois, and Wisconsin—attracted many immigrants. Large concentrations lived throughout the South before the Civil War, including Wheeling, West Virginia; Mobile, Alabama; Richmond, Virginia; Charleston, South Carolina; Louisville, Kentucky; Nashville, Tennessee; New Orleans, Louisiana; and Stuttgart, Arkansas. Some Germans went west, as did John Sutter, on whose land the discovery of gold touched off the California gold rush.

The "German Athens"

If New Orleans was the definitive French city of the United States in the 1850s, then Milwaukee, Wisconsin, was the definitive German city. Two-thirds of the city's 13,000 inhabitants in 1850 were foreign-born, and Germans accounted for two-thirds of this foreign-born number. The city became the distributing center of German settlers throughout the north central states.

In contrast to the coarseness and dullness of most frontier towns, Milwaukee was an oasis of culture in the 1850s. Its musical and literary cultural level shone so brightly that travelers called it the "German Athens."[13] The city possessed numerous German organizations, including a highly respected German American Academy, a freethinkers club, a Sangerbund (singing society), a theatre, and a Turnvereine, which blended physical fitness and German patriotism. A brewery, beer gardens, pork stores, mutual aid societies, and fire and militia companies were other aspects of the German presence.

German Diversity

Nineteenth-century German immigrants defied categorizing because of many differences within their own group, which impeded any sense of pan-German ethnicity. A significant cultural gap existed between the Catholics, mostly from the southern and southwestern provinces, and the Protestants, who were mostly from the northern provinces.[14]

Yet the Protestants themselves comprised distinct subcultures. The Calvinists—Baptists, Presbyterians, and Reformed—did not share the cultural nationalism espoused by the German Lutherans, and all of these religious groups were less culturally isolated than the Pietists— Amana, Amish, Hutterites, and Mennonites—who lived in separate but closely knit (*gemeinschaft*) communities.

Other distinctions among the Germans were occupational and residential patterns. In rural areas throughout the land, Germans turned uncleared, partly cleared, or waste lands into productive farms with their agricultural aptitude. These industrious and conservative Germans were knowledgeable in livestock, dairying, and crop-raising, but they were far less cosmopolitan than their city-dwelling compatriots.

The latter were the artisans and merchants who settled in Germantown sections in virtually every American city. As their numbers increased, their many social and cultural activities sometimes replaced the pre-eminence of an earlier group, as in St. Louis, where French music and customs yielded to those of the Germans. Not all Germans in the cities were economically secure people enjoying social and cultural activities, however. Some lived in abject poverty and struggled each day just to survive.

For most German immigrants, the reunification of Germany in 1871 intensified their sense of German ethnicity. The common German language reinforced that awareness and militated against going to a non-German church regardless of faith. A German Reformed Church not Dutch, a German Lutheran Church not Norwegian, or a German Catholic Church not Irish made one feel more comfortable by practicing the faith in one's native language. A common expression in those times for German Catholics was "language saves the faith," and so German-language masses continued despite protests by the Irish American–dominated church hierarchy to Rome.[15]

NATIVE AMERICANS

White attitudes toward Native Americans were mixed in the 19th century. Whereas some simply wanted them out of the way, idealists sought to integrate the indigenous peoples through assimilation. Various missionary groups attempted to make them into individualist, English-speaking Christian farmers instead of communal, foreign-speaking "heathens" who depended on hunting and subsistence agriculture.

Assimilation Efforts

Some Native Americans in the old Northwest Territory did convert to Christianity and attempted to assimilate. In doing so, they found themselves to be a dually marginal people because they were now social outcasts from their own tribes, victims of ridicule and even physical abuse, and also not accepted by the Whites. Confronted by a double dose of discrimination, many chose to return to their old ways rather than suffer a lifetime of social isolation.

By 1820, hundreds of thousands of Whites lived in Georgia, Tennessee, and the brand new states of Alabama and Mississippi. With their food source and lifestyle endangered by White encroachment, five tribes—the Cherokee, Chickasaw, Choctaw, Creek, and Seminole—tried to keep their lands by adopting the White man's way of life. Greater power comes to those who assimilate into a society rather than live on its fringes, and these tribes thus sought power through integration to control their destinies, rather than face loss of power through resistance and thus have no voice in their future. Because of the tribes' conversion to their culture and Christianity, White Americans gave them the ethnocentric appellation of the "Five Civilized Tribes."

"As Long as Grass Grows or Water Runs"

Living on rich, fertile land at a time of agricultural growth, particularly in cotton, the tribes stood in the path of further White settlement. President Jackson sent agents to negotiate, offering them lands west of the Mississippi River "in possession of land of their own, which they shall possess as long as grass grows or water runs."[16]

For those tribes not pressured into agreeing, Jackson ordered the military to expel them from their lands and to force-march them into Oklahoma Territory to live.[17] Despite a U.S. Supreme Court ruling in favor of the tribes, Presidents Jackson and Van Buren, the Congress, and the public sided with economic expansion instead of cultural accommodation. By 1838, Indian removal was complete except for the Seminole, who, aided by runaway slaves who had married into the tribe, waged guerilla warfare until 1842, when they, too, were defeated and removed to Oklahoma. In the old Northwest Territory, only the Sauk and Fox, led by Chief Black Hawk, fought against removal until their defeat in 1832. Like the Delaware, Kickapoo, Miami, Ottawa, Peoria, Potawatomi, Shawnee, Winnebago, and Wyandot tribes before them, the Sauk and Fox also were moved across the Mississippi.

As a witness to one small part of this expulsion, Tocqueville offered this poignant commentary:

> It is impossible to conceive the frightful sufferings that attend these forced migrations. They are undertaken by a people already exhausted and reduced; and the countries to which the newcomers betake themselves are inhabited by other tribes, which receive them with jealous hostility. Hunger is in the rear, war awaits them, and misery besets them on all sides. To escape from so many enemies, they separate, and each individual endeavors to procure secretly the means of supporting his existence by isolating himself, living in the immensity of the desert like an outcast in civilized society. The social tie, which distress had long since weakened, is then dissolved; they have no longer a country, and soon they will not be a people; their very families are obliterated; their common name is forgotten; their language perishes; and all traces of their origin disappear. Their nation has ceased to exist except in the recollection of the antiquaries of America and a few of the learned of Europe.[18]

All that now remained east of the Mississippi were the Iroquois of upstate New York, whose land was not coveted, and remnant bands from the expelled tribes who had escaped detection. Most Native Americans now lived in the western half of the nation on lands that were supposed to be theirs forever.

The End of Forever

"Forever" was less than 20 years. Acquisition of Oregon in 1846 and the Southwest in 1848 extended the U.S. border to the Pacific Ocean. Native Americans found new pressures for their land from a relentless White migration, encouraged by the discovery of gold in California in 1848, the Homestead Act of 1862 giving 160 acres of free land in the Great Plains to migratory Whites, and completion of the transcontinental railroad in 1869.

Skirmishes, massacres, and major battles erupted throughout the West. Deliberate, large-scale slaughter of the buffalo made them nearly extinct, devastating the culture and economy of the Plains tribes. In time, the independence of all the tribes ended, and they began a new life as dependent wards of the government, segregated on open-air slums called reservations.

Because ethnic Americans, mostly German and Irish, served in the U.S. army in numbers greater than their proportion in the population, they played a major role in the bloody Indian wars of the 19th century. Military service offered them a well-paid job without discrimination and enabled them to assert that they were "real" Americans. Adapting to the cultural biases of their new country, they saw it as their duty to kill the "bloodthirsty savages."

THE AFRICANS

Of the 1.8 million African Americans in 1820, all but about 230,000 were slaves. By 1860, the slave population increased to almost 4 million, and free Blacks grew to about 488,000. Virtually all of this growth was due to a natural population increase because Congress outlawed international slave trade in 1808.

Southern Blacks

Three separate cultures evolved in the South among (a) the non-slave-owning Whites primarily living in the back country, (b) the plantation owners, and (c) the slaves. Even among the slaves, diversity existed. Most were field hands working from sunup to sundown, but a small number were domestic servants or skilled workers. Of the tens of thousands of skilled workers, some lived and worked on plantations, but many were artisans hired out in the cities. In some cities, notably New Orleans, these artisans had a remarkable degree of free physical movement and personal behavior, but they were slaves nonetheless.[19]

In 1860, about 4 million African Americans lived in the South compared to 7 million Whites. In South Carolina and Mississippi, Blacks far outnumbered Whites, whereas in Georgia, Florida, Alabama, and Louisiana, the two races were about evenly divided in numbers. Only in Virginia, Arkansas, and Texas did Whites outnumber Blacks, by about a three-to-one ratio.

Life as a slave was a blend of labor exploitation, sexual exploitation, illiteracy, limited diet, and primitive living conditions. Only in their private times of leisure in the evening or on Sundays and holidays could slaves find respite from the relentless demands of bondage. It was then that they could hunt, fish, gamble, visit, gossip, sing, dance, picnic, or attend church. Essentially, slave culture revolved around three elements: family, music, and religion.

The family was the primary institution of slave society despite the breakup of families through sale or transfer of ownership or White sexual exploitation of Black women. The typical slave household had two parents, fulfilling their traditional gender roles with the male as disciplinarian and head of the family and the female in charge of their home and children.

We have several clues to the strength of Black family norms in the antebellum South. Their sexual mores allowed premarital sex but condemned adultery. This commitment of a man and woman to one another, first legitimized in the "jumping over the broomstick" ceremony, was reinforced by tens of thousands of former slaves legalizing their marriages through an official ceremony after the Civil War. Moreover, many actively searched for children, spouses, and parents after the war to reunite separated families.

African music has a rich history and variety. Beginning with the recorded observations of Hanno the Carthaginian in the 5th century BCE, many have written about the varied African musical instruments, including flutes, lutes, fiddles, lyres, reed pipes, drums, xylophones, and musical bows. African music also is different from Western music in that one cannot separate music from dance or bodily movement; even the playing of an instrument involves a complex combination of body movements.

Music is a reflection of the life and times of a people. In their slave society, African music was an important component of work, leisure, and worship. Using the forms, tones, and rhythms of their heritage, African Americans expressed their emotions and feelings through songs and spirituals. Frederick Douglass—whose rise from an illiterate slave to an articulate abolitionist writer and speaker is an inspiration to anyone born into poverty—noted the importance of music to his brothers still in bondage: "Slaves sing most when they are most unhappy. The songs of the slave represent the sorrows of the heart, and he is relieved by them, only as an aching heart by its tears."[20]

Religion was another outlet where slaves could express their deep feelings, bond together, and find hope. Traditional African cultures are rooted in a worldview of continuous interaction between spiritual forces and the community. Thus, it was a logical step for slave religion to blend the spiritual and secular worlds, connecting themselves to both a glorious past and a more rewarding future. Converting mostly to the Baptist and Methodist faiths because they permitted Black clergy, African Americans used their Christian faith to sing the joys of God's love for all and of the promise of glory and salvation in heaven.[21]

Northern Blacks

Theoretically, Northern Blacks were free but, in reality, they were not equal. Most states passed laws denying them the right to vote, serve on juries, or migrate from another state into theirs. Segregation was the norm in public facilities and residential areas. Job discrimination was widespread. Confined primarily to menial occupations, the Northern Blacks also fought a losing battle in the northeastern cities against the inroads of Irish competition.

Socially ostracized, disenfranchised, and economically discriminated against, Northern Blacks created their own sub-society. Parallel social institutions, comparable to those of White ethnics, sprung up. Besides Black churches, there were the fraternal and mutual aid societies. These organizations offered educational programs and medical and burial services, and they provided forums to air grievances and enhance self-esteem.

THE CHINESE

As with all immigrants, a combination of push-pull factors brought the Chinese to America in the mid-19th century. Chinese from Kwangtung Province, more so than from other regions of their homeland, were more easily able to reach the gold rush country in an effort to recoup their losses from flood, famine, and the Taiping Rebellion (1850–1864). Only 88 Chinese immigrants entered the United States between 1820 and 1853, but in 1854, 13,100 arrived, attracted by the discovery of gold. When the 1850s ended, more than 41,000 Chinese had come, followed by another 64,000 in the 1860s.

Most Chinese came to the United States in the 19th century as sojourners, intending to work for a limited time and then return home. Few women came; about 1 in 20 arrivals from China was a female. The men worked as miners, farm laborers, and fishermen. Soon many were employed as railroad workers and builders of dams, levees, and irrigation systems.

Obviously, the Chinese brought a new element to an already diverse U.S. society. They were a non-Western, non-Christian people whose appearance (race, clothing, and hair), belief system, food, language, music, and other cultural attributes clearly set them apart from the rest of society.

Another distinction was their social structure.[22] Traditional clans were a primary source of identity and emotional ties to family.

Settlement patterns depended on clan location because each tended to take up residence in selected areas. The *hui kuan* associations were mutual aid societies that represented six sending regions of China. With wider influence than the clans and often mediating disputes between clans, the *hui kuan* played a key role in helping Chinese newcomers find work and lodging; they also lent money, provided health care and burial arrangements, and met other social needs as necessary.

The tongs, or secret societies, brought a disruptive element to the Chinatowns. Involved in such organized crime activities as gambling, heroin, opium, and prostitution, the tongs challenged clan and *hui kuan* leadership, resulting in frequent bloody clashes. Because the tongs were better organized, they were more effective at offering welfare assistance to the sick, disabled, and unemployed, as well as life insurance, thus mixing fear and support to gain influence.

These three groupings—clans, *hui kuan,* and tongs—provided the Chinatowns with an infrastructure that resulted in self-sufficient ethnic communities. Ignored by politicians because they could not become citizens and vote, the Chinese in 19th-century America preserved their way of life much as, for example, Germans in isolated rural communities sought to preserve theirs by different means.

THE MEXICANS

Beginning in the 1820s, thousands of American settlers crossed the Louisiana border into the Mexican land of Texas, starting hundreds of cotton plantations in that fertile region. A decade later, more than 25,000 Americans lived in eastern Texas. Their presence set a chain of events in motion that would result in the U.S. annexation of Texas from Mexico, war with Mexico, and the subsequent acquisition of New Mexico and California territories. With the signing of the Treaty of Guadalupe Hidalgo in 1848, nearly 100,000 new ethnics became part of the American population.[23]

The new Americans were mostly a blend of a small group of wealthy landowners and a much larger group of artisans, ranch hands, or farmers who lived in an area also occupied by tens of thousands of Native Americans. Soon, widespread land fraud, expensive litigation, or forced land sales under violent duress caused almost all the Mexican American elite to lose their land titles to squatters or emerging White land barons for little or no money. As for the tribes, federal troops would eventually subdue them as they had others.

Northern California and Texas were the locales of the most violent episodes of interethnic conflict with the Spanish-speaking Catholic residents. Banditry, riots, terrorism, vigilantism, and even open warfare were common throughout the 1850s. In southern California and New Mexico, ethnic relations were more peaceful because arid conditions there attracted far fewer White settlers. Completion of the southern transcontinental railroad in the 1870s, however, brought in many new settlers and a repetition of the cycle of ethnic hostility and loss of land titles to the Whites.

Although some landowning Mexicanos managed to keep their property, most did not. Gradually, the Mexican Americans took on the status of a colonized people. School segregation, political disfranchisement, and economic dependence as laborers for the now-powerful Whites changed the Mexican Americans into essentially a suppressed minority. One telling statistic about the impact of colonization and poverty on family organization was the increase in Mexican American female-headed households, which numbered one-third of the total by 1880.

INTERGROUP CONFLICTS

As already mentioned, numerous interethnic clashes had occurred throughout the 19th century in the West and Southwest between Whites and Mexicans or Native Americans. Elsewhere, during this period other intergroup conflicts arose. Upset over the large influx of Chinese, Irish and German Catholics, and other foreigners, a right-wing reactionary group formed, calling itself the Supreme Order of the Star Spangled Banner. Dubbed "Know-Nothings" for their refusal to talk about their secret activities, they lobbied extensively for strict immigration laws and discrimination against Catholics.

Often accompanying their vicious hate campaign was brutal violence, with mobs raiding Irish and German homes, churches, schools, and businesses. Arson, vandalism, beatings, and murders occurred throughout the 1850s, with virtually every large northeastern city experiencing major disturbances.[24]

Organizing as the American Party, they elected 75 congressmen in 1854. By the next year, they had elected six governors and many local officials. In 1856, their presidential candidate, ex-President Millard Fillmore, ran a distant third to James Buchanan and John C. Fremont, although he did receive about 22 percent of the vote. Afterward, this movement faded into oblivion as North-South antagonisms mushroomed into civil war. Unfortunately, this would not be the last time that American minorities faced right-wing extremists.

THE NEXT HORIZON

In this era, the large numbers of Asians, Hispanics, and Europeans, particularly Germans and Irish, brought significant cultural diversity into the land. Some assimilated, but the numerous pockets of ethnic pluralism returned an expanded America to a newer version of its earlier colonial patchwork ethnic quilt. On the negative side, the violence perpetrated by anti-foreign or anti-Indian forces and the exploitation of racial minorities scarred the American minority saga. Yet it also was a time when the national conscience was stirred into various social reforms, including the end of slavery, and when feminists organized and launched a campaign for women's rights, achieving in this era only limited success. Of course, much more was to come.

The Civil War curtailed immigration, but did not stop it completely. When the awful carnage ended and the nation was reunited, immigration resumed even stronger than before. Whereas it had taken 40 years before the war to absorb more than 5 million immigrants, that figure was surpassed in just 20 years, with the arrival of 5.1 million between 1861 and 1880.

Irish immigration, however, had peaked and was now about half what it had been in the 1850s. German immigration dropped too, but not as much, and exceeded the Irish by more than 630,000 between 1861 and 1880. Other groups began to make their presence felt more, most notably the Chinese, French Canadians, Russians, Scandinavians, and Swiss. By 1880, the U.S. population exceeded 50 million, more than five times what it had been in 1820. It was filled now with millions of Irish and German Americans; tens of thousands of Chinese, Mexican, and Native Americans; plus many other White ethnics, none of them Anglo-Americans, and most of them still unassimilated.

Although the process was incomplete, this era was drawing to a close and a new one was beginning. In 1890, the U.S. Census Bureau would declare that the frontier no longer existed; in urban areas, steel girders and elevators would dramatically alter the cityscapes and population density, and inventions such as the telephone (1876) and incandescent light (1880) would revolutionize life at home.

An industrializing America would now roar into an industrial age, with new factories opening almost daily. The world would become a smaller place, thanks to advances in transportation and communications. Steamships would soon fill their holds with human freight as millions of "new immigrants" from Asia, Europe, and the Middle East would seek the American Dream. The America to which they came would be enormously different from what earlier immigrants had found, and these new immigrants would be vastly different from what Americans had known of immigrants. Physically and culturally distinct, the newcomers would bring even greater diversity, challenges, and progress to the American scene than ever before.

NOTES

1. Kevin Starr and Richard J. Orsi, *Rooted in Barbarous Soil: People, Culture, and Community in Gold Rush California* (Berkeley: University of California Press, 2000), p. 49.

2. U.S. Census Bureau, *Historical Census Statistics on Population Totals by Race, 1790 to 1990,* Working Papers Series No. 56 (September 2002), Table 19.

3. See, for example, Susan F. Martin, *A Nation of Immigrants* (New York: Cambridge University Press, 2011), pp. 101–4.

4. See Alejandro Portes and Rubén Rumbaut, *Immigrant America: A Portrait,* 3d ed. (Berkeley: University of California Press, 2006), pp. 224–32.

5. Alexis de Tocqueville, *Democracy in the United States* (North Charleston, SC: CreateSpace, 2011; originally published in 1835), pp. 290–1.

6. Harriet Martineau, *Society in America* (Charleston, SC: Nabu Press 2010; originally published in 1837), p. 183.

7. In Carl Wittke, *We Who Built America,* rev. ed. (Cleveland: Case Western Reserve University Press, 1967), pp. 207–8.

8. Frederick Law Olmsted, *A Journey through Texas, or a Saddle Trip on the Southwestern Frontier* (Ann Arbor: University of Michigan Library, 2006; originally published in 1860), pp. 169–83, 276–8.

9. Charles Dickens, *American Notes for General Circulation* (North Charleston, SC: CreateSpace, 2011; originally published in 1842), p. 172.

10. Wittke, *We Who Built America,* p. 318.

11. Charles E. Rosenberg, *The Cholera Years: The United States in 1832, 1849, and 1866,* 2d ed. (Chicago: University of Chicago Press, 1987).

12. See Margaret Lynch-Brennan, *The Irish Bridget: Irish Immigrant Women in Domestic Service in America, 1840–1930* (Syracuse, NY: Syracuse University Press, 2009).

13. Don Heinrich Tolzmann, *Wisconsin's German Element,* reprint ed. (Baltimore: Clearfield, 2001), p. 21.

14. Jay P. Dolan, *The Immigrant Church: New York and German Catholics, 1815–1865* (Terre Haute, IN: University of Notre Dame Press, 1993).

15. James Buckley, Frederick Christian Bauerschmidt, and Trent Pomplun, eds., *The Blackwell Companion to Catholicism* (Malden, MA: Blackwell, 2011), p. 196.

16. Andrew Jackson quoted in Howard Zinn, *A People's History of the United States,* reprint ed. (New York: Harper Perennial, 2010), p. 134.

17. Dale Van Every, *Disinherited: The Lost Birthright of the American Indian* (New York: Avon Books, 1966).

18. Tocqueville, *Democracy in America,* Vol. 1.

19. Ira Berlin, *Slaves without Masters* (New York: The New Press, 2007).

20. Frederick Douglass, *Narrative of the Life of Frederic Douglas* (New York: Simon and Brown, 2011; originally published in 1845), p. 20.

21. Henry H. Mitchell, *Black Church Beginnings: The Long-Hidden Realities of the First Years* (Grand Rapids, MI: William B. Eerdmans Publishing Company, 2004).

22. Stanford M. Lyman, *Color, Culture, and Civilization* (Champaign: University of Illinois Press, 1995), p. 244.

23. Manuel G. Gonzalez, *Mexicanos: A History of Mexicans in the United States,* 2d ed. (Bloomington: Indiana University Press, 2009), p. 80.

24. John Higham, *Strangers in the Land* (New Brunswick, NJ: Rutgers University Press, 2002; originally published in 1955), chap. 1.

6

Diversity in the Industrial Age

Today in America, unions have a secure place in our industrial life. Only a handful of reactionaries harbor the ugly thought of breaking unions and depriving working men and women of the right to join the union of their choice. I have no use for those—regardless of their political party—who hold some vain and foolish dream of spinning the clock back to the days when organized labor was huddled, almost as a helpless mass.

—*President Dwight D. Eisenhower*

These "breaker boys" at a 1913 Pennsylvania anthracite coal mine are separating slate rock from coal after it was brought out of the mine. For 10–16 hours a day, their hazardous work with fast-moving conveyor belts could result in amputations or death.

Astounding changes occurred between 1871 and 1920. In just one decade, the 1880s, railroad companies built 76,000 new track miles, increasing the total to about 164,000 by 1890 and thereby creating an efficient transportation system that welded the nation into a unified, enormous market.[1] In addition, the spectacular growth of cities dramatically altered the American way of life, and industrialization brought the majority of the labor force into manufacturing, creating thousands of jobs and a labor shortage.

The influx of 26.3 million immigrants in this period filled America's desperate need for labor. Whether they worked in the mines, on railroad construction, or in the factories and mills, the immigrants helped the nation come of age industrially. In a pattern somewhat similar to today, immigrants were obliged to take jobs of low status, low pay, long hours, and difficult work that were shunned by the native-born. By their presence, the immigrants represented the paradoxical duality of opportunity and exploitation.

The 84-hour work week (14 hours a day, 6 days a week) was common. Jobs offered no vacations, sick pay, or pension plans. Child labor was commonplace, and entire families often worked to provide a subsistence-level family income. Lighting, ventilation, and heating were poor; in the factories, moving parts of machinery were dangerously exposed, leading to numerous horrific accidents, but there was no workers' compensation for those injured on the job. A worker who objected to working conditions was likely to be fired and blacklisted. Exploited by the captains of industry, the immigrants became deeply involved in the labor-union movement, so much so that to tell the story of one without the other is virtually impossible. Labor strife in this era led many native-born Americans to call for immigration restrictions. In 1921, a new law did exactly that, severely curtailing immigration from all areas except northern and western Europe.

Until then, large-scale immigration enabled industrialists to keep wages low and circumvent labor union organization efforts. A split labor market between groups evolved, as employers hired newcomers as strikebreakers or as lower-paid workers to replace higher-paid ones.[2] The result was ethnic antagonism of native-born or older immigrant workers against the new arrivals for either taking their jobs away or else depressing their wage scale.

The country's growth continued, both territorially and numerically. By 1900, another 7 states had joined the Union, bringing the United States to a total of 45 states (see Map 6.1). The turn of the century saw the U.S. population tallying 76.2 million, nearly one in seven of them foreign-born.

MAP 6.1 U.S. Territories and States, 1900

THE LARGER CONTEXT

In this era, the United States became an industrial giant and had a major influence on the international community. Sometimes its actions impacted the world scene, as when it altered sea travel by building the Panama Canal (1903–1914) or when it defeated Spain in the War of 1898 and acquired Spain's island possessions in the Caribbean and Pacific. At other times, global forces beyond the control of the United States—such as the social upheavals in southern, central, and eastern Europe or World War I—dramatically affected the country by changing migration patterns, which in turn affected its population composition and intergroup relations.

An especially harsh peasant life in Europe, coupled with political and economic unrest often squashed by tyrannical regimes, were push factors that prompted thousands to flee their homelands for the promise of "Golden America." Many European governments encouraged the large-scale exodus because it relieved the pressures they faced from overpopulation, the decline of feudalism, a changing agrarian economy, chronic poverty, and political unrest.

The initial impetus for Jewish migration (its U.S. population rose from 250,000 in 1880 to almost 3 million by 1920) was a pogrom (organized massacre) that followed the assassination of Czar Alexander II (1881). Although no Jews were involved in the regicide, the czarist government used them as a scapegoat to divert people's attention from long-festering social, political, and economic grievances.

MINORITY FAMILY ECONOMIES

Gender played an important role in family economic activities. Whereas the men sought employment in a variety of occupations, cultural norms dictated that married women should not work outside the home. Indeed, less than 5 percent did so in 1890, often only because their husbands were disabled, missing, or unemployed.[3] Typically, the wife's role was to maintain the house. If family needs required her income because the children were too young to work, then she would take on work at home (such as laundry or sewing) or else care for boarders (a common practice given the high number of male immigrants).

The world of work for women thus fell mostly to the young and single. More than half of all gainfully employed women at the turn of the century were between 16 and 24 years of age. These young women were often employed in factories or mills in "suitable" positions as machine tenders or seamstresses perhaps, or else as assemblers, inspectors, packers, and so on in various types of plants.[4]

About one-third of all employed female workers were blue-collar workers. Another third were domestic workers: maids, cooks, nannies, and so on. In the North, many were single Irish or Scandinavian women who had journeyed without family to begin life anew. In the South, African American women held similar positions. The final third of female workers were usually not first-generation Americans. This category of employed women comprised such white-collar positions as nurse, teacher, or sales clerk.

Children, usually at about age 8 or 9, often went to work in the mills and mines. With no child labor laws yet to protect them, they worked the same long hours under harsh working conditions as did the adults, but usually for one-tenth an adult's wages. Economic necessity dictated their working, however, for without the children's small wages, families could not survive.

In nonurban settings—whether the family be African, Asian, Hispanic, White ethnic, or native-born American—the entire family unit worked every day, each family member—man, woman, and child—performing necessary tasks for the welfare of all. Here, too, the work was hard, although one's labors were at least within a family environment.

An expanding economy and population, and the institution of child labor laws (not applicable to agriculture), brought about an increase in jobs for women. Included in this significant rise in female participation in the nonfarm labor force were married women as well. By 1920, 1 in 5 paid workers was a woman, and 1 in 10 married women—twice that of 1890—had become a wage earner.

POPULATION DIVERSITY

In addition to the great influx of southern, central, and eastern Europeans in this period, it also was a period of high immigration from northern and western Europe and other parts of the world. For example, government records show the arrival of 1.7 million Canadians, 840,000 Asians, 277,000 Mexicans, 307,000 West Indians, and 90,000 Central and South Americans. In cities, towns, and reservations, America's racial minorities lived segregated and socially isolated from White America. Some were former slaves or their descendants. Others were a conquered people. Still others were voluntary immigrants seeking their fortune. All shared, however, a common fate, working in occupations that did not provide for upward mobility.

People of color provided much of the hard labor (and the technical skills) that built up the agricultural base and the mineral-transport-communication infrastructure necessary for industrialization and modernization, whereas Europeans worked primarily within the industrialized, modern sectors. The initial position of European ethnics, although low, was such that it allowed for movement up the socioeconomic pyramid. The placement of non-White groups, however, imposed barrier upon barrier on such mobility, freezing them for long periods of time in the least favorable segments of the economy.[5]

The "new" immigration, encouraged by a rapidly expanding economy, brought considerable cultural diversity into the country. Previously little-known nationality groups now flocked to the nation's shores, establishing their ethnoreligious cultural marks. By the turn of the century, most northeastern cities would contain two-thirds or more of a foreign-born population.

Yet even as pluralism manifested itself in new or revitalized ethnic communities, ethnicity was beginning to fade among other groups. Second- and third-generation Americans of northern and western European ancestry were less inclined to retain an ethnic identity. Although they had not yet become fully assimilated, the Irish and Germans were gaining political power and moving toward economic equality with older groups. The native born of Dutch, French, and Scandinavian ancestry were more likely to have attained structural assimilation even as new arrivals from those areas replenished the ethnic mosaic.

In short, the dual realities of assimilation and pluralism were once again evident. The following pages offer a brief look at some of the various groups that comprised that diversity.

AFRICAN AMERICANS

After the Civil War, interracial cooperation offered promise of a new era in race relations in the South. Blacks and Whites worked side by side in coal mines and lumber camps and on waterfront docks, their efforts encouraged in the mid-1880s by the interracial unionism of the Knights of Labor. White and Black dirt farmers formed separate Farmers' Alliance organizations, but the two worked together for agrarian reform. They united behind the Populist Party in 1891, but vicious opposition and voter fraud resulted in defeat almost everywhere. The embittered poor Whites turned against their Black allies as the cause of their losses, strongly encouraged in this direction by the White conservative elite.

Out of this struggle was born a malicious form of White supremacy, determined to establish a rigid color line. As George M. Fredrickson succinctly said,

In the late nineteenth century, when blatant racism was reaching the extreme point of its development, the resurgent white supremacists of the South put new and more stringent laws on the books. Not only were anti-miscegenation statutes re-enacted or reaffirmed, but more rigorous definitions of whiteness were put into effect. By the beginning of the twentieth century most southern states were operating in accordance with what amounted to a "one-drop rule," meaning in effect that a person with any known degree of black ancestry was legally considered a Negro and subject to the full disabilities associated with segregation and disfranchisement.[6]

Poll taxes, initiated in some districts in 1877 to disenfranchise Black voters, now spread. Mandatory literacy tests were another effective means because about 75 percent of Black Americans were illiterate. However, illiterate poor Whites whose grandfathers had been eligible to vote in 1860 were exempted by "grandfather clauses." Beginning in Florida in 1887, mandatory segregation laws regarding train passengers were passed; other states soon followed. When the U.S. Supreme Court upheld such laws in its 1896 *Plessy v. Ferguson* decision, the "separate but equal" doctrine became institutionalized. Between 1901 and 1910, most southern states passed a wide array of Jim Crow laws, bringing racial segregation into all places of public accommodation.

Racism manifested itself in its ugliest form in violence. From 1892 to 1921, almost 2,400 Blacks were lynched, most of them in the South. The growing presence of Blacks in the cities and perceptions of them as an economic threat led to deadly race riots erupting in Georgia, Illinois, Indiana, and Ohio from 1904 to 1908. Fear of economic competition triggered another deadly race riot in East St. Louis in 1917. When union organizers placed a newspaper ad claiming that local industries were recruiting Blacks to reduce White wages, the workers attacked the Black ghetto. In the aftermath, 39 Blacks and 9 Whites had been killed. Two years later, riots exploded in 26 cities, leaving 38 killed in Chicago and 6 dead in Washington, DC.[7]

The promise of better education and jobs kept luring Black migrants to the North. Their numbers were not that noticeable next to the large European inflow, but the 80,000 migrants from 1870 to 1890 increased to 200,000 from 1890 to 1910, bringing the northern Black population to about one-tenth of the total at the turn of the century.[8] Economic hard times and boll weevil destruction of cotton crops prompted more to head north in the next decade, raising the northern Black population from 850,000 in 1910 to 1.4 million in 1920.

Labor union hostility in the North and de facto segregation created a dual society there, just as de jure segregation had done in the South. Black churches and other parallel social institutions formed the bedrock of the segregated racial community. A Black middle class, many of them graduates of Black colleges, emerged and achieved success in business and the professions. Black artists and writers creatively depicted Black life in America, while musicians contributed blues and jazz to the popular culture.

Southern Blacks remained mostly a rural people, struggling within a system designed to keep them subjugated. Northern Blacks were an urban people, some of them poor, others working or middle class. A 1918 Census Bureau analysis showed that 79 percent of all Black males older than age 10 were gainfully employed, with 49 percent of them in agricultural pursuits. Economist Robert Higgs reports that, between 1867 and 1900, Black incomes more than doubled, increasing more rapidly than White incomes. He adds, however, that in absolute numbers, the Black income level in 1900 lay far below the White level:

> Even if the Blacks could have steadily raised their income per capita twice as fast as the Whites, about 70 years would have been required to close the gap. Black income per capita probably did not exceed four-tenths of the white level in 1914.[9]

Black exclusion from political influence and public discrimination in education and in law impeded their economic development. But even if there had not been racial discrimination, argues Higgs, the years of the industrial age were not sufficient to enable Blacks to acquire the literacy, skills, experience, and capital needed to close the economic gap with Whites. These "swift competitors" had too large of a head start.

ASIAN AMERICANS AND PACIFIC ISLANDERS

Between 1871 and 1920, the Asian American population changed from a fairly small, mostly Chinese group to a significantly large, multi-Asian and Pacific Islander presence. Japanese, Filipinos, Asian Indians, and Koreans came to the U.S. mainland, as tens of thousands of others went to Hawaii, most to work there on the sugar and pineapple plantations.

Each of these non-Western groups brought, and kept fairly intact, a racial and cultural diversity throughout the western states. Despite Asian American differences in nationality, language, and culture, to most Americans, they all looked alike and so they all must be alike, non-assimilable and undesired. Not surprisingly, fear, resentment, antagonism, and violence soon marked Asian-White relations.

Some Americans viewed the Chinese presence as a serious threat to the popular notion of the United States as a melting pot. Assimilationists could content themselves with the pronouncement that the Germans and Irish, once seen as a threat to the national fabric, at least were physically similar to the northern and western European Americans, unlike the racially distinct Asians.

National leaders fanned the flames of racial bigotry. U.S. Senator James G. Blaine, who narrowly lost the presidency to Grover Cleveland in 1884, declared in an 1879 Senate speech, "The Asiatic cannot go on with our population and make a homogeneous element."[10] Pressured by labor unions and newspapers, Congress enacted in 1882 the first national human embargo on a particular race. The Chinese Exclusion Act, subsequently made more restrictive and twice renewed, would remain in effect until immigration reform in 1965. Japan also came under legislative restrictions. In 1924, spurred by the efforts of Senator Henry Cabot Lodge and Secretary of State Charles Evans Hughes, Congress specifically excluded immigrants from Japan in the Immigration Act of 1924.

What can we make of these actions? It is too simplistic to attribute them solely to racial bigotry, although it certainly was a factor. From an interactionist perspective, non-Western differences in physical appearance, language, belief systems, customs, stoicism, and observable behavior affected social distance perceptions and resultant interaction patterns. Once removed from any affinity to the dominant group, the Asians were more likely to generate tensions, violent outbreaks, and governmental restrictions.

It would be a mistake, however, to confine interracial problems only to racist motivations and/or perceived cultural dissonance. Economic competition played a major role, as indicated by the rising intensity in demands for Chinese exclusion during the depression of the 1870s, when a lull in railroad construction brought the Chinese back into California. In another example, Roger Daniels describes a "crusade against Japanese contract labor" in the 1890s by the *San Francisco Morning Call,* which claimed that Japanese immigrants were taking work away from Americans.[11]

Organized labor continually viewed the Asians as a threat to the American worker and lobbied extensively against their immigration. Indicative of its position is a resolution passed at the 1893 American Federation of Labor (AFL) convention that stated the Chinese bring to the United States "nothing but filth, vice, and disease."[12]

HISPANIC AMERICANS

In the second half of the 19th century, a greater need for agricultural labor developed because of an increase and expansion of cotton, fruit, and vegetable farms. Because the Chinese Exclusion Act of 1882 curtailed one source of labor, growers enticed Mexicans to leave their poverty-stricken country to earn money by working on American farms.

One must understand the cultural milieu in their native land in order to comprehend the Mexicans' situation in the United States for more than 100 years. Most Mexicans were poor, illiterate peasants, virtually serfs, who eked out an existence laboring for the *haciendados,* the large landholding aristocracy of Mexico. Exploited by the hacienda owners and the Mexican government for years, and ignorant of the language and laws of this country, the Mexicans worked in the United States under servile conditions for meager wages. Reflecting the degree of poverty in their native country is the fact that, although they worked for low wages here, they were still earning a great deal more than they could at home.

In the last two decades of the 19th century, approximately 300,000 Mexicans living in the American Southwest continued to experience serious challenges brought on by thousands of Anglo-Americans and European immigrants coming to settle in the region. Victims of drought, discriminatory taxes, foreclosures, questionable local judicial rulings, and violent intimidation, many lost their lands. Economic changes also victimized Mexican Americans as the large commercial farms of agribusiness, with their extensive investments in machinery and irrigation systems, priced the small farmers out of business.

Decline of their *rancho* system played havoc with their traditional values, which had long sustained the cohesiveness of a paternalistic, extended family system. A nuclear family pattern slowly emerged, accompanied by an increase in common law marriages and consensual unions. In urban areas such as Los Angeles, a startling increase in female-headed families occurred; by 1880, one-third of the Mexican American families were matriarchal, most living in substandard conditions. Reduced to the status of low-paid laborers, Mexican Americans became stereotyped as lazy and backward. Living in the barrio of a city or town, or in rural isolation, they were virtually a colonial people lacking in economic or political power.

Elsewhere, the Hispanic presence was small. About 1,500 Puerto Ricans lived in the continental United States by 1910. Florida was home to most other Hispanics at this time, although in New Jersey, a small Cuban community across the Hudson River from New York City continued to thrive since its 1850 beginnings.

NATIVE AMERICANS

This era was a bleak one for the indigenous peoples of the United States. In the mid-19th century, the government had embarked on a policy of containment as a means of controlling the Native Americans and encouraging westward expansion. Using military force, the government displaced many tribes and resettled them on wasteland reservations, where they remained unless new settlement plans or the discovery of valuable natural resources resulted in further displacement. This program of forced segregation and dependency, compounded by attempts at forced "Americanization," reduced Native Americans to the status of a subordinate colonized people.

Officially made dependent wards of the government in 1871, confined to reservations out of the White man's way, they would soon lose even two-thirds of these reservation lands through deceitful and fraudulent real estate transactions. This followed passage of the ill-conceived Dawes Act of 1887, which attempted to divide tribal lands into individual tracts in an effort to "civilize" the inhabitants.

Whites' fears of a resurgence of Native American beliefs and practices, prompted by a Native American spiritual revival known as the Ghost Dance Religion, led to the tragic massacre at Wounded Knee in 1890 that killed 150 defenseless Sioux. It was the last violent episode, as the government continued its efforts at Anglo conformity through education and Christian missionary work. The northern Plains Indians were given the southern section of the Dakota Territory, and the southern Plains Indians were placed in Oklahoma Territory along with the Cherokee, Chickasaw, Choctaw, Creek, and Seminole. The Navajo and Apache were on reservations in the Southwest, whereas other tribes were scattered in the Rockies and beyond.

Reservation life changed the tribes from self-reliant harvesters of nature's bounty to dependent wards of the government, obliged to rely on food shipments for sustenance. With their food-producing, often nomadic, lifestyle nullified, Native Americans also found their cultural, familial, and communal well-being subverted as well. Their social structure, with active roles for all within the tribe, collapsed under an imposed passive role. Loss of their independent male role as leaders, hunters, providers, protectors, and warriors denied the men any means of maintaining self-esteem. As an escape from their harsh reality, hopelessness, and despair, many thousands of Native American men turned to drink and drugs.

Despite laws against Native American possession of alcohol, it was readily available, even supplied by government agents to keep the reservations tranquil. Alcoholism became a problem, as did the chronic use of the hallucinogen peyote, a derivative of the cactus plant. Its use spreading through several decades from the Mescalero Apache to virtually all tribes, peyote became an institutionalized part of the Native American Church. With no control of their lives, Native Americans struggled to maintain their sense of identity and oneness with the universe by any means possible.

As the Native Americans lived their lives in a reduced state of dependency, their population shrank to about 237,000 by 1900. (It had been 600,000 in 1776.) During the late 19th and early 20th centuries, they remained pockets of diversity, ignored by most of society, pacified through alcohol by government agents, and encouraged by assimilationist idealists and missionaries to divest themselves of their diversity and embrace "white civilization."[13]

MIDDLE EASTERN AMERICANS

About 3,000 Arab immigrants came in the 1880s, followed by more than 30,000 in the 1890s. Another 70,000 followed until the outbreak of World War I in 1914. Most came from Syria and Lebanon, but because they lived in a region under the control of the Ottoman

Empire, their passports designated them as "Turks." Not until 1899 did a separate category for "Syrian" appear on immigration rosters. Although about 85 percent came from Lebanon, identification of "Lebanese" did not gain acceptance until the 1930s.

About 10 percent were Muslims, a small number were Jewish, and almost all the rest were Christians fleeing religious persecution from the Turks. The Christians divided into Maronites, Melkites, Orthodox, and Presbyterians. Their theological differences translated into social and structural separation in their ethnic communities in the United States, as they had in the Middle East. What bonded them together was a conviction that those sharing similar beliefs belonged to a social order qualitatively different from the rest. They looked on themselves not as Syrians, but as coreligionists from a particular village. Americans lumped them together as the single entity of Syrian, much as they had combined other provincial groups into single nationality groups. As with other ethnic groups, these first-generation immigrants soon saw themselves as Americans perceived them.[14]

Most immigrants settled in a "Syrian belt" stretching westward from the textile mills of southern New England and New York–New Jersey through the steel towns in Pennsylvania and Ohio to the automobile factories in Detroit. In each of these regions near the factories where they worked, the Syrians established their ethnic communities. Some Syrians became itinerant peddlers or salesmen. Once financially secure, they became shopkeepers, wholesalers, and fabric or department store owners. By 1911, Syrians were in almost every branch of commerce, including banking and import-export houses, and the government reported that Syrian American median income was only slightly lower than the $665 annual income of adult native-born White males.

NORTHERN AND WESTERN EUROPEAN AMERICANS

For many countries situated in the northwestern part of the European continent, the late 19th and early 20th centuries marked the time of their largest numbers of emigrants leaving for the United States. Belgium, Denmark, England, Holland, Norway, Scotland, and Sweden sent more emigrants at this time than in any other period.

Because more than 8.1 million immigrants arrived from this part of the world between 1880 and 1920, northern and western European cultural diversity was as marked a presence as that of other nationality groups. English immigrants, for example, numbered 1.5 million from 1881 to 1920, and other parts of Great Britain accounted for almost an additional half million.

Almost a million Swedes, more than a half million Norwegians, and almost a quarter million Danes came. Germany sent more than 2.4 million immigrants, and Ireland supplied more than 1.5 million. More than 100,000 Belgians, 170,000 Dutch, and 216,000 French also came.

With large numbers coming in each of these four decades, the tight clusters of these ethnic communities made the vigor of their everyday ethnicity even more pronounced. In the 1880s, for example, the 5.2 million immigrants included approximately 1.5 million Germans, 655,000 Irish, 645,000 English, 177,000 Norwegians, 392,000 Swedes, 150,000 Scots, 88,000 Danes, 53,000 Dutch, and 50,000 French. From 1901 to 1910, the 8.8 million immigrants included about 388,000 English, 341,000 Germans, 339,000 Irish, 250,000 Swedes, 190,000 Norwegians, 120,000 Scots, 65,000 Danes, 48,000 Dutch, and 41,000 Belgians.

New Irish arrivals, in typical chain migration pattern, often settled near family or friends. Consequently, by the turn of the century, almost 7 million Irish Catholics were concentrated in the urban Northeast, living in "Paddy's Villages" or shantytowns usually located in older, less desirable residential sections of most cities. Experiencing job and social discrimination because of their religion, their full absorption into the mainstream was at least one generation away.

More than 9 million Germans, diverse in religions and backgrounds, lived in both rural and urban clusters. Most major cities throughout the Northeast had Germantown sections, but the greatest number remained in the German triangle of the Midwest (the area between Milwaukee, Cincinnati, and St. Louis). Wherever they lived, German Americans, particularly first generation, functioned in a culturally isolated ethnic world where a wide array of parallel social institutions helped maintain their language and customs.

The Midwest—particularly Illinois, Iowa, Michigan, and Wisconsin—also attracted the recent Dutch immigrants because of favorable soil and climate conditions. More than 1.5 million Danes, Finns, Norwegians, and Swedes lived on farms or in towns of the northern Midwest, further stamping a vibrant Scandinavian imprint upon that region.

The residence in New England of more than a half million French Canadians and in Louisiana of about a quarter million Cajuns reinforced conditions that allowed for the establishment of persistent ethnic subcultures lasting into present times. In addition, more than 150,000 French immigrants arriving elsewhere between 1871 and 1900 spiced Gallic diversity even more.

SOUTHERN, CENTRAL, AND EASTERN EUROPEAN AMERICANS

Whether for economic, political, or religious reasons, these "new" immigrants came to "Golden America" to seek a better life. They included Armenians, Greeks, Italians, Portuguese, and Turks from the southern part of the European continent; Czechs, Hungarians, Poles, and Slovaks from the plains of central Europe; Austrians and Swiss from the high mountain country; Latvians and Lithuanians from the Baltic area; Byelorussians, Ruthenians, Ukrainians, and others from the western regions of czarist Russia; and Jews from all parts of eastern and central Europe, especially Russia. Even within these groups, much diversity could be found. Within the Slavic group, for example, were Bohemians (Czechs), Bulgarians, Croatians, Dalmatians, Montenegrins, Serbs, Slovaks, Slovenians, and still others. Each had their own identities and cultures, which they attempted to preserve in their adopted country.

Arriving in record numbers, these nationality groups were strikingly different in appearance, culture, customs, language, political experiences, and ideology. Physical appearance—whether the darker features of those from the Mediterranean region, or the eastern European women with kerchiefs on their heads, or Jewish men with yarmulkes and full beards—set them apart from native-born Americans. Because most were Catholics, Jews, or Orthodox Christians, Protestant America once again reacted with disdain at this large display of diverse groups whose religious buildings and clergy were daily reminders of a change in U.S. society.

The largest nationality group was the Italians, who numbered more than 4.1 million arrivals between 1881 and 1920. Settling mostly in "Little Italys" in cities large and small, immigrants from the same region—sometimes even the same village—clustered in the same city sections. This chain migration pattern resulted in the creation of cohesive neighborhoods with village, family, and communal orientations built around their parallel social institutions of church, newspapers, social organizations, and stores. Although assimilation would gradually occur—particularly among their children pursuing *la via nuova*—in those communities, Italian was the daily language and ethnicity an everyday reality, leading many native-born Americans to view negatively the presence of so many "unassimilable" newcomers.

Native-born Americans, mostly of northwestern European descent, were aghast at the heavy immigration of dissimilar cultural types and blamed the new arrivals for all existing social discontents. They condemned them for the increase in crime, although every objective investigation proved that the crime rate among first-generation Americans was lower than for the rest of the country. (The increase occurred more typically among the second generation.) Labor disputes and calls for political and economic reform furthered criticism of the "un-American agitators." Hundreds of thousands came as sojourners, or "birds of passage" as some called them. They came not to stay, but to make enough money to return home and to buy land, redeem the family mortgage, or provide dowries for sisters or daughters. They had less interest in learning English, getting involved in the labor movement, or acculturating. Greeks, Poles, and Italians particularly were sojourners. Half of all Italians to arrive in the 1880s and 1890s returned home, creating a "shuttle migration." Often, between 1908 and 1920, the number of Italians returning home reached between 60 and 70 percent of the new arrivals.[15] More than 500,000 Poles returned between 1900 and 1915, as did tens of thousands of Greeks.

Gradually, many sojourners decided to stay. Others returned to the United States with their wives and children. As these people joined other family groups putting down roots, their birth rates—considerably higher than for those of multiple-generation Americans—became a cause for nativist alarm. Some cited population statistics to project the "old" Americans becoming a minority to the "inferior" newcomers. Eugenicists like Madison Grant, president of the New York Zoological Society, argued in *The Passing of the Great Race* (1916) for those of Anglo-Saxon, Nordic, and Teutonic origins to marry only among themselves to prevent racial hybridism and reversion to the "lower type" through contamination of their "racial purity."[16]

INTERGROUP CONFLICTS

Nativist hostility and violent clashes marked the industrial age as they had the earlier part of the 19th century. In addition to the race riots previously mentioned, interethnic conflicts also arose. Organizations such as the American Protective Association (APA) and the

Ku Klux Klan drew widespread popular support in their campaigns for a "pure" America.[17]

The APA began in Iowa in 1887. By 1893, it claimed about 1 million members in 20 states, primarily in the midwestern "Bible Belt." An anti-Catholic organization, it particularly attracted the Scots-Irish, as well as Germans, Scandinavians, and English. Committed to an English-only school curriculum, removal of Catholic teachers and school board members, longer naturalization periods, restrictive immigration, and election of Protestant officeholders only, the APA claimed 100 members serving in the 54th Congress (1895–1896).

The Ku Klux Klan, reconstituted in 1915 after being sympathetically portrayed in D. W. Griffith's silent film classic *Birth of a Nation,* reached a membership of almost 5 million by 1926. Membership was strongest in Indiana and Ohio, with loyal support from thousands of Pennsylvania Dutch Klansmen, who held intense feelings against Roman Catholics. Dedicating itself to White supremacy, Protestant Christianity, and Americanism, the new Klan used intimidation, violence, and politics to influence voters, employers, schools, and textbook content, seeking moral regulation and a stabilization of the old order.[18]

American entry into the war in 1917 touched off an anti-German, patriotic hysteria. This ranged from renaming sauerkraut "liberty cabbage," to German Americans losing their jobs, to mob attacks on German establishments and communities. Anything German was eradicated: German-language publications, school courses, church services, concert music, street names, and organizations.

In each instance, these reactionary movements flourished and faded within a few years. Internal struggles, corruption charges, and the free-silver issue undermined the APA. Corruption among the leadership of the Ku Klux Klan and restrictive immigration laws lessening public concern hastened its decline. The end of World War I in 1918 soon enabled the German American community to reassert its ethnic marks of organizational activities, although its cultural resilience never sprang back fully to its former vitality.

THE NEXT HORIZON

A new flurry of immigration after the war brought calls anew for restrictions. Passage of the National Origins Quota Act of 1921 reduced immigration to 3 percent of any nationality living in the United States in 1910. Amended in 1924 to a temporary limit of 2 percent of those here in 1890, the limit was raised again to 3 percent in 1929 with a ceiling of 150,000 total immigrants. Because the law favored northern and western Europeans, supporters hailed this legislation as a way to prevent further dilution of the U.S. population and its cultural composition. In their desire to "keep America American," nativists succeeded in ending the Great Migration.

Yet as Charles Dickens once wrote, "Change begets change." The labor market still needed workers in good economic times. With few Europeans to fill expanding needs, Mexicans and Puerto Ricans would meet the demand for new labor, setting in motion a greater Hispanic migration than ever before.

Ahead lay the Roaring 20s, the Great Depression, and another world war, which would bring in about 400,000 displaced persons afterwards. It was a paltry number, however, compared to past immigrant totals or to the nation's 150.7 million people in 1950.

Even though in 1930 almost one of three Americans was foreign-born or the child of immigrant parents, ethnicity became less visible. With few new immigrants to renew them, ethnic communities would fade, causing a new generation of Americans to forget the great cultural diversity that had been such a dynamic part of U.S. society. Once again, as in the early 19th century, low immigration in the 1920s and throughout the 1930s, together with the pervasive acculturation process, were slowly creating a culturally homogeneous population. Although assimilation remained the ongoing process it always had been, the ebb in immigration gave it preeminence over the ever-present reality of pluralism.

This time, however, there would be differences. Some groups—the Armenians, Greeks, and Jews—would quickly enter the middle class. Others—like the Italians, Poles, and Slavic peoples—would mostly remain in working-class occupations for another generation. So, too, would Asian Americans, African Americans, Mexicans, and Native Americans—victims of racial discrimination and internal colonization—mostly struggle to survive in poverty or near-poverty circumstances.

Further ahead lay suburbanization, the end of the Cold War, the Vietnam War, the civil rights movements, space exploration, the fall of communism, and the information age. Significantly, also ahead would be a new immigration law and a third wave of immigration that would once again bring widespread diversity to the land and test anew its people's acceptance of that diversity.

NOTES

1. Rudolph Daniels, *Trains across the Continent*, 2d ed. (Bloomington: Indiana University Press, 2001), p. 75.

2. See Selig Perlman, *A History of Trade Unionism in the United States* (Charleston, SC: Nabu Press, 2010; originally published in 1923).

3. U.S. Census Bureau, *The Report of Population of the United States at the Eleventh Census, 1890*, Vol. 1, Part 2 (Washington, DC, 1897), pp. 414, 417, 420, 423, and 426.

4. See Alice Kestler-Harris, *Out to Work*, 20th ed. (New York: Oxford University Press, 2003).

5. Robert Blauner, *Still the Big News: Racial Oppression in America* (Philadelphia: Temple University Press, 2001), p. 54.

6. George M. Fredrickson, *White Supremacy: A Comparative Study of American and South African History* (New York: Oxford University Press, 1981), p. 130.

7. Harper Barnes, *Never Been a Time: The 1917 Race Riot That Sparked the Civil Rights Movement* (New York: Walker and Company, 2008).

8. See W. E. B. DuBois, *The Philadelphia Negro: A Social Study* (Charleston, SC: Nabu Press, 2010; originally published in 1899).

9. Robert Higgs, *Competition and Conflict: Blacks in the American Economy, 1865–1914* (New York: Cambridge University Press, 2008), p. 126.

10. *Congressional Record* (February 14, 1879), quoted in Vincent N. Parrillo, *Strangers to These Shores*, 10th ed. (Boston: Allyn and Bacon, 2011), pp. 266–7.

11. Roger Daniels, *The Politics of Prejudice* (Berkeley: University of California Press, 1999), p. 20.

12. American Federation of Labor, *Proceedings* (1893), p. 73.

13. Frederick E. Hoxie, *A Final Promise: The Campaign to Assimilate the Indians, 1880–1920* (Lincoln: University of Nebraska Press, 2001).

14. Philip M. Kayal and Joseph M. Kayal, *The Syrian-Lebanese in America* (New York: Twayne, 1975).

15. See Dino Cinel, *The National Integration of Return Italian Migration, 1870–1929* (New York: Cambridge University Press, 2002).

16. Madison Grant, *The Passing of the Great Race* (Charleston, SC: Nabu Press, 2010; originally published in 1916).

17. See Donald J. Kinzner, *An Episode in Anti-Catholicism: The American Protective Association* (Seattle: University of Washington Press, 1964); Kenneth Jackson, *The Ku Klux Klan in the City, 1915–1930* (New York: Oxford University Press, 1967).

18. Thomas R. Pegram, *One Hundred Percent American: The Rebirth and Decline of the Ku Klux Klan in the 1920s* (Chicago: Ivan R. Dee Publisher, 2011).

7

Diversity in the Information Age

Our nation is the enduring dream of every immigrant who's ever set foot on these shores, and the millions still struggling to be free. This nation, this idea called America, was and always will be a new world—our new world.

—President George H. W. Bush, 1990

The Electronic Numerical Integrator and Computer (ENIAC), was the first programmable electronic digital computer, making its debut in 1946. Weighing 30 tons and measuring 150 feet wide, it had 20 banks of flashing lights, with 17,468 vacuum tubes, 70,000 resistors, and 10,000 capacitors.

As early as 1948, the invention of the transistor signaled the dawn of an electronic revolution. In the 1950s, numerous advances—the discovery of the structure of the genetic material DNA, the first successful transplant of an organ (the kidney), the development of an effective polio vaccine and of an oral contraceptive, the building of atomic energy plants, and the successful orbiting of Sputnik, the first artificial earth satellite—all expanded the horizons for human achievement.

The 1960s, an incredible decade of turbulence and reform, also heralded new accomplishments once the sole province of science fiction. We developed the laser beam, transplanted hearts, and launched communication satellites instantly linking the world with images and sound from anywhere. Sending men into space and landing on the moon fired our imaginations even more. In the 1970s came microprocessors, test tube babies, space shuttles, and the eradication of smallpox. On the heels of those advances arrived VCRs, CDs, and personal computers in the home and workplace, utilizing the Internet and the information highway.

A DIFFERENT AMERICA

The high-tech age dramatically altered U.S. society just as the industrial age once did. Previous emigrants from agrarian Europe had to make a triple adjustment to a new culture, an urban environment, and an industrialized society. Many of today's emigrants also make a triple adjustment, but for some the third part is often a bigger leap in trying to adjust from a preindustrial background into a postindustrial society.

Gone are many unskilled and semiskilled jobs that once enabled newcomers to gain even a toehold in their new society. Most of any remaining factory and mill jobs, once plentiful in the cities a short distance from where immigrants clustered in ethnic urban neighborhoods, are now often in industrial parks away from where many of today's immigrants can afford to live. Other new types of jobs now exist in the building, landscaping, and food service sectors, but many are low-paying, dead-end jobs.

Some immigrants, however, arrive possessing entrepreneurial skills or the education and training needed for higher status, higher paying positions. Their income enables them to settle in residential areas unaccustomed to the presence of first-generation Americans, particularly racially and culturally distinct Asians. Many rural and suburban areas now have a racial and cultural diversity once mostly confined to our cities.

Today's diversity is visible everywhere, not just in a few geographic locales. Some states receive more immigrants than others, and some have greater numbers of one or more groups than others, but no state is immune to the influx of developing-world immigrants. Each of the 50 states now contains an unprecedented mixture of racial and ethnic groups that reflects current immigration patterns.

For Americans lulled by previous decades of lower immigration totals and new arrivals primarily from the traditional sending countries of Europe, the presence of so many different groups and languages is strange, but it is déjà vu for this nation. Some of the groups may be new to the U.S. scene, but the patterns of acculturation and ethnogenesis among them and of negative dominant responses are replays of yesteryear.

However, this latest manifestation of pluralism also comes with some new ingredients. Government policy now supports pluralism instead of forced assimilation. Bilingualism in ballots, driver education manuals, education, and other public aspects are controversial realities. Social legislation from the 1960s ensures minority rights and opportunities as never before. Because diversity is more visible and protected than ever, some Americans fear the loss of an integrative, assimilationist force in the land.

THE LARGER CONTEXT

In this era, the United States became a global, hegemonic power, particularly after the collapse of the Soviet Union in 1991. Changes in immigration laws, declining birth rates in Europe, and numerous push factors in the developing world—high birth rates, weak economies, and political unrest, to name a few—resulted in a new migration flow to the United States. Asia and Latin America surpassed Europe as the primary sending areas of new immigrants, a process intensified by the chain migration pattern of family members reuniting with those who arrived before them. Living conditions in Mexico prompted an unauthorized migration flow northward across a convenient, porous border. The violence of wars in Vietnam, Bosnia, and Kosovo (and civil wars in Angola, El Salvador, Peru, and Sierra Leone) forced refugees to flee and played an additional role in further changing the population composition of the United States.

Technological advances led to the evolution of a global economy, enabling companies to market their goods and services throughout the world. The lower labor costs in newly industrialized countries (NICs)—notably Brazil, China, India, Malaysia, Mexico, the Philippines, South Africa, Thailand, and Turkey—gave them a comparative advantage over more developed countries (MDCs) in exporting their products, thereby stimulating rapid economic growth in those emerging economic powers. As a postindustrial society, the manufacturing sector of the United States declined. Once dominant in global exports, the United States now ranks third behind China and Germany. Japan, France, South Korea, and Italy complete the list of the top seven countries.[1] This development has a global impact on the American economy and job opportunities for both the native-born and foreign-born population.

Globalization—whether through economic changes, rapid air travel, instant telecommunications, or borderless Internet activity—has shrunk the world irrevocably. Practically everyone everywhere is now aware of the diversity of people and cultures elsewhere. Foreign lands no longer seem so remote, prompting in many the desire to travel or migrate. Multinational companies are the norm, as are transnational families maintaining strong links to their homeland, as well as building new lives in their adopted country. Despite their inevitable adapting to their new culture, recent immigrants find through technology the means to retain their own multicultural reality through a psychological nearness to others they left behind, as well as in the reinforced ethnic vitality they experience among compatriots who have made the same migrating journey.

THE HUMAN ELEMENT

This exciting world of scientific advancement is, of course, only one part of the human dimension, and in many ways, other aspects of life are unchanged from past generations. People in the world still suffer from hunger, deprivation, persecution, and repression. They still dream of a better life for themselves and their children. For many, that dream has a name: America.

In July 1963, when President John F. Kennedy urged an end to national quota restrictions in a special message to Congress, he initiated a change in our immigration policy that culminated with President Lyndon B. Johnson symbolically signing the new bill in 1965 at the base of the Statue of Liberty. With his signature, he ended a discriminatory immigration policy that emphasized place of birth and not individual worth or family reunification.

Unexpected Consequences

Most government officials expected the new legislation to open the doors to increased European migration. After all, an extensive waiting list for visas then existed in many European countries severely restricted under the old quota system. Yet in a typical year, the British Isles, for example, sent less than 40 percent of its allotted quota.

Immigrants from some countries—namely, Greece, Italy, Poland, Portugal, Spain, the Soviet Union, and Yugoslavia—did increase notably. However, the "push" factors to leave were now greater in other parts of the world, and soon European migration was quickly eclipsed. By the 1980s, European immigration represented only 10 percent of the total, with countries such as Greece, Italy, and Yugoslavia declining significantly in the number of emigrants leaving for the United States.

In the 1960s, emigrants from the Caribbean and Latin America outnumbered those from Europe for the first time and have done so ever since. European immigration was more than two-and-a-half times Asian immigration in the 1960s, but only slightly more than half the Asian total in the 1970s. In 2010, Europe accounted for 9 percent of all legal immigration, Asia for 39 percent, and the Caribbean and Latin America for another 39 percent. Canada, Africa, and Oceania accounted for the remaining 13 percent.[2]

INSTITUTIONALIZING MINORITY RIGHTS

Significant legislation passed in the 1960s brought American ideals about equality closer to reality for minorities long denied their rights. The Civil Rights Act of 1964 was the most far-reaching law against racial discrimination ever passed. It dealt with voting rights, employment practices, and any place of public accommodation, whether eating, lodging, entertainment, recreation, or service. It gave broad powers to the U.S. Attorney General to intervene in private suits regarding violation of civil rights and it directed federal agencies to monitor state and local recipients of federal funds and withhold monies wherever noncompliance was found.

In 1965, Congress simplified judicial enforcement of the voting laws and extended them to state and local elections. In 1968, new legislation barred discrimination in housing and gave Native Americans greater rights in their dealings with courts and government agencies. Affirmative action, initiated by an executive order in

1963 by President Kennedy, became a powerful tool toward reducing institutional discrimination in hiring, promotion, and educational opportunities for minority group members or women.

Since then, minority groups in the affirmative action protected categories—Asians, Blacks, Hispanics, women, the elderly, disabled, and gays—made important gains, as delineated in the following sections on specific groups. For women, majority or minority, we note some progress now.

Females have achieved near parity with the males of their race in the level of educational attainment. A greater proportion than ever before are in the labor force, with growing numbers of women entering male-dominated occupations, including such advanced degree professions as medicine, dentistry, law, and engineering. Whereas only 9 percent of women earned bachelor's degrees in business and management in 1971, about half now do. Even in the historically male-dominated domains of mathematics and statistics, where women earned 13 percent of the degrees in 1971, they now earn 43 percent and are steadily increasing in numbers.[3] The 112th Congress (2011–2013) has the most female senators (17) in its history, while house representatives number 72, one fewer than the previous Congress. The number of women serving in state legislatures is four times greater than the number 20 years ago. Although only 2 of 9 justices currently serving on the U.S. Supreme Court are women, thousands of others hold judgeships at the federal, state, county, and local levels.[4]

These gains and many others too numerous to mention are encouraging, yet many disquieting signs exist as well. Workplace gender bias contributes to the continuing wage gap. In 2011, White women earned 82.5 percent as much as their male counterparts, more than Asian women (70.1 percent), but less than Black (90.2 percent) and Hispanic women (92.9 percent).[5]

For decades, women faced a "glass ceiling" that limited their upward mobility into top corporate management positions. That situation is slowly changing. In 2011, women were chief executive officers (CEOs) of 18 of the Fortune 500 companies, an all-time high.[6] In 1995, women held only 2 percent of the chief financial officer (CFO) positions at the country's 500 largest corporate firms. In 2011, they held 9 percent, a figure that has been holding steady since 2007.[7] With women in most major companies constituting about half of managers, the possibilities loom large that many other women will soon be breaking through to the top positions.

Women of racial minority groups face the double problem of racism and sexism. As in generations past, women from affluent, mainstream groups enjoy greater advantages and are often social activists in quest of gender equality. Many women have not yet reached that destination, but their journey is nearer its destination than ever before.

THE EUROPEANS

Although Europe is no longer the principal sending region for immigrants to the United States, it still continues to send a sizable number. Between 2000 and 2010, about 1.44 million European immigrants arrived. Included were approximately 153,000 British, 140,000 Russians, 149,000 Ukrainians, 117,000 Poles, 89,000 Bosnia-Herzegovinians, 78,000 Germans, 54,000 Romanians, and 39,000 Bulgarians.[8] Although the nation's population composition is changing, 1 in 7 Americans claimed German ancestry in 2010, 1 in 10 claimed Irish, and 1 in 20 Italian.[9]

California, Texas, and New York, in that order, are typically the primary places of intended residence for today's German arrivals. For the Irish, it is New York, Massachusetts, and California. Polish immigrants prefer Illinois, New York, and New Jersey, whereas former Soviet Union immigrants like better the states of California, New York, and Illinois. British immigrants mostly choose California, New York, and Florida.

States with the highest density of people with English ancestry are Utah, Maine, and Idaho. Highest German densities are North and South Dakota, Wisconsin, and Minnesota. Highest Irish densities are Massachusetts, New Hampshire, and Rhode Island. Other significant ancestry densities are the Italians in Rhode Island, Connecticut, New Jersey, and New York; the French in Vermont, New Hampshire, Maine, and Rhode Island; and the Polish in Wisconsin, Michigan, Connecticut, Illinois, and New Jersey.

ASIANS AND PACIFIC ISLANDERS

The Information Age has witnessed Asia surpassing Europe as a sending area of immigrants to the United States. In the 1960s, about 1 in 10 immigrants came from Asia. In the 1970s, however, Asians became one in every three immigrants, a ratio even slightly higher now. As they once naively did with the Native Americans and the southern, central, and eastern European immigrants, today many Americans view Asian Americans as a single cultural entity because they are of the same race. In fact, they are quite different from each other in their histories, languages, religious beliefs, and cultural attributes.

The earliest of the Asian immigrant groups to put down roots in the United States, the Chinese have become a strong presence, numbering now more than 3.8 million. Although Chinese Americans live in all 50 states, their greatest concentrations are in California and New York, with high aggregates also found in Massachusetts, Illinois, New Jersey, and Texas. Chinese Americans have a higher percentage of college graduates than the total U.S. population (52 to 28 percent) so, not surprisingly, their ratio in the management and professional occupations is also higher (54 to 36 percent).[10] However, their poverty rate is only slightly lower (13 to 14 percent), suggesting somewhat of a bipolar socioeconomic distribution.

Other than Mexican Americans, no other foreign-born group is as heavily concentrated in one state as in California where nearly one-third of the 3.2 million Filipino population lives. Other states where large clusters of Filipinos live are Hawaii, New York, Illinois, New Jersey, Washington, Texas, and Virginia. Mostly Roman Catholics, American-born Filipinos tend to have less education and fewer occupational skills than do newcomers from the Philippines, and so many work in low-paying, private-sector jobs. Some of the new arrivals find work in professional and technical fields, especially in health care. Because of licensing and hiring problems, many are underemployed and unable to secure jobs comparable to their education, skills, and experience. Filipino Americans are fragmented linguistically, politically, and socially. Although they have strong loyalty to their family and the church, they generally avoid group separatism or an ethnic advocacy group. Although fraternal and social organizations do offer ethnic interaction opportunities, most Filipinos seem more desirous of broader participation in non-ethnic associations.

Asian Indians are another sizable presence, now numbering about 2.8 million. California is home to the largest cluster of Asian Indians, with other high population totals found in New York, New Jersey, Illinois, and Texas. Most Asian Indian immigrants are Hindi-speaking, but many others arrive who speak Gujarati, Punjabi, or Bengali. Two-thirds of all working Asian Indians are in managerial or professional occupations, greater than any other group in the United States, including Whites. They also are the most highly educated of all U.S. groups; about 71 percent of all adults over age 25 are college graduates, compared to 29.5 percent of all Americans.[11] About 20 percent of the nation's convenience stores, gas stations, or family-managed hotels and motels are operated by Asian Indians, giving them a family-labor economic niche. This ethnic group has the smallest proportion of its members in low-paying, low-status jobs.

Vietnamese Americans, now exceeding 1.5 million, live in all 50 states. Half of them live in California, with other sizable numbers in Texas, Virginia, Washington, New York, and Pennsylvania. Their acculturation is similar to other Asian groups. The older adults—particularly the women, who are less likely to be in work situations interacting with outgroup members—display little grasp of English or American ways, but the children and younger adults, more exposed to American life, learn quickly, and their educational attainment levels are comparable to the national average.[12]

Korean Americans are the fifth largest Asian American group, with their immigration presently exceeding 20,000 annually. Among first- and second-generation Korean Americans, about one-third live in California, with other large concentrations in New York, New Jersey, Texas, Virginia, Washington, and Maryland. About 70 percent of the 1.3 million Korean Americans are Christians, mostly Methodist and Presbyterian. Church affiliation is about four times greater than in Korea because the church also serves as a communal bond for ethnic identity and culture.[13] Koreans can be found in a variety of occupations, but one striking aspect is their self-employment rate of about 12 percent, far greater than any other group.[14] One out of eight Korean Americans is thus a business owner. These family-owned businesses are found in both cities and suburbs, more likely serving other minority customers or mainstream Americans than fellow Koreans.

In 1970, Japanese Americans constituted the largest Asian American group, totaling 591,000. However, with negative population growth in Japan, its emigrants to the U.S. are presently about 9,000 annually, which is far below other Asian-sending nations. Today, however, Japanese Americans rank sixth, behind the groups just mentioned. As with other Asian groups, the largest concentration of Japanese Americans resides in California. Other high population areas are New York, Hawaii, Texas, and Washington. Although a significant presence in some states, Japanese Americans are the most widely dispersed of all Asian groups throughout the 50 states. Younger Japanese Americans seem more interested in their structural assimilation, as indicated by their high rates of outgroup dating and marriage. To illustrate, about 1.3 million Japanese Americans resided in the U.S. in 2010, but their numbers drop by nearly 40 percent when the ancestry is Japanese alone.[15]

More than 275,000 Cambodians, 234,000 Laotians, and 234,000 Thai also call the United States home. Many of the first wave were refugees, but more recent arrivals are either part of the U.S. family reunification program or else immigrants motivated by the same forces that attract others. A new wave of refugees from Afghanistan is beginning to make its presence felt in many communities; about 25,000 Afghanis arrived between 2000 and 2010. Also comprising part of the cultural diversity of Asian Americans are more than 365,000 Pakistanis, about half of whom live in California. The United States is also the residence of more than 77,000 Afghanis, 114,000 Bangladeshi, 87,000 Indonesians, and 11,000 Malaysians.[16]

BLACK AMERICANS

Use of the term *African American* is somewhat problematic because we must distinguish among those who are American-born of long-ago African ancestry, those who are recent African immigrants, and those who are from an Afro-Caribbean background. Even within these three main groupings, enormous diversity exists in the lives of the different social classes of American-born Blacks and in the languages, cultures, and adjustment patterns of Black immigrants from the different countries. Moreover, as with other racial groups, social stratification creates separate worlds for the American-born, and ingroup loyalty and social isolation among many first-generation Americans often keeps them apart from others.

U.S. society is far from eliminating racism as a serious social problem, and Black Americans still remain disproportionately represented among the nation's poor, with all the attendant problems of that sad reality. Despite the spending of billions of dollars on social welfare programs and economic incentives, one-fourth of Black Americans remain mired in poverty. Yet this is not the complete picture. Black America is really two societies: one poor and the other nonpoor. Thanks to civil rights legislation and other social reforms, remarkable gains have been made, especially in education and occupational representation. Of no small significance also is the election in 2008 of Barack Obama, the first non-White in world history to be elected national leader in a predominantly White nation. Nevertheless, a disturbing gap remains between Black Americans and White Americans.

One of the more encouraging social indicators for Black Americans is educational attainment, but even here the message is mixed. From a 1980 high school dropout rate of 16 percent, compared with

11.3 percent for Whites, both rates are now lower though a gap still remains—9.3 percent for Blacks and 5.2 percent for Whites in 2010. In 1970, 4 percent of Blacks and 11 percent of Whites completed college; by 2010, this level was achieved by 17.9 percent of Blacks and 29.5 percent of Whites, or a quadrupling of the Black rate to a near tripling of the White rate. Black enrollment in college among 18- to 24-year-olds increased from 19 percent in 1980 to 38 percent in 2010. However, this increase only slightly narrowed the gap with that of White students, whose college enrollment grew from 27 percent to 45 percent in the same period.[17]

Black representation in managerial and professional specialties is steadily growing, now at about 23 percent for males and 33 percent for females, compared to the 35 and 41 percentages, respectively, for Whites. About 19 percent of the males and 31 percent of the females are in sales and office positions, figures relatively similar to the 18 and 34 percentages for Whites.[18]

The continued increase in the number of Black elected officials is another positive indicator. With 41 of 435 representatives in the 112th Congress, Blacks are nearing a total proportionate to their population ratio, although none presently serves in the U.S. Senate. More than 9,000 elected Black officials now serve in the U.S. or state legislatures, in city or county offices, and in law enforcement or education. This number has grown consistently for more than three decades.

On the negative side are the data for Blacks living in the central cities: higher rates of poverty, unemployment, infant mortality, miscarriages, and mortality than Whites. Of particular concern is the high proportion of female-headed families. Of the 8.9 million Black families in 2010, women headed 29 percent of them, compared with a total of 13 percent female-headed White families. Adding strength to some Black American families, however, is the extended family household. About 14 percent of children under age 18 with only the mother present live in a household with at least one grandparent present as well.[19]

Many Black immigrants add to the diversity found among the U.S. Black population. About 91 percent of the more than 881,000 Haitian Americans now in the United States are Roman Catholics and two thirds of them live in Florida and New York. Other states with a higher percentage of Haitians than the national average are Massachusetts, New Jersey, and Connecticut. Most live in tightly clustered neighborhoods in large family households. Speaking Haitian Creole, 3 in 5 are foreign born with a limited command of English. Most work in low-paying jobs in service industries or as farm laborers, and the Haitian American poverty rate is about 50 percent higher than the national average.[20]

Jamaican Americans are the largest non-Hispanic group from the Caribbean now living in the United States. Of the approximately 965,000 here, about three-fourths are foreign-born. Jamaicans continue to grow as a sizable minority group; for instance, about 192,000 arrived between 2000 and 2010. About 40 percent of all Jamaican Americans live in New York. Florida is home to about another one-fourth of the total, with other large Jamaican populations found in New Jersey, Connecticut, California, Maryland, Massachusetts, and Pennsylvania.

Immigration from Africa remained low until the 1980s, but since 1980, about 1 million immigrants have arrived. Nigerians constitute the largest group, with about 265,000 claiming Nigerian ancestry in 2010, compared with 203,000 Ethiopians, 120,000 Somalians, and 91,000 Ghanaians.[21] African immigrants face two handicaps in culturally adjusting to life in the United States. In their homelands they were a racial majority, but here they are not. In various social and work settings, many encounter racism for the first time. Second, because of their cultural distinctions, many Africans do not identify with either American Blacks or Afro-Caribbeans. Successful native-born Blacks interested in helping the less fortunate of their race usually concentrate on the American-born poor, not on newcomers from Africa. As a matter of preference and necessity, the African immigrants seek out one another for mutual support and refuge.

An important lesson emerges from the last point. Culture is the important determinant in how groups relate to one another. Black may be a convenient racial category, but it is a simplistic generalization that ignores cultural differences. Blacks born in Ethiopia, Ghana, Haiti, Jamaica, Nigeria, the United States, or any other country belong to distinctive groups whose cultural differences make them unlike one another and, to some extent, more likely to have social distance barriers between them. Multiculturalism thus takes many forms, both between and within all races.

HISPANIC AMERICANS

Hispanic is a broad term that encompasses the *Hispanos* of the Southwest whose family roots predate the nation's expanding borders, U.S. nationals such as the Puerto Ricans, Spaniards from Europe, Latino immigrants and refugees, and their descendants. This generic term suggests a common Spanish language and cultural influence, but it is deceptive because it ignores the Portuguese Brazilians and the many cultural and class distinctions among the various Spanish-speaking nationalities.

Although some non-Hispanic Americans view the Hispanic American population as a collectivity of similar groups, their differences are consequential enough to prevent the evolution at this time of a cohesive entity. Cultural orientations, social class divisions, and first-generation American ingroup loyalties create considerable diversity within this rapidly growing ethnic group, presently comprising nearly one-sixth of the total U.S. population.

Excluding the Mexican Americans, about 6.8 million people are first- or second-generation Americans from Central or South America. Salvadorans are the largest group, with about 1.6 million, followed by Guatemalans with 1 million and Colombians with about 909,000. Other larger groups include those from Honduras (633,000), Ecuador (565,000), Peru (531,000), and Nicaragua (348,000).[22] Central Americans are diverse and defy generalization, except to say that they tend to be less educated and more susceptible to poverty than all other Latinos. Similarly, differences among South Americans in the economic development in their homelands, rural or urban backgrounds, social class, or racial composition make for a diverse population.

Between 2000 and 2010, more than 318,000 Cubans came to the United States, bringing the total of those with Cuban ancestry to over 1.8 million.[23] Two out of every three Cuban Americans live in Florida, with other large concentrations in New Jersey, New York, and Texas. In Miami, the Cubans have stamped a positive imprint. Its "Little Havana" section is now a 600-block area, and more than 30,000 Cuban-owned businesses operate in the Miami metropolitan area. The Cuban influence has transformed Miami from a winter resort town to a year-round commercial center with linkages throughout Latin America and has made it into a leading bilingual cultural center. Cubans have a lower fertility rate and a much higher proportion of people 65 years old and older than other Hispanic groups. They also have a lower unemployment rate, higher median family income, and greater middle-class composition.

Another major sending country of recent immigrants is the Dominican Republic, which sent more than 329,000 immigrants between 2000 and 2010, bringing the total of those with Dominican ancestry to 1.4 million.[24] Two out of every three live in New York, with other large concentrations in New Jersey, Florida, Massachusetts, and Pennsylvania. Their hefty numbers (nearly 1 million now) and settlement patterns have enabled the Dominicans to establish viable ethnic neighborhoods, often adjacent to Puerto Rican ones. Although the two groups coexist and essentially keep to themselves, intergroup marriages and consensual unions are becoming common. Low educational attainment and limited job skills result in high unemployment rates and poverty-level living standards among many Dominicans.

Most of the 32 million Mexican Americans are concentrated in the southwestern states, with the largest concentrations in California, Texas, and Arizona. However, all 50 states contain appreciable numbers of Mexican Americans, with the largest concentration living outside the Southwest in Illinois. Nine out of 10 reside in metropolitan areas, and some of them are realizing the American Dream in rising educational levels, occupational opportunities, and incomes. However, Mexican American gains as a group have not kept pace with Anglo gains because of the large influx of unskilled, poorly educated newcomers. Almost half of urban Mexican Americans live in central cities where, for many, life in the barrio is one of substandard housing, high unemployment rates, poverty, school dropouts, crime, and gang violence. One source of strength, however, is the family. Mexican Americans' divorce rate is well below the national level, and the percentage of their family units headed by both a husband and a wife is comparable to the national average.

Of the 4.6 million Puerto Ricans living on the mainland, one-third of them live in New York. Other states with large concentrations are Florida, New Jersey, Pennsylvania, and Massachusetts. Puerto Ricans have a higher educational attainment level and lower poverty rate than Mexicans and Central Americans, but lag behind non-Hispanic Americans.[25] As with the Mexican American urban poor, the Puerto Rican urban poor live in areas of limited job opportunities, making them more vulnerable to welfare dependency. Some segments of the Puerto Rican community are doing well. Almost 40 percent of all Puerto Rican families earn as much or more than the national median family income level, and about 10 percent have incomes that classify them as affluent.

More than half of the Hispanic population resides in just three states: California, Texas, and Florida. Their rapid increase (a 43 percent gain from 35.3 million in 2000 to 50.53 million in 2010) accounted for more than half of the total population growth in the United States.[26] Because of a higher birth rate than African Americans, a high immigration rate, and a low average age of these immigrants (nearly 40 percent are under age 21), the Hispanic American population will continue to grow significantly in the foreseeable future.

Their growing numbers have enabled them to gain political power (more than 6,000 elected and appointed public officials nationwide) and have increased their labor market competition, sometimes creating tensions with the African American community.

Perhaps the analogy of the *nopales* is apt here.[27] *Nopales* are cactus with a rather prickly exterior, but they also are edible treats if one proceeds with patience, caution, and determination. In previous eras, a new group's arrival often created tensions with an older minority group, particularly in economic competition, but in time the situation improved as both groups moved past the sharply contested points and "digested" their share of the American Dream. That was not always accomplished simply, but neither was it usually a prolonged encounter. Hopefully, African and Hispanic Americans will similarly move past the prickly experience in short fashion and into that place where both can enjoy the fruits of their labors.

NORTH AFRICANS AND MIDDLE EASTERNERS

Immigration from North African and Middle Eastern countries has been of such sustained strength that these ethnic groups have become a visible presence in many states. More than 506,000 immigrants arrived between 2000 and 2010.[28] Not all are Muslims, particularly the many Christians from Lebanon and Coptic Christians from Egypt.

Of the approximately 1.7 million Americans claiming Arabic ancestry in 2010, two-thirds live in just 10 states, with one-third residing in California, New York, and Michigan. Most (94 percent) live in metro areas; the six largest of these are Detroit, Los Angeles, New York, Chicago, Washington, DC, and northeastern New Jersey. Lebanese Americans are the largest group of Arab Americans residing in most states, except for other larger groups in Georgia, New Jersey, and Tennessee (Egyptians), Rhode Island (Syrians), and Arizona (Moroccans). The largest Palestinian population is in Illinois, and the Iraqi and Assyrian/Chaldean communities are concentrated in Illinois, Michigan, and California.[29]

Another large Middle Eastern group, but neither Arab nor Arabic-speaking, is the Iranians. With their distinct culture and Farsi language, about 60 percent of the more than 463,000 Iranian Americans live in California. Other large enclaves are in the New York and Washington, DC, metropolitan areas. Many are middle-class professionals, and their children are becoming extensively Americanized despite their parents' efforts to preserve their culture.

The 195,000 Turks also are neither Arabs nor Arabic-speaking. Some are working-class tradesmen and laborers who cluster in urban neighborhoods in sufficient numbers to induce the establishment of bilingual programs in neighborhood schools. However, nearly half have a college degree and about one-fourth of Turkish Americans have an advanced degree. As professionals or businessmen, they settle in dispersed patterns in the suburbs.

Over 1,200 mosques now dot the U.S. landscape, two-thirds of them built since 1981. Muslims are but one of many conservative groups in the United States, but in attempting to retain their values and practices, their visibility—particularly since 9/11—often elicits suspicion and hostility, a subject we examine more closely in the next chapter.

NATIVE AMERICANS

By 2010, the Native American population increased 16 percent, rising from 2.5 million in 2000 to 2.9 million, thanks to a birth rate higher than the national average. Their quality of life varies from tribe to tribe. Some reap large profits from gambling casinos, whereas others languish in poverty. Nationwide, the Native American poverty rate hovers at nearly three times the national average. Equally depressing are statistics showing Native American life expectancy about 2.4 years less than the national average, and their infants die at a rate of nearly 10 per every 1,000 live births, compared with 7 per 1,000 for the U.S. total population. Moreover, their death rates are higher than other Americans for tuberculosis (500 percent), chronic liver disease and cirrhosis (260 percent), diabetes (180 percent), homicide (180 percent), and unintentional (alcohol-related) injuries (139 percent).[30]

Twenty-two percent of Native Americans are ages 10 to 19, compared with 14 percent of other U.S. racial/ethnic groups. Yet compared with those same minority groups, fewer Native American teens will graduate from high school (77 percent vs. 84 percent), and fewer still complete college (13 percent vs. 27 percent) given current patterns.[31]

Disputes about water rights, fishing rights, natural resources, landfills, and upwind or upstream pollution of tribal lands continue in many states. However, legal efforts to honor treaty rights have been more numerous and successful in recent years. Those successes have led state officials to respect the growing power of Native Americans and to negotiate directly with tribes in their borders to avoid costly possible court defeats on environmental issues, health policy, child welfare agreements, and water rights.

RELIGIOUS DIVERSITY

The United States is now probably the most religiously diverse country in the world, with more than 1,500 religious groups. About 200 of these are conventional Christian and Jewish denominations, with 29 of them having memberships exceeding 1 million.[32] Although the country remains mostly Christian (78 percent claim this faith), the forces of immigration, intermarriage, and disenchantment with some of the oldest religious institutions are redefining the country's religious composition. For example, the United States now contains 6 times more Muslim Americans (4.8 million), 16 times more Buddhists (3.4 million), 15 times more Hindus (1.5 million), and 28 times more Sikhs (286,000) than it did in 1970.[33] Religions once on the periphery of mainstream Christianity are growing vigorously: Mormons by 188 percent, Jehovah's Witnesses by 187 percent, and the Pentecostal Assemblies of God by 364 percent. In contrast, the once dominant Presbyterian, Episcopal, and Congregational churches have declined in membership by 30 to 43 percent.[34]

A curious paradox now exists. Perhaps the fastest growing group of all is for those opting not to belong to any church, with these "unaffiliated" now totaling 48 million Americans, or 15 percent of all Americans.[35] Nevertheless, religion remains an important aspect of U.S. culture. In a 2011 Gallup poll, 92 percent said they believe in God and, in another poll in 2009, 65 percent said that religion is an important part of their daily lives, a fairly consistent proportion for decades and two to three times higher than in other Western nations.[36] Although the proportion of Americans attending a weekly worship service may appear low at 44 percent, it is higher than Canada (38 percent) and the United Kingdom (27 percent). In contrast, Nigeria (89 percent), Ireland (84 percent), the Philippines (68 percent), Poland (55 percent), Puerto Rico (52 percent), and Mexico (46 percent) have higher weekly church attendance.[37]

The growing diversity in religion and its increased importance for many often have a pronounced effect on numerous societal issues and on race and ethnicity. Such "hot-button" topics as abortion, gay marriage, Nativity displays on public property, and school prayer, for instance, fuel intense and bitter debate, political pandering, and extensive lobbying. Erection of an Islamic center near Ground Zero in New York City or of non-Western houses of worship in mostly Christian suburban communities can trigger a backlash of resentment and hostility. Seemingly minor issues, such as Sikh males insisting on maintaining their religious beliefs in wearing a turban and having the right to be, say, a police officer, can spark controversy and criticism.

In many ways, U.S. society is more religiously tolerant than in past centuries. However, the efforts of some religious groups to impose their values about some of these issues on the rest of society create both division and conflict. A multicultural society continually faces the moral challenge of encouraging norms and laws for the common good while respecting the different religious values of others.

THE NEXT HORIZON

A new wave of immigrants arrives on U.S. shores in pursuit of the same dreams of a better life that motivated millions of other immigrants before them. A new generation of native-born Americans, the descendants of those older immigrants, observes the present immigration with apprehension, concern, and alarm about what they fear is an undermining of the American culture and character. That also was the past nativist reaction to previous immigrations.

Some demographers, historians, and politicians point with alarm to tomorrow's reality, given today's trends. Misgivings about the multiple losses of White numerical superiority, preeminence of Western culture and the Judeo-Christian heritage, and preservation of the existing social order are heard from many sections of the country. There is distress about group separatism and use of languages other than English. On another front, feminist advocacy also draws negative responses in some quarters.

Some of the resistance is from well-intentioned individuals who view the changes as altering the nation's identity too dramatically. Some of that concern is rooted in racial fears, as the White majority sees its numerical superiority and its economic and political dominance threatened by the continued arrival of so many non-White immigrants.

At the heart of most of these feminist, ethnic, and racial issues is the struggle for power. Challenges to the status quo—as vocal and visible minority groups seek economic, political, and social power— prompt resistance by those unwilling to yield their advantages. Their real fears of loss of hegemony are masked in dire predictions about loss of societal cohesion.

Multiculturalism is evident in the land once again, and we can find many examples of both accommodation and conflict. Which trend will prevail? Will our future be one of greater discord or greater unity? What does lie beyond the next horizon? Fortunately, we have some clues from our past and present that may offer us a glimpse of that future. In the remaining chapters, we seek that understanding.

NOTES

1. "Exports (Most Recent) by Country," Nationmaster.com. Available at www.nationmaster.com/graph/rel_chu_att-religion-church-attendance #source. (Accessed January 5, 2012.)

2. Office of Immigration Statistics, *2010 Yearbook of Immigration Statistics* (Washington, DC: U.S. Government Printing Office, 2011), Table 2.

3. National Center for Education Statistics, *Digest of Education Statistics 2010* (Washington, DC: U.S. Government Printing Office, 2011), Table 286.

4. Center for the American Woman and Politics, Eagleton Institute of Politics. Available at www.cawp.rutgers.edu/. (Accessed January 2, 2012.)

5. U.S. Department of Labor, "Usual Weekly Earnings of Wage and Salary Workers: Third Quarter 2011," USDL 11-1501, October 20, 2011. See, for example, Mark Trumbull, "For Women, Glass Ceiling Still an Issue," *Christian Science Monitor* (February 8, 2007): 1, 11.

6. Patricia Sellers, "Fortune 500 Women CEOs Hits a Record 18," CNN Money. Available at http://postcards.blogs.fortune.cnn.com/2011/10/26 /fortune-500-women-ceos/. (Accessed January 5, 2012.)

7. Marielle Segarra, "Women CFOs: Still at 9%." Available at www.cfo .com/article.cfm/14581369. (Accessed January 5, 2012.)

8. U.S. Department of Homeland Security, *2010 Yearbook of Immigration Statistics* (Washington, DC: U.S. Government Printing Office, 2011), Table 3.

9. U.S. Census Bureau, *2010 American Community Survey* (Washington, DC: U.S. Government Printing Office, 2010), Table B04003.

10. Ibid., Table S0201.

11. Ibid.

12. Ibid.

13. See, for example, Okyun Kwon, "The Role of Religious Congregations in Formation of the Korean American Community of the Washington, DC Area," in *Korean-Americans: Past, Present, and Future,* ed. Ilpyong J. Kim (Elizabeth, NJ: Hollym International Corporation, 2004), pp. 239–70.

14. U.S. Census Bureau, *2009 American Community Survey* (Washington, DC: U.S. Government Printing Office, 2009), Table S0201.

15. U.S. Census Bureau, *The Asian Population: 2010* (Washington, DC: U.S. Government Printing Office, 2012), Table 5, p. 14.

16. Ibid.; U.S. Department of Homeland Security, *2010 Yearbook of Immigration Statistics*.

17. National Center for Education Statistics, *Digest of Education Statistics 2010* (Washington, DC: U.S. Government Printing Office, 2011), Table 212.

18. U.S. Census Bureau, *2010 American Community Survey*.

19. U.S. Census Bureau, *America's Families and Living Arrangements: 2011* (Washington, DC: U.S. Government Printing Office, 2011), Table C4.

20. U.S. Census Bureau, *The Population with Haitian Ancestry in the United States: 2009*, American Community Survey Briefs, October 2010.

21. U.S. Census Bureau, *2010 American Community Survey*.

22. U.S. Census Bureau, *American Fact Finder*, Hispanic or Latino by Type: 2010, Summary File 1, QT-P10.

23. Ibid.; U.S. Department of Homeland Security, *2010 Yearbook of Immigration Statistics*.

24. Ibid.

25. U.S. Census Bureau, *The Hispanic Population of the United States: 2010* (Washington, DC: U.S. Government Printing Office, 2011), Table 26.

26. U.S. Census Bureau, *The Hispanic Population: 2010*, 2010 Census Briefs, C2010BR-0, May 2011.

27. My thanks to Gonzalos Santos at California State University, Bakersfield for suggesting this concept.

28. U.S. Department of Homeland Security, *2010 Yearbook of Immigration Statistics*.

29. Arab American Institute, "Quick Facts about Arab Americans." Available at www.aaiusa.org/pages/demographics. (Accessed January 5, 2012.)

30. National Center for Health Statistics, "Health Characteristics of the American Indian or Alaska Native Adult Population: United States, 2004–2008," *National Health Statistics Reports*, 20 (2010).

31. U.S. Census Bureau, *2010 American Community Survey*, Table S0201.

32. Eileen W. Lindner, ed., *Yearbook of American and Canadian Churches, 2011* (Nashville, TN: Abingdon Press, 2011).

33. Ibid.

34. "U.S. Denominations," Association of Religion Data Archives. Available at www.thearda.com/Denoms/families/index.asp. (Accessed January 5, 2012.)

35. Lindner, *Yearbook of American and Canadian Churches*.

36. Gallup, "More than 9 in 10 Americans Continue to Believe in God," 2011. Available at http://www.gallup.com/poll/147887/Americans-Continue -Believe-God.aspx (Accessed on January 5, 2012); "State of the States: Importance of Religion," 2009. Available at www.gallup.com/poll/114022/ state-states-importance-religion.aspx. (Accessed January 5, 2012.)

37. "Church Attendance (Most Recent) by Country," Nationmaster.com. Available at www.nationmaster.com/graph/rel_chu_att-religion-church -attendance#source. (Accessed on January 5, 2012); Pew Forum on Religion and Public Life, "Religion among the Millenials," February 17, 2010. Available at http://pewforum.org/Age/Religion-Among-the-Millennials. aspx#attendance. (Accessed January 5, 2012.)

8

Diversity in Today's World

There is not a Black America and a White America and a Latino America and an Asian America; there's the United States of America.
—*President Barack Obama*

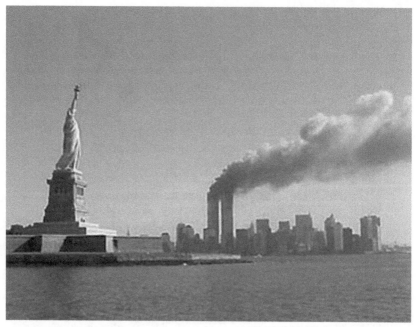

"September 11," a U.S. National Park Service photo (2001), depicts the Statue of Liberty facing the burning World Trade Center soon after the double impact from hijacked airliners.

Although it has been an issue of concern for practically every generation, multiculturalism in today's world is perhaps even more controversial, particularly when combined with fears about terrorism or resentment about the presence of large numbers of illegal immigrants. Although neither problem is really new, certainly in the modern era both have emerged as major everyday issues that impact society's response to the foreign born.

TERRORISM

Deadly acts of violence against the dominant society had a long, sad history in the United States, beginning with those between Native Americans and Whites during both the colonial period and the westward expansion. In the late 18th century, fears of the exportation of the Reign of Terror following the French Revolution prompted the Federalists under President John Adams to pass the Alien and Sedition Acts in an effort to suppress a perceived threat from the foreign-born and their sympathizers. Killings and other violent actions by Know-Nothings and the Ku Klux Klan were acts of terrorism by the dominant group against minorities, while the same type of actions by the Molly Maguires and anarchists were terrorist acts by minorities against the dominant group. In 1886, when a bomb exploded in Haymarket Square in Chicago during an immigrant labor demonstration, killing a police officer and wounding 70 others, a nationwide xenophobic reaction set in, linking for a long time in the minds of many Americans the words *foreigner* and *radical*.

All of that, however, was in the past, long ago, and did not traumatize the public personally as much as what happened in our lifetimes. The horrendous and tragic events of September 11, 2001, had a pronounced effect on the U.S. national psyche. Until then, two generations of Americans had never experienced any foreign attack on their native soil, and even for an earlier generation that could recall the Japanese attack on Pearl Harbor on December 7, 1941, that action was against a military target in the mid-Pacific, not against civilian targets on the mainland. If there has been one universal comment in the United States by those old enough to remember, it is this: Our lives were changed forever on that day.

The Larger Context

Putting aside suspicions and fears of vulnerability to terrorism for the moment, two other elements about multiculturalism in Europe require mentioning. First, Muslims have been a presence in Europe for more than 1,200 years, not only in Spain, but also originally in Armenia, Georgia, and parts of the Byzantine Empire. For centuries, they peacefully coexisted with Christians and Jews and made significant cultural and scientific contributions to European civilization.[1] Second, European colonialism in numerous Muslim countries (France in Algeria, Lebanon, Morocco, and Tunisia; Italy in Eritrea, Ethiopia, and Libya; and the United Kingdom in Egypt and Pakistan, among others) encouraged migration to those European lands in the postcolonial period. Third, the strong push-pull factors involving quality-of-life improvement have motivated tens of thousands of Muslims in the past two decades to migrate to Europe.

Finally, migrations and changing borders throughout Europe in the past 100 years may have brought varying ethnic mixtures within national populations, but that often did not result in the same multigenerational integration found in the United States. The laws of many European countries define citizenship eligibility by bloodlines and not residence, thereby institutionalizing the perception of nonmainstream group members as permanent outsiders. Multiculturalism, therefore, is more a display of minority separatism than of mainstreaming. Racial and ethnic heterogeneity, therefore, when combined with misgivings about national loyalties in many European countries, makes for a less cohesive society than in those countries such as Canada and the United States, where a long history of receiving large numbers of immigrants has created a cultural milieu that allows for easier absorption (see Figure 8.1).

The events of 9/11 had a sobering impact throughout the world, not just in the United States. The other major immigrant-receiving nations (Australia, Canada, and the United Kingdom) began exercising greater caution in their immigration processing, as well as initiating surveillance on suspected radical foreigners to guard against any attack within their borders. When the United States, joined by some of its Western allies, invaded and occupied Iraq, the European allies increased their vigilance against radical Muslims seeking revenge.

It was not enough. On March 11, 2004, terrorists carried out a coordinated series of train bombings in Madrid, killing 191 people and wounding more than 1,800. Other European governments went on even higher security alert status. On July 7, 2005, the terrorists

FIGURE 8.1   Foreign-Born Citizens, Selected Countries, by Percent, 2010
Source: Eurostat, "Foreign Citizens Made Up 6.5% of the EU 27 Population in 2010," new release
(July 14, 2011).

struck again, this time attacking the London public transport system. Within 50 seconds of one another, three bombs exploded on three London Underground trains, and a fourth bomb exploded nearly an hour later on a bus. The bombings killed 52 people, plus 4 of the radical Islamic terrorists, and injured about 700. Two weeks later, a second set of explosions occurred on the London Underground and a bus, but this time, fortunately, no one was killed.[2]

Since then, all Western nations have cast a wary eye on their Muslim populations, with several European countries (France, Italy, and the United Kingdom) deporting radical Islamic clerics they viewed as promoting subversive activities. Beefed-up security measures at airports and other counterintelligence surveillance measures have since prevented other major acts of terrorism in developed countries, but the danger of future attacks remains an always-present danger and, as such, an ongoing basis for suspiciousness about foreigners. In the United States, the 9/11 attack provoked many emotional responses, including initial shock and disbelief, followed by outrage and a demand for justice, together with a determination never to be so vulnerable again. How did the events of that day affect multiculturalism in the United States?

U.S. Government Responses

In October 2001, the U.S. government reacted decisively both within and outside its borders. Most of the world supported its military action in Afghanistan to overthrow the Taliban, flush out terrorist mastermind Osama bin Laden (successful 10 years later), and punish those who protected him. However, the 2003 preemptive war against Iraq, ostensibly to prevent Saddam Hussein from using the "weapons of mass destruction" (later proven to be nonexistent) and to remove from power a supporter of terrorism, was far more controversial, both at home and abroad.

Other government actions in the United States, designed as protective actions in the name of national security, also generated controversy and debate about their infringement on civil rights and liberties. The controversial USA PATRIOT Act—signed into law on October 26, 2001—significantly increased the surveillance and investigative powers of law enforcement agencies in the United States. For example, it authorized searches of such personal data as library use, as well as financial or travel history, without informing the person(s) under investigation. As a result, the Act did not provide for the system of checks and balances that traditionally safeguards civil liberties. Opponents particularly worried about its effect on the civil liberties of immigrants.[3] Here is where this law may be most dangerous, as it allows for detention of immigrants for an indeterminate amount of time, or even deportation, simply on suspicion alone or presumed association with a terrorist organization (such as giving donations). By permitting such governmental discretionary actions without a judicial hearing, these provisions remind us of another controversial law, the Alien Act of 1798 discussed in Chapter 4. Although several court rulings declared sections of the law unconstitutional, Congress expanded and renewed the act several times and it remains the law of the land.

The Department of Homeland Security (DHS), created in 2002, is the unifying core of a vast national network of organizations and institutions involved in efforts to secure the nation. This includes border and transportation security, immigration, emergency preparedness and response, infrastructure protection, and the Secret Service. As the DHS continues various initiatives to fulfill its mission, some of its domestic actions still encounter resistance from civil libertarians and multiculturalists intent on preserving minority rights.

Here is a partial list of its early actions that provoked criticism[4]: (a) Arab and Muslim alien residents (noncitizens) had to register at federal offices; government officials then deported those with expired visas or faulty papers, allowing no appeal. (b) Those suspected of terrorist links were rounded up and held incommunicado, often for months. As many as 1,200 people were detained for an extended period without any criminal charge lodged against them and, in most cases, without any basis in immigration law. (c) Racial profiling—taking race or ethnicity into account in deciding whom to stop, question, frisk, and so on—occurred as law enforcement officials placed Arab and/ or Muslim Americans under intense scrutiny, especially at airports. (d) The DHS also initiated the required photographing and finger-printing of all new arrivals from parts of the world associated with terrorism and anti-Americanism.

American Public Responses

How did the events and aftermath of 9/11 affect the public's attitude about multiculturalism? A tiny minority of Americans responded with personal attacks on people assumed to be Arab and/or Muslim, as well as with verbal abuse, vandalism, and threatened boycotts of Arab-owned local businesses. At first, many first-generation Arab Americans found their loyalties questioned, especially after the discovery that several of the hijackers had lived beforehand in the United States for several years as "sleeper terrorists." In addition, conservative and/or nativist groups called for severe immigration restrictions, but these limits never occurred.

More common, however, were other reactions. In areas with large concentrations of Arab Americans—such as Dearborn, Michigan, and Paterson, New Jersey—those residents put up banners in their streets denouncing the attacks, displayed U.S. flags at their homes and places of business, and donated blood for the victims. In local communities throughout the United States, Jews, Christians, and Muslims joined together in interfaith prayer services to demonstrate their solidarity with one another.

Civic, political, and religious leaders all urged tolerance and avoid-ance of blaming all for the actions of a few. Letters to the editors of newspapers and calls to radio and TV talk shows were overwhelmingly supportive of Arab and Muslim Americans as people "who came to join us," while denouncing the radical few "who came to hurt us." As the Arab American Institute reports, "The vast majority of Americans were disgusted by and ashamed of such acts of hatred and misdirected anger [by that] 'tiny minority.'"[5] Significantly, Americans of all persuasions took proactive steps to come to the aid of Arab and Muslim Americans and offer their sympathy and support at a time when all Americans were dealing with the shock and trauma inflicted on the nation.[6]

Of particular note is how local and state governments responded differently from the federal government. The city councils of New

York, Los Angeles, Chicago, and Philadelphia—along with nearly 250 other municipalities and three state legislatures (Vermont, Hawaii, and Alaska)—passed resolutions denouncing provisions of the USA PATRIOT Act and called for their repeal. Whatever threat these governing bodies felt, they were closer to direct public input and expressed a more protective stance on the rights of targeted minorities caught up in a federal government effort to make the nation more secure.

Clearly, the community response was not the same as the federal response. Some argued that the federal government trampled on civil liberties in its combative efforts to root out all internal threats. A large segment of the public—although traumatized by the terrorist acts—refused to support any broad measures against all members of these ethnic groups. This reluctance, illustrated by the actions of so many city councils (and in national studies that I will discuss in a few paragraphs), reveals an important aspect of U.S. culture: Americans' values and attitudes are more tolerant than ever before of the "different others" in their midst, more accepting of individuals, and less willing to stereotype an entire group.

In fairness, it also must be said that President George W. Bush and other national leaders urged the public not to blame all Arabs and Muslims for the actions of a few "criminals." Early and forceful statements by President Bush made it clear that the federal government would not tolerate acts of violence against any Americans because of their skin color, religious affiliation, or ethnicity. The political leadership at all levels offered the voice of reason and tolerance, and it prevailed. Nevertheless, the sweeping countermeasures to combat terrorism suggested a broader "us-them" mentality than displayed by the general populace.

Several court rulings in 2004 struck down key parts of the USA PATRIOT Act as overly broad and unconstitutional. The rulings affected provisions that (a) barred giving expert advice or assistance to groups designated as international terrorist organizations on the grounds that this part was in violation of the First and Fifth Amendments, (b) denied detainees held as "enemy combatants" the right to challenge their confinement through the U.S. courts, and (c) allowed the FBI to demand information from Internet service providers without judicial oversight or public review. This judicial curtailment of excess by the executive and legislative branches of government speaks well of the nation's ideals of protecting the rights of all minorities even under such stressful circumstances. Embedded in U.S. culture is a respect for, and protection of, individual rights and freedom, the cornerstone of a multicultural society that even 9/11 cannot erase.

It was not that 9/11 had a negative impact on people's attitudes about multiculturalism, but rather that people's attitudes about multiculturalism had a positive impact on their responses to the diversity in their midst despite the terrorists. Americans of all races, creeds, and ethnic backgrounds united in a bond of solidarity, making sincere and sustained efforts to emphasize their commonalities. As idealistic as that statement may sound to some, these actions nevertheless occurred. Evidence of this reality was shown in two of the largest national studies ever conducted that measured Americans' acceptance of others, the first of which coincidentally occurred soon after this national tragedy.

Measuring Social Distance

The most recent national study, conducted in 2012, captured the attitudes of more than 3,100 undergraduate and graduate students, ranging in age from 18 to 35, at 24 colleges and universities throughout the United States. A replication of social distance studies created by Emory Bogardus that had been conducted five times in the 20th century between 1926 and 1977, this new study was itself a replication of a 2001 national study conducted in the aftermath of 9/11.[7]

Quite simply, the survey presented a list of 30 groups and asked respondents to give anonymous choices as to the degree of closeness they would allow for each group. On a 7-point scale, these choices included members of a group marrying into one's family (1.0), being part of a close social circle (2.0), a neighbor (3.0), a coworker (4.0), a citizen (5.0), a visitor only (6.0), or excluded from entering the country (7.0). The closer a group was accepted, the less its social distance and the lower its social distance score.

Combining individual responses to get average mean scores, the results indicated how willing Americans were to accept others who were "different." As shown in Table 8.1, the respondents—not surprisingly—relegated Arabs and Muslims to the bottom of the list, expressing greater social distance between them than for all other groups. Significantly, however, these two groups received lower (i.e., more socially acceptable) mean scores than those received by at least 8 of the 30 groups in the 1977 study. What this tells us is that, although a few Americans assigned group blame to all Arabs and Muslims and/or committed hate crimes against them, that mind-set did not extend to most respondents in either the 2001 or 2012 study. Their making a distinction between the ethnicity of the terrorists and others who were Arabs and/or Muslims resulted in such lower scores than given to past low-ranked groups that it is indeed an impressive finding. Americans

Table 8.1 Social Distance Rankings in 2012*

Rank	Group	Score	Rank	Group	Score
1.	Americans	1.14	16.	Dominicans	1.68
2.	Italians	1.29	17.	Other Hispanics/Latinos	1.68
3.	British	1.33	18.	Chinese	1.70
4.	Canadians	1.35	19.	Cubans	1.71
5.	African Americans	1.41	20.	Jews	1.71
6.	Irish	1.41	21.	Russians	1.71
7.	French	1.47	22.	Jamaicans	1.72
8.	Greeks	1.48	23.	Mexicans	1.77
9.	Germans	1.49	24	Japanese	1.77
10.	Indians (American)	1.56	25.	Vietnamese	1.84
11.	Polish	1.60	26.	Koreans	1.84
12.	Africans	1.60	27.	Indians (India)	1.89
13.	Dutch	1.61	28.	Haitians	1.89
14.	Puerto Ricans	1.62	29.	Arabs	2.18
15.	Filipinos	1.67	30.	Muslims	2.24

Source: Vincent N. Parrillo and Christopher Donoghue, "The Social Distance Study Ten Years Later: Preliminary Findings from a New National Study." Paper presented at the annual meeting of the Eastern Sociological Society, New York City, February 24, 2012.

*These are preliminary findings and subject to revision when all data have been analyzed.

may have felt less close to Arabs and Muslims after 9/11, but nonetheless not as distant as other generations felt to other foreigners in their midst.

No one should give too much importance to exact ranking of specific groups in the 2012 study, given the close scores, because these may be the result of sampling variability. Still it is interesting to note the intermixing of Whites and people of color in the top two-thirds of the list. This finding suggests that, in the multicultural U.S. society, a high level of social acceptance exists regardless of color. Those from a Judeo-Christian background typically rank higher than those from non-Western religious backgrounds but, even then, the differences in social distance scores are not that pronounced.

Another interesting finding was the higher level of acceptance of Italian Americans than of other Euro-American groups, including the English, Irish, and Germans. Statistical analyses of the data reveal that this placement occurred in part because of their high level of acceptance by Black and Hispanic Americans, as well as by White Americans, in comparison to other Euro-American groups.

ILLEGAL IMMIGRATION

As these chapters have revealed, each generation of Americans has faced the reality of a foreign-born presence in its midst. When immigration reached epic proportions in the three waves occurring since the nation's founding—first between 1820 and 1860, then between 1880 and 1920, and now in the current era—there was no shortage of negative commentary or calls for closing the gates. Exacerbating the reaction in today's world are the millions of undocumented foreigners throughout the United States. Their presence clouds the discussion, as many people fail to make a distinction between legal and illegal immigrants. The next chapter includes a comparative examination of legal immigration over the generations. Here, because concerns about illegal immigration in general also touch on worries about terrorism, we will focus on that aspect of the immigration debate.

The Larger Context

Worldwide, millions of people have illegally migrated from countries with poor living conditions into countries offering a better quality of life. Some of the more obvious examples are Eastern Europeans throughout Western Europe; Africans in Italy; Albanians in Greece; Central Americans in Mexico; Colombians in Venezuela; Bolivians, Chinese, and Peruvians in Brazil; Bangladeshis in India; sub-Saharan Africans in Libya; Zimbabweans in South Africa; Central Asians in Turkey; Yemenis in Saudi Arabia; and Mexicans in the United States.

Negative reactions to undocumented aliens typically stem from such factors as cultural differentiation, job competition, quality of life, and/or respect-for-law beliefs. The large-scale presence of illegal immigrants has triggered numerous reactions: building a barrier along the border (Saudi Arabia, United States); the rise of anti-foreign, nationalist political parties (Denmark, France, Italy); anti-foreign violence (Germany, South Africa); actual or proposed amnesty programs (Italy, Poland, Spain, United Kingdom, United States); and government crackdowns and arrests (Britain, Ireland, Japan).

Illegal immigration also is a matter of serious concern in Europe. The European Union (EU) reports that a half million illegal immigrants enter the EU every year.[8] Government-funded researchers in the United Kingdom estimate that about 533,000 illegal immigrants and 85,000 of their UK-born children are in their country.[9] France may have as many as 400,000 people who are illegal, Germany about 500,000, and in Italy, where government leaders do not give estimates, thousands arrive each month. Although most Western European countries turn back or deport tens of thousands of undocumented immigrants each year, in 2005, Spain bucked this trend by granting legal status to about 600,000 illegal immigrants from Africa, Latin

America, and eastern Europe who applied for residence permits.[10] Sweden (population 9.4 million, with 15 percent foreign-born in 2010) appears to be among the least xenophobic EU countries. Whereas other member nations have clamped down on immigration, it officially received immigrants in record numbers. It accepted about 99,000 foreign nationals in 2010, only slightly lower than its record high of 102,000 in 2009. Many were Iraqi refugees fleeing their homeland or Somalis and Poles looking for work.[11] With a long history of neutrality in armed conflicts since the end of the Napoleonic Wars in 1815, it lacks any fears of terrorist attacks and has long been a place of refuge for asylum seekers.

Unauthorized Immigrants in the United States

What galvanizes public debate about immigration, especially during these recession years, is the number of authorized foreign-born people living in the United States, estimated in 2011 to be 11.2 million. This population grew rapidly from 1990 to 2006, which generated at that time opposing legislative proposals for amnesty or a crackdown on "illegals" (neither enacted) and the building of a barrier fence along the Mexican border (643 miles built as of 2010).[12] However, up to 45 percent of all undocumented immigrants are individuals who did not leave after their temporary worker, student, or tourist visas expired.[13]

Calls for reform come at a time when parts of the U.S. economy are dependent on the labor of undocumented migrants. Mostly Latinos, these unskilled workers have spread to a wide range of industries. Comprising 3.7 percent of the total U.S. population in 2010, undocumented immigrants constituted 5.2 percent if its labor force.[14] Construction attracts 21 percent of undocumented workers, and another 30 percent work in the services sector. An additional 15 percent are production and installation workers (see Figure 8.2). Thus, two-thirds of unauthorized immigrant workers have occupations in these three fields, compared to 31 percent of U.S.-born workers.[15]

For several decades the estimated proportion of Mexicans as undocumented migrants has hovered at about 59 percent of the total. Central Americans and Southeast Asians are the next largest groups (11 percent each), followed by South Americans (7 percent), and those from Canada, the Caribbean, and Europe (4 percent each).[16]

Attempted border crossings result in most apprehensions of undocumented immigrants, unlike those who slip in undetected after overstaying their visas. In the United States, Mexicans predominate among undocumented immigrants (83 percent of all apprehensions in

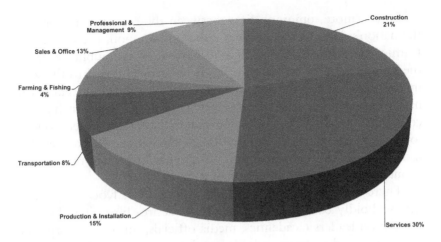

FIGURE 8.2   Undocumented Immigrants in U.S. Labor Force, 2008
Source: Jeffrey Passel and D'Vera Cohn, "A Portrait of Unauthorized Immigrants in the United States," Pew Hispanic Center (April 14, 2009).

2010). Guatemalans, Salvadorans, and Hondurans account for another 11 percent of those apprehended.[17]

Public Attitudes

Attitudes about immigration give us a partial understanding of the attitudes about multiculturalism. By comparing immigration attitudes before and after 9/11, we can get a sense of its impact on the acceptance and practice of multiculturalism.

A quick review of the national polls might lead one to conclude that public views have changed significantly, but how they have changed is quite a revelation. Right after 9/11, Gallup public opinion polls found that support for reducing immigration indeed jumped sharply, from 38 percent in September 2000 to 58 percent in October 2001. This spike upward, however, has since declined, with those wanting a decrease in legal immigration falling to 41 percent in a 2010 CBS News/New York Times poll. Still, a 2007 NBC News/Wall Street Journal poll revealed that, although 46 percent of respondents thought immigration helped more than it hurt the country, another 44 percent believed the opposite.[18] These findings bring us to an important point: Just as previous chapters reported mixed responses to multiculturalism prior to 9/11, so, too, do they appear afterward. 9/11 appears not to be a causative factor in any significant change in attitudes about multiculturalism.

Furthermore, opinions differ between the mass population and the nation's elite. In a December 2002 opinion poll, the Center for Immigration Studies found that 60 percent of the public regarded the present level of immigration to be a "critical threat to the vital interests of the United States," compared with only 14 percent of the nation's leadership—a gap of 46 percentage points. Despite such public concern, federal officials have continually either advocated policies to increase the flow of immigration or else embraced policies that indicate a desire to continue immigration at its present numbers of about 1 million newcomers annually.

There are two reasons that national leaders advocated policies that so boldly contradicted the public's desire. First, they listened to opinion leaders (academics, media officials, union and corporate executives, and religious and think tank leaders), and only 14 percent of these leaders viewed current immigration levels as a problem. So, although federal officials were not following the desires of the public, they were in tune with the views of the top leaders of America's institutions. Second, the public did not view the immigration issue as such a major concern as to mobilize to challenge current policies. When asked in 2012 to name the most important problems facing the United States, immigration ranked fifth, far below unemployment, government spending, the federal deficit, and health care.[19]

Throughout the country's history, American ambivalence about immigration has been common. Because of their perceived differences and threats to U.S. culture and societal cohesion, immigrants were seldom welcomed with open arms at any time. The altruistic, sometimes romantic, notions expressed by contemporaries or by those viewing the past have constantly been in contrast to people then expressing realistic concerns about the impact of immigrants on the economy or geographic areas in which they were heavily concentrated.

That ambivalence still remains, but it does so to no greater degree now than in earlier years. 9/11 has less to do with these split feelings than do economic conditions and concerns about illegal immigration, not legal immigration. In difficult economic times when unemployment rises, the old fear of immigrants taking jobs away from Americans resurfaces, naturally giving rise to stronger anti-immigration sentiments.

Right now, illegal immigration is the primary concern among most Americans. Public opinion polls in 2010 generally showed about two-thirds of all respondents wanting illegal immigration reduced and expressing displeasure over government efforts to do so. Among the factors influencing this public attitude is concern about terrorists slipping into the country to do us further harm. However, in addressing the issue of undocumented immigrants already in the country, Americans were more divided over what to do. Only one in eight favored deportations, with the rest saying such an option was unrealistic given the many millions living here and contributing to the economy. Although a majority favor citizenship for undocumented immigrants, they are far from agreement on the means of doing so.[20] Such divisiveness, compounded by political partisanship in Congress, led President Obama to issue a controversial order to halt deportations for those here for five years who arrived before age 16.

Illegal immigration clouds the topic of multiculturalism. However, if we remove it from the debate, we find that the current views on legal immigration are no different now than before 9/11, suggesting that, from this perspective at least, neither have they changed about multiculturalism. Another partial indicator giving some support to this conclusion is a 2007 ABC News national poll, in which more than three-fourths of the non-Hispanic respondents said they come into contact with people who mostly speak Spanish (55 percent "often" and 23 percent "sometimes"), and yet two-thirds said it does not bother them.[21]

Another immensely important development that has been affecting multiculturalism since 9/11 is the expanding global economy. Aided by instantaneous telecommunications and rapid air travel, the recent global transformations have led to the creation of social ties and networks no longer bound by national boundaries. The easy flow of people and money back and forth between countries allows individuals to maintain dual identities, with strong cultural ties and the capacity to make contributions to both places. Their labors contribute to the Gross Domestic Product (GDP) of their host country and their sending some of their earnings back home greatly aids family quality of life in their native country. In 2011, for example, Mexicans working in the United States sent $23 billion back home, making them the country's third largest source of foreign income after automobile and oil exports.[22]

This transnationalism of sustained ties of persons and networks anchors immigrants in multiple sites. Instead of a permanent move from one country to another, many of today's immigrants retain interconnected and intense, even legitimized, links (cultural, economic, familial, and political) than ever before. As a result, the traditional interpretations of assimilation and integration seem less relevant than in the past.[23] We need to understand multiculturalism in a much larger context given the reality that we are more and more living in a "global village."

WHAT ABOUT TOMORROW?

The world remains a dangerous place. When it comes to political and terrorist events, no one can speak with certainty about the future, but those concerns remain foremost in the minds of most Americans and Europeans, in turn affecting attitudes and reactions to Muslim immigrants, although almost all of them reject terrorism. Today, then, multiculturalism is far less the area of public concern than are the issues of global terrorism and immigration. Indeed, on radio and TV talk shows, in congressional debates, and in the 2012 presidential election, some politicians have played to public fears, even biases, in the hope of gaining political capital.

The theme of this book, of course, is not about politics or terrorists. It is about diversity, about multiculturalism, and here we can make some reasonable projections about the future. Although arguments about assimilation versus pluralism continue in the land, we also have witnessed the triumph of the ideal of multiculturalism over the evil of reprehensible acts of indiscriminate killing. No curbs on immigration occurred in reaction to the terrorism. No assignment of group blame took place. Other than a few isolated actions immediately after 9/11, no retaliatory measures against Arab and Muslim Americans occurred. Instead, Americans ignored the differences of race, religion, and place of birth to unite in recognition of a reality they sometimes forget: *e pluribus unum* ("from the many, one").

We are a diverse people. We always have been, and we most likely always will be. We are an imperfect society, to be sure, and we do not always get along with one another. That is part of the growing pains of a society attempting to be all-inclusive and its people not always knowing how to achieve its ideals. Still the U.S. Constitution and culture provide a framework wherein all individuals have equal protection under the law, as well as opportunities to attain a better life for themselves. It is the dream that still attracts so many new immigrants, and it is the cultural and structural reality that not only gives substance to the possibilities of realizing that dream, but also enables multiculturalism to flourish in the land, even though not everyone accepts it.

The issue of multiculturalism may remain controversial, but it passed an incredible test in the aftermath of 9/11. No doubt the future holds other challenges. However, the reality is that, in this shrinking world of ours, a multicultural reality is the one that future generations and we must face. How we do that, how we harness that diversity into strength, is the real challenge ahead of us.

NOTES

1. Ekmeleddin Ihsanoglu, "Is Islam an Intruder in Europe?" Keynote address at Institut Francais des Relations Internationales Conference, Paris, January 29, 2007. Available at www.ifri.org/files/Moyen_Orient/Speech_ Ihsanoglu_290107.pdf. (Accessed January 7, 2012.)

2. U.S. Department of State, *Country Reports on Terrorism*. Available at www.state.gov/g/ct/rls/crt/index.htm. (Accessed January 7, 2012.)

3. An excellent analysis of the USA PATRIOT Act and related links can be found at the Electronic Privacy Information Center. Available at www.epic.org /privacy/terrorism/usapatriot. (Accessed January 7, 2012.)

4. For information about remaining provisions that civil rights activists insist must be removed, see http://www.aclu.org/reform-patriot-act. (Accessed January 7, 2012.)

5. Arab American Institute, "Healing the Nation: The Arab American Experience after September 11." Available at http://aai.3cdn.net /64de7330dc475fe470_h1m6b0yk4.pdf. (Accessed January 7, 2012.)

6. Ibid.

7. Vincent N. Parrillo, *Strangers to These Shores*, 10th ed. (Boston: Allyn and Bacon, 2011), pp. 5–7; Vincent N. Parrillo, "Updating the Bogardus Social Distance Studies: A New National Survey," *The Social Science Journal*, 42 (2005): 257–71.

8. EurActive Network, "Illegal Immigration, Asylum, and Border Control" (April 24, 2006). Available at www.euractiv.com/security/illegal -immigration-asylum-border-control/article-117508. (Accessed January 8, 2012.)

9. Ian Gordon, Kathleen Scanlon, Tony Travers, and Christine Whitehead, *Economic Impact on the London and UK Economy of an Earned Regularisation of Irregular Migrants to the UK* (London: Greater London Authority, 2009), p. 48.

10. Jason De Parle, "Spain, Like U.S., Grapples with Immigration," *New York Times*, June 2008. Available at www.euractiv.com/en//justice/article -117508. (Accessed January 7, 2012.)

11. Statistics Sweden, "Immigration Rate Still High." Available at www.scb .se/Pages/PressRelease_305658.aspx. (Accessed January 8, 2012.)

12. "US-Mexico Border Fence/Great Wall of Mexico." Available at www .globalsecurity.org/security/systems/mexico-wall.htm. (Accessed January 8, 2012.)

13. Pew Hispanic Center, "Fact Sheet: Modes of Entry for the Unauthorized Migrant Population." Available at www.pewhispanic.org/2006/05/22/modes -of-entry-for-the-unauthorized-migrant-population/. (Accessed January 8, 2012.)

14. Jeffrey Passel and D'Vera Cohn, "Unauthorized Immigrant Population: National and State Trends, 2010," Pew Hispanic Center (February 1, 2011). Available at www.pewhispanic.org/2011/02/01/unauthorized-immigrant -population-brnational-and-state-trends-2010/. (Accessed January 11, 2012.)

15. Jeffrey Passel and D'Vera Cohn, "A Portrait of Unauthorized Immigrants in the United States," Pew Hispanic Center (April 14, 2009). Available at www .pewhispanic.org/files/reports/107.pdf. (Accessed January 11, 2012.)

16. Ibid.

17. U.S. Department of Homeland Security, *2010 Yearbook of Immigration Statistics* (Washington, DC: U.S. Government Printing Office, 2011), Table 34.

18. All poll data are found at www.pollingreport.com/immigration.htm. (Accessed June 26, 2012.)

19. Ibid.

20. Ibid.

21. Ibid.

22. "Mexicans Living in U.S. Sending More Money Home." *Bloomberg News* press release (April 5, 2012).

23. Nina Glick Schiller, Linda Basch, and Cristina Blanc-Szanton, "Transnationalism: A New Analytic Framework for Understanding Migration," in *Towards a Transnational Perspective on Migration: Race, Class, Ethnicity, and Nationalism Reconsidered,* eds. N. Glick Schiller, L. Basch, and C. Blanc-Szanton (New York: New York Academy of Sciences, 1992), pp. 1–24.

9

Intergenerational Comparisons

Each generation goes further than the generation preceding it because it stands on the shoulders of that generation. You will have opportunities beyond anything we've ever known.

—*President Ronald Reagan*

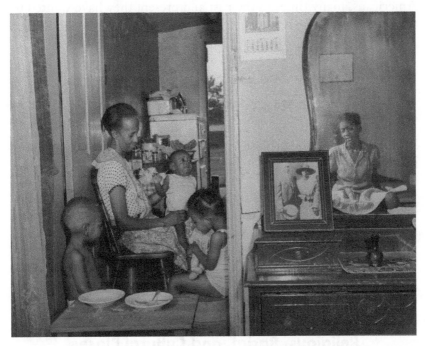

"Generations" by noted photographer Gordon Parks (1942) depicts Mrs. Ella Watson of Washington, DC, with three grandchildren and her adopted daughter, together with a photograph either of her parents or herself and her husband.

Each generation of Americans experiences anew the influx of immigrants arriving in pursuit of the American Dream. Each new generation also contains native-born Americans not only denied fulfillment of that dream, but also witnesses to newcomers who succeed where they do not. This has been the case since colonial beginnings and appears likely to continue far into the future. It is an old story and yet incredibly fresh each time to those who live or observe it.

When we examine what prompted people, past and present, to forsake their homelands and begin new lives elsewhere, we find a remarkable consistency in their motives.[1] Many people entered on their own initiative, lured by the promise of a better life. Others were recruited by labor agents, enticed by the media, or encouraged to leave by their own governments seeking a lessening of social unrest or economic distress. Still others, forced to flee their native lands as refugees, had little choice.

Whatever the reason and whenever the time, the United States has always served as a destination for these adventurous, desperate, or determined people. Yet despite the immigrant ancestry of most Americans, many times in the past and present they have wanted to pull in the welcome mat for new immigrants.

WHY ARE VOICES RAISED AGAINST IMMIGRATION?

Too often the native-born react with fear and anxiety, perceiving some groups as "unassimilable" and their presence in large numbers as a threat to societal cohesion.[2] Other Americans are apprehensive about these groups' possible integration, believing that such an eventuality would somehow destroy or undermine the "purity" of the American character. So it was with U.S. ambassador to England Rufus King, who wrote in 1797 to Secretary of State Timothy Pickering that the Irish immigrants would "disfigure our true national character."[3] Ever since, others have expressed concerns about this or that group of immigrants as wrong for the nation's well-being.

Religious, Racial, and Cultural Biases

Sometimes these reactions revealed a religious bias: against Quakers, Shakers, or Catholics in the 18th century; against Catholics, Jews, or

Mormons in the 19th century; and against Catholics, Jews, or Sikhs in the early 20th century. Other negative responses reflected a racial bias: against African and Native Americans throughout the nation's history, and against Asians and dark-complexioned southern Europeans in the late 19th and early 20th centuries. Sometimes it was a bias combination: religion and race (Rastafarian) or culture and religion (Irish and Italian). Today, other nativist voices express the old fears about other religiously, racially, or culturally different newcomers: Muslims, Asians, or Latinos.

Economic Competition

Past or present targets also have induced alarm because others see them as a danger to their own livelihood. This perceived economic threat may result from the scarcity of jobs, affirmative action hiring or promotion policies, or the recruitment of cheaper labor or strike breakers. Since the mid-19th century, employers have often used newly arrived groups, including once migrating Black Americans, to keep wages low or to break a strike.

The resulting ethnic antagonism can be of three types. Native-born Americans may resent the immigrant influx, as when West Coast labor unions in the late 19th and early 20th centuries fought against Asian workers. An interethnic rivalry may develop, such as the importation of Syrian-Lebanese immigrants in an effort to break the 300-mill shutdown in the Paterson, New Jersey, metropolitan region in 1913, caused by striking European immigrant textile workers. Same-group members can pose a third variation of an immigrant economic threat. For example, the actions of unscrupulous employers in exploiting undocumented Mexican workers has had a negative influence on the wages earned by native-born and legal Mexican Americans.[4]

The "Tipping Point"

Sometimes biases are so deeply ingrained that people will respond negatively to the presence of even one member of a despised outgroup. More often, however, if the number of outgroup members is few, people tend to be more receptive to less-alike strangers or at least indifferent or begrudgingly tolerant. When the numerical increase reaches the tipping point, hostile responses become more likely. As Luigi Laurenti's classic study on property values and race revealed, that tipping point has no exact number; it is a perceptual stage when the ingroup believes "too many" of "those people" are in its midst and "something needs to be done."[5]

Today Isn't Yesterday, or Is It?

If 10 generations of Americans have followed similar patterns of response to immigrants who have subsequently blended into the mainstream, why can't we recognize that fact and be less fearful about today's newcomers?

Today's nativists dismiss any effort to compare past immigrant concerns with their own. Past objectors, they argue, were narrow-minded bigots opposed to people who have since proven their ability to assimilate. They contend that today we are "inundated" with racially different Asians who lack a Judeo-Christian heritage and whose culture is radically different from ours.

Hispanics, they add, are holding onto their language and customs, thereby presenting a real threat to the cohesiveness of U.S. society.

With the 2000s now the period of the greatest number of immigrants ever to arrive (11.4 million between 2000 and 2010), and with about four in five coming from developing-world countries, nativists consider current immigration as a serious threat to the population composition of U.S. society as we have long known it. Furthermore, a lower national birth rate among the native-born, combined with a higher birth rate among the foreign-born, provides immigrants with a stronger impact on natural population growth. Moreover, they contend that the nation has not satisfactorily dealt with the unemployment and poverty of its native-born Americans, so continuing to admit large numbers of immigrants intensifies further an already difficult problem.

Questions about America's racial mix, natural population increase, unemployment, and poverty do offer some new wrinkles to old arguments and need to be addressed. However, despite nativist disclaimers of new and different elements, these arguments share many commonalities with those of similar-minded alarmists of previous generations. All have seen newcomers as a threat to the "purity" of the American character and to the stability and economic welfare of the society. All have seen the newcomers as inferior additions and complained about their retention of language and customs. All have assumed acculturation and assimilation would not occur. As Rita J. Simon states,

These have been the arguments used against all of the "current cohorts" from the time the new immigrants began arriving, first from Ireland, then a decade or two later from Southern and

Eastern Europe.... Contemporary immigrants are no less popular than the immigrants who began coming to this country after the Civil War and for all the years in between. The only popular or valued immigrants are those who came long ago, whenever "long ago" happened to be.[6]

I would suggest that, when nativists argue that today's situation is far different from past years, their perception reflects the Dillingham Flaw. They tend to view past fears as ignorant or irrational nativism against White ethnics who actually shared far more similarities with their hosts than any differences. However, what we perceive today as mutual similarities were not viewed as such in those times. It is past perception—not present-day perception—that matters when examining past behaviors.

So are things different today or not? We need some comparative data to determine where the truth lies. To relate the present with the past, let's focus on four aspects of nativist fears: the significance of immigration totals, the foreign-born presence, racial population changes, and assimilation.

IMMIGRATION RATE

As specified by the Immigration Act of 1990, an annual limit of 700,000 immigrants currently exists. Because immediate family members are not included in these caps, yearly totals have actually been higher, as they were in 2011, when 1.06 million legal permanent residents entered the United States. That total is actually lower than in other recent years, although since 2005, more than 1 million immigrants have been arriving.[7] Such numbers provoke that nativist alarm but, by themselves, these are misleading statistics. Much more helpful in understanding the impact of immigrants on society is the immigration rate. This measurement tool allows for comparisons of different eras while enabling us to specifically address vague nativist fears that the United States is being overwhelmed by a large influx of foreigners. It thus serves as a concrete aide in objectively describing a reality that may or may not differ from perceptions.

The immigration rate per 1,000 persons in the general population is computed by dividing the sum of the annual immigration totals by the sum of annual U.S. population totals for the same number of years. Collection of such data began in 1820, when new regulations required shipmasters to submit passenger lists to customs officials.

FIGURE 9.1   Immigration Rate, 1830–2010

Source: U.S. Census Bureau, *Statistical Abstract of the United States: 2011* (Washington, DC: U.S. Government Printing Office, 2010), Table 43, p. 46.

What is particularly useful about this measurement tool is that it allows us to relate immigration totals to population totals and to do so in a way that provides a comparative means for analysis. Immigrant totals for any particular year or decade become more relevant if we know the size of the population the newcomers are joining. To illustrate, if 1 million people enter a society that totals 50 million people, the immigrants' presence will be more keenly felt than if 1 million people enter a society that has a population of 250 million.

The 2000s were the decade with the highest total number of immigrants arriving. However, in terms of its immigration rate of 3.5, the 2000s actually tie for tenth highest out of 19 decades (Figure 9.1). Immigrants in the 2000s were about one-third of the proportion found in 1901–1910, and so the influx of 8.8 million immigrants in that decade resulted in an immigration rate of 10.4 in comparison to the 3.5 immigration rate for 2001 to 2010.[8]

What are we saying? First, the earlier waves of immigrants in each of the decades between 1841 and 1920 had a more immediate effect on the nation's population composition. That is, the ratio of immigrants to the population receiving them was greater in the past. Such a higher ratio means that those immigrants from 1840 to 1920 proportionately and visibly changed America's population mix to a greater degree than the recent immigrants have.

Second, a major factor in examining the immigration rate is immigration law. With the current ceiling of 700,000 immigrants annually, the general population will experience natural increases annually while the immigration cap remains constant. The result therefore must be an eventual decline of the immigration rate in the years to come, as the population (denominator) increases while the number of immigrants (numerator) remains fairly constant. Until new legislation raises that immigration cap, we can expect a steady reduction in the immigration rate, one measurement of foreign impact on the host society.

Immigration Rate Caveats

Although the legal immigration rate is a helpful comparative measurement, it cannot stand alone. Too many other factors need to be considered as well. Perhaps most important is how much immigration contributes to population growth in an era of declining birth rates. Because immigrants have a higher birth rate than the native-born, their group numbers will grow at a faster rate. For example, between 2000 and 2010, the Mexican American population grew by 7.2 million by births and grew by an additional 4.2 million from new immigrants.[9] More broadly, between 1990 and 2010, immigration directly contributed one-third of U.S. population growth and—when adding in the U.S.-born children and grandchildren of immigrants—immigration contributed half of U.S. population growth.[10]

We also must consider illegal immigration in any discussion of the presence in the United States of the foreign-born. Although undocumented immigrants have always been a presence since the first immigration laws, their numbers—now estimated at 11.5 million—are close to a record-high level. An estimated 4.5 million children of these undocumented immigrants are U.S.-born and an additional 1 million are foreign-born, making the expense of their education a major source of controversy.[11]

Another consideration is that the United States is now a postindustrial society. Many manufacturing jobs no longer exist that immigrants with few skills and limited command of English could once attain. The ability of a nation to absorb its newcomers is thus dependent on how well they can find their niche in the workplace, as well as on the proportion of immigrants to the total population. Research shows that legal and illegal immigration adds one-tenth of one percent to the Gross Domestic Product (GDP), the value of goods and services produced in the United States. Since the GDP was $15 trillion in

2010, that would suggest that foreign-born workers contributed about $15 billion to the U.S. economy.[12] Both legal and illegal immigrants not only work, but also pay taxes, including sales and income taxes, but also they consume tax-supported services, notably education and health care provided by state and local government. In areas with large concentrations of immigrants, these costs can offset their economic contributions.

FOREIGN-BORN POPULATION

A companion set of data to immigration rates is the foreign-born population in various time periods because it represents the cumulative totals of immigrants residing in the United States. By determining what percentage of the total population is foreign-born at any given time, we can discern the extent of their presence as a basis for comparing the past with the present.

The 1850 census revealed a foreign-born U.S. population of 1.7 million, the first decade with more than 1 million immigrants recorded (compared to about 600,000 in the 1830s and about 143,000 in the 1820s). Hence, 1850 serves as a good starting point for examining times of higher immigration.

Because immigration rates were higher in the past than in the present, as we have just seen, it is therefore not surprising to see that the foreign-born segment of the population has been higher in 10 of the past 15 decennial censuses, consecutively from 1850 to 1940. Figure 9.2 shows that the percentage of foreign-born living in the United States between 1860 and 1930 was greater than in 2010. In the 1890 and 1910 censuses, one in seven was foreign-born; in 1860, 1870, 1880, 1900, and 1920, it was one in eight. In 2010, the foreign-born population totaled 40 million, or 12.9 percent of the population, a lower percentage than existed between 1860 and 1920.[13]

At the beginning of the 20th century, most cities in the Northeast contained a foreign-born population that comprised two-thirds to three-fourths of the cities' total populations. In contrast, the cities in 2010 with the most foreign-born populations were Miami (56.5 percent), Los Angeles (39.5 percent), New York (35.9 percent), and San Francisco (34.4 percent).[14] Although these are significant proportions, they pale alongside the data of 100 years ago.

From another viewpoint, the aforementioned 40 million foreign-born are the largest numerical total ever, but in proportion to the entire population, that figure ranks eighth among the past 17 decades.

FIGURE 9.2 Foreign Born as a Percent of Total U.S. Population, 1850–2010
Source: U.S. Census Bureau, 2010 American Community Survey.

Because these statistics do not include U.S.-born children raised in immigrant family households, the proportion of those living in various ethnic subcultures has been greater, especially among past generations, when family size was typically larger than today. Regardless of acculturation patterns, the different languages, customs, and traditions from the old country have always prevailed to some extent among a sizable part of U.S. society, and more so in the past than in the present.

At its lowest point in 1970, the foreign-born component has since been moving upward again, reflecting the recent increases in the immigration rate. Similarly, the foreign-born percentages will continue to rise for a while, but will eventually level off and decline for the same reasons enumerated earlier for the immigration rate.

RACE IN AMERICA

U.S. race relations have a violent, exploitative past and an often-troubled present. Racism finds many forms of expression ranging from verbal putdowns to killing, producing disturbing consequences not only for its victims, but also for society itself in economic, health, and social welfare costs.

At first, only Whites among the native-born enjoyed the privileges of citizenship and voting rights, and only White aliens could become naturalized citizens. In time, following the pain of the Civil War, the 14th Amendment (1868) granted citizenship to anyone born or naturalized in the United States, and the 15th Amendment (1870) extended voting rights to every male regardless of race or color. After an arduous struggle, non-White exclusion yielded under force of law to inclusion.

Advances against other areas of exclusion—notably in education, employment, housing, and public accommodation—occurred only two generations ago, growing out of the civil rights movement of the 1960s. Gaining legal rights and political participation did not necessarily mean social acceptance, however. Just as Crèvecoeur overlooked the disenfranchised racial U.S. minorities of his time, so, too, have many White Americans avoided any inclusion of non-Whites in their daily lives. Lack of interaction helps perpetuate stereotypes and allows racial prejudice and discrimination to thrive.

Although succeeding generations of America's people of color have made significant gains in education, employment, income, and political participation, problems remain. Many forms of institutionalized racism have been eliminated, but structural discrimination—the differential treatment of racial groups that is entrenched in our social institutions—remains, such as in racial profiling. Poverty is another area: about 27 percent of African Americans as well as 27 percent of Hispanic Americans lived in poverty in 2010, more than twice that of Whites.[15]

Racism manifests itself in negative reactions to the number of immigrants in general who are non-White, or of one race such as Asians, or of one group such as Haitians. It finds expression also in fears that the racial mixture of U.S. society is changing too dramatically.

If we look at some of the data about past and present racial groups in the United States, we can dispel some generalizations and unfair comparisons (the Dillingham Flaw) that engender unfavorable responses to the presence of people of color. Our focus once again will be on proportional representation within the total population through the years. Is the non-White to White ratio greater than ever? Exactly how is our society changing in its racial mixture?

After increasing proportionately since 1790 and peaking in 1940 at 89.8 percent, the nation's White population has since been decreasing steadily (Figure 9.3). In 2010, the total White population (including Hispanics) was 72.4 percent, the lowest proportion of the

FIGURE 9.3   U.S. Population by Race as a Percent of Total U.S. Population

Source: U.S. Census Bureau, *Historical Statistics of the United States, Part II*, Series Z-20-132 (Washington, DC: U.S. Government Printing Office, 1976); *Statistical Abstract of the United States: 2011* (Washington, DC: U.S. Government Printing Office, 2010); "Quick Facts," *2010 American Community Survey*.

total population since the 79.3 percent of Whites living in the United States in 1790.[16]

A smaller percentage of Whites existed in 1790 because of the greater percentage of Blacks. African Americans then constituted almost one in five residents (18.9 percent), which was their peak year. Thereafter, elimination of the slave trade in 1808 and mostly White immigration slowly but steadily reduced the African American proportion until it reached its lowest point in 1940 at 9.8 percent. Before then, in 1870, the 12.7 Black percentage was comparable to the 12.6 percentage in 2010.[17] Continued immigration from the Caribbean and Africa will likely affect this ratio in the future.

Virtually nonexistent in the United States in 1790, Asians and Pacific Islanders have been steadily increasing in numbers and proportion since their first tallies in the 1860 census. Since the liberalization of immigration regulations in 1965, their growth has been dramatic, and their visible concentration in certain regions of the country—particularly on the east and west coasts and in the Chicago metropolitan region—makes their 5 percent of the total population in 2010 seem much greater to residents of those areas.

After experiencing a calamitous decline in population from first contact with Europeans until the 20th century, Native Americans have a high birth rate and are now steadily increasing their numbers. Their recent population growth has stabilized their proportional place in U.S. society at 1 percent.

What can we conclude from this information? Perhaps one surprise is that the United States is less Black today than it was from 1790 to 1890. However, it is also true that the White population percentage of the total is shrinking and the Black population percentage is increasing. Also, the increase in Asians and Native Americans—when combined with the increase in African Americans—means that the United States today is more of a multiracial society than ever before. What will the changing racial composition mean for the future of race relations? As the ratio of Whites declines, they will no doubt become more aware of their race instead of just paying attention to the visibility of other racial groups. Will this lead to greater understanding or to a racial backlash? The answer is still to be determined.

In the last chapter, we will explore more fully the implications of current birth and migration rates on the future of U.S. society, including racial composition.

MAINSTREAM AMERICANS

Rarely are cultures or societies static entities. In the United States, the continual influx of immigrants has helped shape its metamorphosis. Part of this tempering has been the evolving definition of the mainstream ingroup or identifying who was "really an American."[18]

In the initial conception of mainstream Americans, the English comprised virtually all of this ingroup. Gradually, this ingroup expanded from English American exclusivity to British American or White Anglo-Saxon Protestant, thus including the Scots-Irish and Welsh previously excluded. Triggering this re-conceptualization was the rapid Americanization of these groups after the Revolutionary War and nativist reaction to the first large-scale wave of immigrants whose culture, religion, and—in the case of the Irish—peasant class set them apart from the mainstream.

By 1890, the "mainstream American" ingroup did not yet include many other northwest European Americans. Although some multigenerational Americans of non-British ancestry had blended into the mainstream, millions of others had not. These Americans remained culturally pluralistic, their separateness resulting from race, religion, or geographic isolation. In addition, more than 9 million foreign-born—one in seven, perhaps one in five if we include their children—also then lived outside this mainstream society.

In 1890, the "melting pot" had not yet absorbed the 80,000 Dutch, 200,000 Swiss, or 1.2 million Scandinavians in the Midwest, most of whom had arrived after 1870. Likewise, the 150,000 French immigrants, 200,000 Cajuns in Louisiana, and 500,000 French Canadians in New England and the Great Plains remained culturally, linguistically, and religiously separated from the larger society. So, too, did many of the 8 million Germans in the rural Midwest or who were concentrated in many large cities. Their poverty and Catholic faith kept 6 million Irish in the Northeast and 300,000 Mexican Americans in the Southwest in social isolation. About 7.5 million African Americans, 248,000 Native Americans, and 110,000 Asians also lived as mostly impoverished racial minorities separate from the mainstream.[19]

Race, culture, and/or social class origins thus shaped group relations in the United States in 1890, keeping the nation a patchwork quilt of cultural diversity. All three variables influenced perceptions, receptivity, and interaction patterns.

In the 1890s, the tide of immigration changed. The turning point came in 1896, when immigrants from the rest of Europe surpassed those from northern and western Europe. These "new" immigrants soon caused a redefinition of a mainstream American, bringing those of northern and western European origins (including Australian and Canadian) into this classification in contrast to the newer, "less desirable" newcomers. This redefinition did not necessarily reflect cultural or structural assimilation in 1890, however. Figure 9.4 suggests the perceptual reality of that time and how it had changed by 1920.

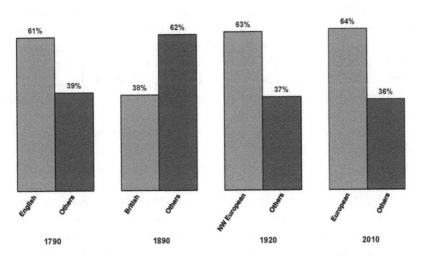

FIGURE 9.4 Mainstream Americans by Ancestry Group, Selected Years

Source: Based on data from U.S. Census Bureau, *Historical Statistics of the United States, Part II*, Series Z-20-132 (Washington, DC: U.S. Government Printing Office, 1976).

By 1970, a new turning point in immigration occurred, with immigrants from less developed countries outnumbering those from more developed countries. Once again, partly through a reaction to this change and partly due to acculturation, education, and upward mobility, the concept of mainstream American expanded. This time it included anyone of European, Australian, or Canadian origin, thus setting them apart from the people of color—both the new arrivals and the still non-integrated African Americans and Native Americans.

Mainstream American Caveats

Admittedly, these mainstream American and outgroup classifications in Figure 9.4 are somewhat arbitrary. For example, some non-English were clearly mainstream Americans in 1790, such as Welsh Americans William Floyd, Button Gwinnett, Thomas Jefferson, Francis Lewis, and Lewis Morris—all signers of the Declaration of Independence. However, many 18th- and 19th-century segregated Welsh settlements of Quakers, Baptists, or Congregationalists remained scattered in numerous regions where Welsh-language newspapers, even books, helped maintain a distinct ethnic minority group. Similarly, 19th-century German industrialists such as H. J. Heinz, Frederick Weyerhauser, John J. Bausch, and Henry Lomb typify non-British individuals who wielded considerable power and influence; still, most Germans remained socially isolated in rural or urban subcommunities.

The 2010 mainstream category also is an arbitrary oversimplification because it overlooks the religious and cultural differences among White ethnics that set them apart from fully assimilated European Americans. For example, mainstream Americans view the Amish, Mennonites, and Hasidic Jews as culturally distinct groups living within their own subcultures outside the mainstream. Therefore, the categories cannot be taken literally.

Even so, these categories still serve a useful purpose. They address the perception, acceptance, social distance, and therefore the basis on which people react positively or negatively to physically or culturally distinct others. Some people included in the mainstream group may not actually be a part of it and vice versa, yet these groupings offer an approximation of those seen as "Americans" and those who still remain as outsiders. The social distance scores reported by Emory Bogardus and other researchers since 1926 are a helpful indicator of these groupings. Comparatively, the studies reveal a lessening of social distance among all groups through the decades, but nevertheless a consistent clustering of many non-White groups further away in social acceptance than White ethnic groups.[20]

Of course, one can create other configurations and numbers. For example, one could introduce social stratification as a variable and make an effective argument for social class designation affecting mainstream acceptance and thereby altering the ingroup-outgroup memberships. Such a position has some merit, although it opens the door for counterarguments involving racism and structural assimilation, which would affect acceptance regardless of social class. Even so, with a smaller proportion of people living in poverty today than in 1890, and fewer in 1890 than in 1790, the pattern shown in Figure 9.4 of an increased proportion of mainstream Americans through the centuries would likely remain and perhaps be even greater.

These statistics serve as a guide to our understanding and not as an absolute identification. Avoiding the Dillingham Flaw and instead identifying mainstream Americans through the eyes of each period's contemporaries, we find that the expanding American identity has resulted in a greater ingroup totality today than ever before. Despite recently expressed fears about the United States becoming a polyglot society of dissimilar people (a historically recurring anxiety), the nation's mainstream group has expanded, not contracted.

The "Wall"

What do we learn from this focus on mainstream Americans? As the nation's population mix has changed through the generations, so, too, has its definition of national cultural identity. Groups once excluded, once considered unassimilable and even sometimes reviled, became included. In time, this socially constructed new reality seemed natural, especially with the appearance of a new group perceived as "different" and/or as economic competitors. A long, sometimes conflict-ridden process unfolded. Eventually, the newer group also became part of the ingroup and was replaced by another outgroup.

The concept of an expanding mainstream American identity is similar to the history of walled medieval cities. Only so many inhabitants could fit within the protective wall that surrounded the city. The lack of available space forced newcomers to settle outside in faubourgs (the first suburbs), where they could participate in the city's daily activities, although they were not really a part of the city.

Hawking their wares as merchants inside the city's gates, they no doubt were resented by some as economic competitors. When trouble came in the form of marauders, all united in a common cause, but the newcomers were more likely to suffer the most in loss and destruction of their property outside the walls. In time, as the outsiders became a more integral part of the city, a new encircling wall was built farther out as the old wall was torn down. With the previously excluded inhabitants now safely ensconced within the city's new walled perimeter, others would soon settle outside and begin the process anew.

The wall is an apt metaphor. In intergroup or gender relations, too often we still build protective walls of isolation, avoidance, or exclusion. Whether physical or social, walls do more than separate people: They limit one's field of vision, restrict movement, create a "they" and "we" mentality, and inspire conflict. Walls of prejudice keep people apart from one another, making those on one side more susceptible to victimization, as those faubourg dwellers once were. Just as economic growth brought the medieval walls down, so, too, does it help bring down our walls of prejudice. Conversely, economic decline helps erect walls between groups as people compete for jobs.

The social barriers we erect can sometimes be just as insurmountable and long lasting as many of those medieval walls still standing these many centuries later. Sometimes, however, those walls can be scaled, their gates opened, and the ramparts destroyed. It is a paradoxical tribute to the dynamics of U.S. society that its cultural identity walls of exclusivity have been weak enough to be overcome several times, thereby producing a stronger nation and a more vibrant American character than could have existed without such expansiveness.

PERCEPTION AND REALITY

Americans' perception of the foreign-born population is affected by how they become aware of that diversity within the United States. The growing presence of first-generation Americans in previously homogeneous small-town and suburban locales brings a changed reality into the residents' taken-for-granted world. How that translates into interaction patterns helps determine whether the interactions are positive or negative. However, news about "illegal aliens" almost always triggers a negative response, because Americans typically resent people violating their laws who cost them money as well.

Concern about unauthorized immigrants is nothing new. After passage of the Chinese Exclusion Act in 1882, Americans reacted strongly against the problem of Chinese illegally entering the United States through British Columbia. Today, with a porous border with Mexico, unauthorized crossings are constant. Federal agents apprehend more than 500,000 aliens each year, but tens of thousands of others successfully elude detection.[21]

Controversy about these unauthorized immigrants—particularly with the education, health, and social welfare costs they create—distorts the public image of authorized immigrants, resulting in mixed public opinions on the issue of immigration. For example, in a December 2011 Fox News national poll, 63 percent of respondents said they favored an increase in the number of legal immigrants allowed to come into the United States as long as they agreed to work, pay taxes, and obey the law. In contrast, a 2011 USA Today/Gallup poll found 55 percent of respondents opposed to passage of a law that would give illegal immigrants living in the United States a path to legal status. A 2010 NBC News/Wall Street Journal poll found the same percentage similarly opposed.[22]

Those expressing negative views frequently cite reasons such as immigrants lacking job skills and using too many tax-supported services, factors that are more likely to be associated with unauthorized immigrants than the immigrants whose skills or family sponsorship clears them for admission legally. Unfortunately, many Americans do not make a distinction between these two different groups of newcomers.

THE LARGER CONTEXT

The United States is certainly not the only country undergoing a significant foreign-born influx that prompts native-born citizens to compare their present-day scene with their nation's past. For example, many Western European countries, mostly homogeneous in the past, now find themselves confronting the large-scale presence of racially and culturally distinct others. This situation has necessitated changes in government policies to maintain societal cohesion in the face of such unprecedented diversity.

Following World War II, England experienced a major change in the size of its non-White population. Numbering in the low thousands in 1945, by 1970, they numbered about 1.4 million, one-third of them actually born in the United Kingdom.[23] Enacting strict controls on immigration in the 1970s and confronting race riots in the early 1980s, the British government sought to improve the situation. Because many Britons viewed the new minorities as outsiders, even though growing numbers of the second- and third-generation minority citizens were U.K.-born, the government acted to change this mind-set. Since passage of the Race Relations Act (1976), all official reports use the term *ethnic minority* instead of *immigrant*. The law also expanded the concept of discrimination to include indirect discrimination (any seemingly neutral rule that has an indefensibly discriminatory effect). Amended in 2000, this law also holds police accountable in racial matters. Although problems remain, race relations have improved and 12 non-White citizens now serve in the British Parliament. In 2010, the foreign-born population was 6.5 million, or 11.5 percent of the total population. The largest groups were Asian Indians, Poles, Pakistanis, Irish, and Germans.[24]

Industrialization in early-20th-century France attracted millions of Italian, Polish, and Spanish immigrants to work in the factories. Yet despite their common Catholic faith and shared continental heritage, they were not easily able to join the French mainstream. In a country that for many years enforced a language policy even against regional dialects, foreigners discovered that Franco-conformity (assimilation) was the only allowable choice, not pluralism. Today, about 3.1 million immigrants (8.2 percent of the population) live in France, most of them from Muslim North Africa.[25] With so many foreigners differing in appearance, language, religion, and values, many French worry that their nation is losing its cultural identity. Riots in 2005, 2007, and 2009 by alienated Muslim youth were a clear signal that the fabric of French society was, at the least, badly frayed. The 2004 government ban on headscarves (still in effect and enforced primarily in schools) was supported by 69 percent of the populace, another indicator of the difficulties that multiculturalism is presenting in France.[26]

In Germany, an acute labor shortage after World War II prompted the government to invite foreign guest workers from several countries to help rebuild the country. Most notably, beginning in 1961, it officially invited Turkish workers to replace East Germans no longer able to work in the factories after the communists built the Berlin Wall. These "temporary immigrants" elected to stay and soon sent for their families. Under previous German law, children born to foreigners in Germany were still not citizens, so over time even the third generation born there remained outsiders, typically living in ethnic enclaves, socially segregated from the mainstream.

Although many in the second and third generations only know Turkey secondhand, prevailing societal norms prompted them to assume their parents' nationality. Numbering about 2 million, they comprise more than one-fourth of Germany's foreign-born population (11.7 percent of the total population in 2010). To address the societal schism, in 2000, the government conferred German citizenship on children of all foreigners born in Germany, thereby helping more and more to think of themselves as Turkish Germans, not Turks.[27]

TODAY'S PATTERNS IN PERSPECTIVE

Many Americans believe we are living in the midst of the greatest immigration ever. In actual numbers, that appears to be true, but in relation to the total population, the current immigration rate is lower than that of an 80-year period stretching from 1840 to 1920. Those higher rates meant a much greater ratio of immigrants to the population than at present.

Similarly, today's foreign-born population, so easily visible, is in fact less in relation to the native-born population than in 7 of the last 17 censuses. Put plainly, we have a lower foreign-born ratio today than we had in 70 consecutive years in the nation's history.

We are indeed becoming a more multiracial society, and we have more Africans, Asians, and Hispanics than ever before. The trend toward more people of color will continue. As Whites decline as a percentage of the total, they may feel threatened economically and po-litically, and they could act to reverse or slow down this demographic change. Perhaps California, where Whites first became a minority, will become the bellwether state for a national response. Florida and Texas are other states to watch for nativist reactions.

Acculturation and assimilation have resulted in a greater inclusive-ness of previously excluded groups into the mainstream American category. Up until now, however, that process has not included people of color. If the process is to continue, a sea change in racial attitudes will be required to allow today's outgroup members to become part of the American mainstream. The growing Black middle class, as well as the increase in Black college graduates, managers, and elected of-ficials (most notably Barack Obama) suggest that change may occur.

Our discussions about the statistics relating to immigration, foreign-born census counts, and racial proportions all addressed as-pects of the pluralism that has been, and continues to be, the reality of the United States. Commentary on the expanding definition of mainstream Americans pointed to the ongoing assimilation process that continues through the generations. Besides dispelling myths that current immigration is unprecedented or that the proportion of foreign-born is higher than ever, the data presented here also offer quantitative insights for avoiding the Dillingham Flaw. Peter Berger was right. Things are not necessarily as they seem. The pluralism of today in many ways does not surpass that in our nation's past, and assimilation is not endangered by numbers, because that process has successfully continued as a dynamic force even under more overwhelming proportionate numbers of years past.

Left unsaid in this discussion is whether the agendas of separatist multiculturalists create a real danger to societal cohesiveness regardless of comparative statistics. We turn next to that topic.

NOTES

1. See Vincent N. Parrillo, *Strangers to These Shores*, 10th ed. (Boston: Allyn and Bacon, 2011), pp. 124–5, 222–3, 295–6.

2. See, for example, John Higham, *Strangers in the Land: Patterns of Nativism, 1860–1925* (New Brunswick, NJ: Rutgers University Press, 2002).

3. James M. Smith, *Freedom's Fetters* (Ithaca, NY: Cornell University Press, 1966), p. 25.

4. Douglas S. Massey and Julia Gelatt, "What Happened to the Wages of Mexican Immigrants? Trends and Interpretations," *Latino Studies*, 8 (2010): 328–54.

5. Luigi Laurenti, *Property Values and Race: Studies in Seven Cities* (New York: Praeger, 1976).

6. Rita J. Simon, "Old Minorities, New Immigrants: Aspirations, Hopes, and Fears," *The Annals of the American Academy of Political and Social Science*, 530 (1993): 65, 73.

7. U.S. Department of Homeland Security, *2010 Yearbook of Immigration Statistics* (Washington, DC: U.S. Government Printing Office, 2011), Table 6.

8. U.S. Census Bureau, *Statistical Abstract of the United States: 2011* (Washington, DC: U.S. Government Printing Office, 2010), Table 43, p. 46.

9. Pew Hispanic Center, "The Mexican-American Boom: Births Overtake Immigration," July 14, 2011. Available at http://pewresearch.org/pubs/2058/-immigration-mexican-immigrants-mexican-american-birth-rate. (Accessed January 11, 2012.)

10. Philip Martin and Elizabeth Midgley, "Immigration in America 2010," *Population Bulletin Update*. Available at www.prb.org/pdf10/immigration-update2010.pdf. (Accessed January 11, 2012.)

11. Jeffrey Passel and D'Vera Cohn, "Unauthorized Immigrant Population: National and State Trends, 2010," Pew Hispanic Center (February 1, 2011). Available at www.pewhispanic.org/2011/02/01/unauthorized-immigrant-population-brnational-and-state-trends-2010/. (Accessed January 11, 2012.)

12. Martin and Midgley, "Immigration in America 2010."

13. U.S. Census Bureau, "Quick Facts," *2010 American Community Survey*. Available at www.census.gov. (Accessed January 12, 2012.)

14. Ibid.

15. U.S. Census Bureau, *Income, Poverty, and Health Insurance in the United States: 2010*, Series P60-239, September 2011, Table 4, p. 15.

16. U.S. Census Bureau, "Quick Facts."

17. U.S. Census Bureau, *Historical Census Statistics on Population Totals by Race, 1790 to 1990, and by Hispanic Origin, 1970 to 1990, for Large Cities and Other Urban Places in the United States,* Table A-1.

18. See Martin E. Spencer, "Multiculturalism, 'Political Correctness,' and the Politics of Identity," in "Multiculturalism and Diversity," ed. Vincent N. Parrillo, special issue, *Sociological Forum,* 9 (1994): 547–67.

19. James S. Olson and Heather Olson Beal, *The Ethnic Dimension in American Society,* 4th ed. (New York: Wiley-Blackwell, 2010), pp. 114–5.

20. Emory Bogardus, "Comparing Racial Distance in Ethiopia, South Africa, and the United States," *Sociology and Social Research,* 52 (1968): 149–56; Carolyn A. Owen, Howard C. Eisner, and Thomas R. McFaul, "A Half-Century of Social Distance Research: National Replication of the Bogardus Studies," *Sociology and Social Research,* 66 (1981): 80–97; Vincent N. Parrillo and Christopher Donoghue, "Updating the Bogardus Social Distance Studies: A New National Survey," *Social Science Journal,* 42:2 (2005): 257–71.

21. U.S. Department of Homeland Security, *2010 Yearbook of Immigration Statistics,* Table 33.

22. "Immigration." Available at www.pollingreport.com/immigration.htm. (Accessed January 12, 2012.)

23. British Broadcasting Company, "Short History of Immigration." Available at news.bbc.co.uk. (Accessed January 12, 2012.)

24. "Migrants in the UK: An Overview," The Migration Observatory. Available at http://migrationobservatory.ox.ac.uk/briefings/migrants-uk -overview. (Accessed January 12, 2012.)

25. "Society at a Glance 2011: OECD Social Indicators," OECD iLibrary. Available at www.oecd-ilibrary.org/sites/soc_glance-2011-en/04/03/index .html. (Accessed January 12, 2012.)

26. "The War of the Headscarves," *The Economist* (February 5, 2005). Available at www.economist.com/node/2404691?story_id=2404691. (Accessed January 12, 2012.)

27. Deutsche Welle, "More Ethnic Turks Becoming German Citizens, Study Shows." Available at www.dw-world.de/dw/article/0,,4121209,00.html. (Accessed January 12, 2012.)

10

Is Multiculturalism a Threat?

America rejects bigotry. We reject every act of hatred against people of Arab background or Muslim faith. America values and welcomes peaceful people of all faiths—Christian, Jewish, Muslim, Sikh, Hindu, and many others. Every faith is practiced and protected here, because we are one country. Every immigrant can be fully and equally American because we're one country. Race and color should not divide us, because America is one country.

—President George W. Bush, 2002

Jesse Rudavski's photo of double lightning strikes illustrates the theme of this chapter: determining whether or not what appears on the horizon should be a matter of concern or enjoyed for what and how it presents itself to the beholder.

Multiculturalism is taught in academia, debated in government, promoted by ethnic leaders, reported by the media, and discussed among the citizenry. Few are indifferent to a subject with so many proponents and opponents. Some see multiculturalism as the bedrock on which to build a society of true equality, whereas others see multiculturalism as a sinkhole that will swallow up the foundation of U.S. society.

At its core, the multiculturalism debate is a polarization of the centuries-old dual American realities of pluralism and assimilation into competing forces for dominance. As this book has shown, pluralism has been a constant reality in the United States since colonial times, and assimilation has been a steady, powerful force as well. There have always been both assimilationist and pluralist advocates, as well as both nativist alarmists and minority separatists.

Resentment and hostility about multiculturalism result from several factors. Rapid communication and televised images have heightened public consciousness of the diversity within U.S. society, but without placing it in the continuity of the larger historical context. Government policies and programs, particularly those dealing with bilingualism, become controversial when viewed as more than transitional aids by both pluralists and assimilationists. Vocal advocates for each position arouse strong feelings in their listeners in suggesting an either-or stance of supposedly diametrically opposing forces.

Raising reactions toward multiculturalism to a firestorm level are still other factors. First are the radical positions: anti-immigrant, racist, anti–White male or non-integrationist. Another is revisionist history or literary anthologies that downplay dead White males (DWMs) or Western civilization and heavily emphasize women, people of color, and non-Western civilization. Add furor about political correctness, whether in the guise of speech or behavior codes, curricula offerings, or selective emphases. The result is controversy of a (dare I say it?) white-heat intensity.

Multiculturalism is a stance taken by pluralists. Does that mean it imperils the process of assimilation? Basically, the answer is no, but the explanation is a complicated one. Multiculturalism, as mentioned in the first chapter, is a newer term for cultural pluralism, not a new phenomenon. Large foreign-speaking communities, foreign-language schools, organizations, houses of worship, and even pluralist extremists are not new to U.S. society. Should we, then, not fear this new version any more than its precursor or is this more than a "new suit"? Is this thing we call multiculturalism a clear and present danger?

Before we can address this concern, we need to understand exactly what multiculturalism is.

THE UMBRELLAS OF MULTICULTURALISM

Multiculturalism does not mean the same thing to everyone. Even the multiculturalists do not agree with one another as to what they are advocating. Before we can address the advantages or disadvantages of a multicultural society, therefore, we need to understand these differing viewpoints.

The Inclusionists

During the 1970s, multiculturalism meant the inclusion of material in the school curriculum that related the contributions of non-European peoples to the nation's history. In the next phase, multiculturalists aimed to change all areas of the curriculum in schools and colleges to reflect the diversity of U.S. society and to develop in individuals an awareness and appreciation for the impact of non-European civilizations on American culture.[1]

Inclusionists would appear to be assimilationists, but they are more than this. Assimilationists seek the elimination of cultural differences through the loss of one's distinctive traits that are replaced by the language, values, and other attributes of mainstream Americans. Although inclusionists share assimilationists' desire for national unity through a common identity, they also promote a pluralist or multiculturalist perspective. This notion finds expression by recognition of diversity throughout U.S. history and of minority contributions to American art, literature, music, cuisine, scientific achievements, sports, and holiday celebrations.

In the 1990s, this viewpoint perhaps found its most eloquent voice in Diane Ravitch.[2] She also emphasized a common culture, but one that incorporated the contributions of all racial and ethnic groups so that they can believe in their full membership in America's past, present, and future. She envisioned the elimination of allegiance to any specific racial and/or ethnic group, with emphasis instead on our common humanity, our shared national identity, and our individual accomplishments.

Inclusionist multiculturalists thus approach pluralism not with groups each standing under their own different-colored umbrellas, but with all sharing one multi-colored umbrella whose strength and character reflect the diverse backgrounds but common core culture of those standing under it together.

The Separatists

The group of multiculturalists that generates the most controversy is people who advocate "minority nationalism" and "separate pluralism." They reject an integrative approach and the notion of forming a common bond of identity among both the distinct minority groups and mainstream Americans. Instead of a collective American national identity, they seek specific, separate group identities that will withstand the assimilation process. This form of multiculturalism is the most extreme version of pluralism.

To achieve their objective and create a positive group identity, these multiculturalists seek to teach and maintain their own cultural customs, history, values, and festivals while refusing to acknowledge those of the dominant culture. For example, some Native Americans raise strong objections to Columbus Day parades, while Afrocentrists downgrade Western civilization by arguing that it is merely a derivative of Afro-Egyptian culture—a claim, by the way, that is not historically accurate.[3]

Separatist multiculturalists do not want to stand with others under one multi-colored umbrella. Not only do they wish to be under their own special umbrella, but they also want to share it only with their own kind and let them know why it is such a special umbrella. One may walk the same ground in the same storm, but shelter is to be found under a group's personal umbrella.

What particularly infuriates the assimilationists about the separatists' position is their concern that such emphasis on group identity promotes what Arthur Schlesinger called "the cult of ethnicity." In *The Disuniting of America* (1998), a book widely discussed in both Europe and North America, Schlesinger warned that the Balkan chaos at that time could be America's prologue.[4]

It is precisely that devastating warfare in the Balkans among Bosnians, Croatians, and Serbs in the former Yugoslavia that prompted so many in Canada, Europe, and the United States to speak out against multiculturalists who espoused separate pluralism. The "balkanization of society" is the most common expression that critics of multiculturalism use to suggest the threat to the social fabric supplied by a divisive policy promoting group identity over individual or societal welfare.

When Hispanic leaders from groups such as LULAC insisted on "language rights"—the maintenance of the Spanish language and

Latino culture at public expense—the assimilationists warned of an emerging "Tower of Babel" society.[5] When Afrocentrists such as Molefi Asante and Leon Jeffries emphasized the customs of African cultures over those of the dominant culture, their stress on African ethnicity provoked disapproval from critics such as Schlesinger, who complained that they drive "even deeper the awful wedges between races" by exaggerating ethnic differences.

The Integrative Pluralists

In 1915, Horace Kallen used the metaphor of a symphony orchestra to portray the strength through diversity of U.S. society.[6] Just as different groups of instruments each play their separate parts of the musical score, but together produce beautiful music of blends and contrasts, so, too, he said, do the various populations within pluralist America. Kallen's idea of effective functional integration but limited cultural integration, however, was essentially a Eurocentric vision and reality. People of color were mentioned only incidentally and were typically not allowed to sit with, let alone join, the orchestra.

Harry Triandis added the missing interracial component to this view of integrative pluralism in 1976, and he suggested that the majority culture is enriched by "additive multiculturalism."[7] By this comment he meant that one can become a more complete person by understanding other languages, cultural values, and social settings. He hoped for society becoming more cohesive by finding common goals without insisting on a loss of minority group identities. Arguing that mainstream Americans, secure in their identity, need to develop new interpersonal skills, Triandis maintained that the essence of pluralism is the development of appreciation, interdependence, and skills to interact intimately with persons from other cultures. He added,

> The majority culture can be enriched by considering the viewpoints of the several minority cultures that exist in America rather than trying to force these minorities to adopt a monocultural, impoverished, provincial viewpoint which may in the long run reduce creativity and the chances of effective adjustment in a fast-changing world. (p. 181)

This argument of cultural enrichment from diverse subcultures found another form of expression in *Beyond the Culture Wars* (1993) by Gerald Graff. He suggested that exposure to differing cultural views will revitalize education by creating the dynamics of dialogue and debate. As Socrates once encouraged his students to search for truth through intellectual clashes, so, too, Graff maintained, can multicultural education help students overcome relativism so they can become informed about different positions.[8]

Ronald Takaki echoed Graff's idea by recommending that the university become the meeting ground for different viewpoints so that minds could be opened to greater cultural diversity. His position was that U.S. history, like the country itself, does not belong to one group, and so, a change in the status quo was necessary. Instead of a hierarchy of power headed by a privileged group, greater cross-cultural understanding and interconnected viewpoints would be a healthy change.[9]

Integrative pluralists envision a multitude of distinctive umbrellas each containing a different group, but with the umbrellas' edges attached to each other, so that, collectively, they embrace everyone. Guided equally by the many handles of the interconnected umbrellas, one can look around to see where another group is coming from within the framework of the whole.

THE LARGER CONTEXT

Although the United States has always been a nation of immigrants and a land of diversity, some of its citizens nevertheless have continually spoken and acted against what they perceived as threats from multiculturalism. Similarly, in the other traditional immigrant-receiving nations—Australia, Canada, and England—outcries against multiculturalism have occurred in the past several decades.

In Australia, the debate over multiculturalism centers on the definition of what it means to "be Australian." Initially, political attachment to multiculturalism emerged as counterpoint to diminishing support for sustaining Australia's historically British culture and identity by means of its racist White Australia Policy. In a second phase, emphasis was on reconciliation with the previously exploited indigenous people, Australia's original inhabitants.[10] Facing criticism in the late 1990s over its immigration and multiculturalist policies, the federal government eventually enacted policies that stressed national unity over multiculturalism. Between 1996 and 2007, the rollback of multiculturalism and rise of Islamophobia led to national leaders attacking "political correctness" and blaming it "for keeping Australians with being comfortable with who they are." They urged ethnic/religious schools to teach "Australian values."[11]

Canadian multiculturalism, cited by many admirers as the world's best model of pluralism, nonetheless has its critics who believe it promotes divisiveness. They contend that such policies and practices force individuals to be ethnics forever even if they want to assimilate.[12] Critics cite the demands of the Francophones in Quebec for recognition as a distinct society, First Nations claims of self-government, and class action lawsuits of some ethnic, racial, and religious minorities to protect their ethnic heritage as evidence of multiculturalism undermining societal cohesion.

In England—whose population is one-sixth that of the United States but who received 586,000 immigrants (compared to 1 million to the U.S.)—the cultural stresses have become intense as the British fear the loss of their way of life. Formerly moderate on the issue, Prime Minister David Cameron revealed a change of heart in a 2011 speech:

> Under the doctrine of multiculturalism, we have encouraged different cultures to live separate lives, apart from each other and the mainstream. We have failed to provide a vision of society to which they feel they want to belong. We have even tolerated these segregated communities behaving in ways that run counter to our values…. Frankly, we need a lot less of the passive tolerance of recent years and much more active, muscular liberalism…. There are practical things we can do as well. That includes making sure immigrants speak the language of their new home, and ensuring that people are educated in elements of a common culture and curriculum.[13]

Cameron's remarks echoed those of other Western European leaders also repudiating multiculturalism. In 2010, Germany's Chancellor, Angela Merkel, restated her belief that it had "utterly failed" in her country. French President Nicolas Sarkozy stated his desire for the prevalence of French secularism, saying, "The truth is that in all our democracies we've been too concerned about the identity of the new arrivals and not enough about the identity of the country receiving them."[14]

Perhaps the reason multiculturalism in Europe is far less successful than in Canada and the United States is that it is a far different type of multiculturalism and certainly not one of integrative pluralism. The last sentence in the Cameron quotation reveals that distinction, as he argues for "practical things" already done in North America.

The Canadian and U.S. concept of citizenship is that anyone from anywhere can become naturalized, but the European conception, for the most part, rests on ethnic heritage, language, and culture. I have seen this firsthand through interactions with politicians and nonpoliticians alike in numerous European countries. One can be a third-generation Turk in Germany or Hungarian in Romania, for example, and still not be considered a German or Romanian, respectively, by others or even by oneself. Generally, multiculturalism in Europe means psychological isolation and social distance between groups, rather than any growing cohesiveness.

Current low birth rates mean that not a single European country has people having enough children to replace themselves when they die. Beginning in the 1990s, the resultant influx of foreigners to meet labor demands intensified this us-and-them mentality, generating xenophobic reactions, ethnoviolence, the rise of rightwing reactionary political parties, and efforts at new restrictive immigration laws. Compounding the problem is Islamophobia and the perception of Islam as a religion of intolerance and haven for terrorists. The increased strength of anti-immigrant or nativist political parties in many European countries is testimony to public reaction to the culturally diverse influx.

Europeans use the term *racism* more generally to refer to negative attitudes or actions toward any ethnic group, whereas Americans tend to use its narrower connotation to refer only to physically distinct groups. Yet racism, by its American definition, also is a factor in European xenophobia. As Italy, for example, struggles to absorb its recent influx of developing-world migrants and is dependent on their labors (foreign workers account for 9 percent of the Gross Domestic Product), many non-Whites face exploitation, maltreatment, and violence. In 2011, Human Rights Watch issued a report condemning the state's failure to take effective action to prevent and prosecute racist and xenophobic violence in recent years (nearly 400 in 2009).[15]

ROSES AND THORNS

Cultivated for almost 5,000 years, roses were known to the ancient Persians, Greeks, and Romans. One of our most popular flowers, the rose now comes in more than 8,000 varieties. Yet as beautiful and romantic as most people find roses to be, their thorns can hurt.

Roses seem a particularly apt analogy in any discussion about multiculturalism. Both require warmth and nurturing to bloom fully. The stronger their roots, the more they thrive. A variety of species is common to both, yet universal treatment gives vibrancy to all. Both also contain beauty and danger. Focusing only on the rose when reaching for one on a bush often brings flesh into painful contact with a thorn; focusing narrowly on racial or cultural differences often causes the pain of isolation or conflict.

Some proponents of multiculturalism (the separatists) want to focus on only one variety of "rose" among many, whereas other advocates (the inclusionists) stress the commonality in origin that so many kinds of "roses" share. The third group of multiculturalists (the integrative pluralists) emphasizes the overall beauty of "roses" of different colors and varieties sharing the same "garden." The critics of multiculturalism, however, seem only to see its "thorns."

Completely ignoring the thorns needlessly places one at risk. If we look only at the thorns, we miss the beauty of the rose. If we pay heed to the thorns or remove them, as florists so thoughtfully do for their customers, they cannot hurt us, and our appreciation for the rose remains unspoiled. We now look first at the thorns, the negative side of multiculturalism, and then at the roses, the positive side.

THE "THORNS" OF MULTICULTURALISM

The "thorns" of multiculturalism are primarily those of immigration, language, culture, and race. Other thorns could undoubtedly be named, but these are the most important because it is primarily in them that some Americans find the threat to U.S. society.

The "Immigrant Thorns"

Make no mistake about it. Continuing high immigration fuels the debate about multiculturalism because this subject is about much more than simply preserving national identity. It is about power struggles among groups. It is about economics, jobs, social welfare, and tax dollars.

Concern about large numbers of immigrants arriving each year can instill antipathy in many native-born White and Black Americans toward multicultural policies or programs promoting cultural diversity. With more than 21 million immigrants arriving since 1990, a sizable proportion of the U.S. public thinks there are too many immigrants in the country. Such anti-immigration sentiments have sounded in the land almost continually since large numbers of Irish Catholics began entering the United States in the early 19th century.[16]

Today, Americans have mixed opinions about immigration. A May 2007 CBS News/New York Times national poll, for example, found that 57 percent of respondents said they felt that the most recent immigrants contribute to the country, whereas 28 percent thought they caused problems. Yet in a June 2007 NBC/Wall Street Journal national poll, a more even split occurred, with 46 percent saying immigration helps more than it hurts the United States, whereas 44 percent thought the opposite. On the subject of unauthorized immigration, 61 percent viewed it as "very serious," and another 30 percent said it was "somewhat serious."

One multigenerational pattern about the public response to immigration needs mentioning. Contemporary immigrants of any time period have almost always received negative evaluations by most native-born Americans, many descendants of earlier immigrants once castigated by other native-born Americans. With the passage of time, people view these now "old" immigrant groups as making positive contributions to the cultural and socioeconomic well-being of society as they transfer their negative perceptions to new immigrant groups. Several anti-immigration organizations lobby for restrictive laws to curtail immigration. The largest of these are the American Immigration Control Foundation (AICF), the Foundation for American Immigration Reform (FAIR), and the Center for Immigration Studies (CIS).

Although these and other anti-immigrant groups vary in the intensity of their views, they all see the present immigration as a threat to the United States. Their opposition rests on their belief that immigrants either take jobs away from Americans, often from poor people who are forced onto welfare, or else use tax-supported services in health and education. Either way, these groups insist, the immigrants drive up social welfare costs. Other arguments include the assertion that immigrants strain law enforcement resources, contribute to an overpopulation problem through their higher birth rates, and deplete our natural resources.

Some states—such as California, Florida, Illinois, New Jersey, New York, and Texas, which are the destinations of about 80 percent of all immigrants—clearly feel the impact of immigration more than other states. FAIR estimated that—in the areas of education, medical services, law enforcement and public assistance—illegal immigration cost taxpayers about $113 billion annually.[17] Such reports and claims of high costs for the taxpayer provide ready ammunition for immigration critics.

If multiculturalism means favoring an immigration that places a financial hardship on the American worker and taxpayer, then many Americans oppose multiculturalism.

The "Language Thorns"

Foreigners speaking a language other than English have been a thorn in the side of many Americans for more than 200 years. In 1750, Benjamin Franklin expressed concern about the prevalence of the German language in Pennsylvania, and George Washington wrote to John Adams in 1798 against encouraging immigration because, among other things, the new arrivals "retain the language ... which they bring with them."[18] No doubt these men spoke not only for themselves, but also for a great many of their contemporaries as well.

Such complaints have reverberated down through the generations to the present day. They are now also louder and more numerous given current migration trends. Among today's foreign born, 15 percent speak only English. Of the remainder (including 53 percent of them Hispanics), more than half (52 percent) speak English less than "very well."[19] Immigrant children comprise about one-fifth of the school population, and those with limited English proficiency have difficulty in learning within regular classroom settings and easily lag behind in their academic performance.

With the prevalence of so many non-English-speaking youngsters and adults, Americans have done more than complain. For example, Japanese American S. I. Hayakawa, a former U.S. Senator from California and former president of San Francisco State University, founded U.S. English, an organization dedicated to making English the nation's official language; eliminating or reducing bilingual education programs; and abolishing bilingual ballots, government documents, and road signs. Its president since 1993 has been Mauro E. Mujica, an immigrant from Chile, and in 2012 it claimed 1.8 million members. English-only laws have been introduced in dozens of state legislatures since the late 1980s. Although 13 states rejected English-only legislative proposals, by 2012, 30 states had English as their official language.

Many Americans are impatient with those who are unable to speak English. Their contention is that anyone living in this country should speak its language. Believing that our schools provide the "heat" for the melting pot, they are particularly irked about bilingual education programs. Critics see bilingual programs as counterproductive because they reduce assimilation and cohesiveness in U.S. society while isolating ethnic groups from one another. It is here that opponents use the terms *ethnic tribalism* and *classrooms of Babel* to argue that bilingual education fosters separation instead of cultural unity. Any calls for language and cultural maintenance programs, particularly in the public schools, make the monolingual adherents see red.

If multiculturalism means that English proficiency is not a priority, then many Americans oppose multiculturalism.

The "Cultural Thorns"

A monthly average of 90,000 new immigrants—about 75 percent of them Asian or Hispanic—now arrive in the United States. The steadily increasing size of each new immigrant group sustains and enhances ethnic resiliency in language, ingroup solidarity, and subcultural patterns.

Without this constant infusion of newcomers, acculturation would inexorably lessen each group's cultural isolation. Group members would gradually learn to speak English and function more fully within the larger society. Even if such factors as limited education, poor job skills, and discrimination were present to prevent economic mainstreaming, greater cultural fusion would most likely occur over time.

Instead, we have large-scale immigration from Asian and Latin American countries revitalizing ethnic subcommunities with their language usage and cultural patterns. Differences in physical appearance, non-Western traditions, and religious faiths—together with the prevalence of languages other than English, especially Spanish—suggest to some Americans that, unless immigration is significantly curtailed, American culture and society are in danger of fragmenting.

What makes the cultural thorns even sharper is the new ethnic presence in our small towns and suburbs. Once almost the exclusive sanctuary of homogenized Americans, many small towns and outlying communities are now residential choices for tens of thousands of first-generation Americans of non-European origin. In the more affluent suburbs, educated business and professional persons, seeking out desirable suburban communities with excellent school systems, have brought racial and ethnic diversity to towns unaccustomed to such a multiethnic mix, sometimes erecting a mosque or temple, with its unique architecture, in contrast to other structures in the community.

It is not simply the presence of visibly distinct newcomers that creates tensions. These first-generation Americans live in the community, but they are not of it, because they seldom interact with neighbors. Instead, they maintain an interactional network within their own group scattered throughout the area. This informal social patterning is reminiscent of past European immigrants who lived in recognized territorial subcommunities. However, because these middle-class suburban ethnics live among homogenized Americans, their lack of involvement in community life encourages social distance and grates on others' sensibilities.

Besides a normal first-generation immigrant preference to associate with one's own people, some pragmatic elements deter suburban ethnic social interactions. Often, the wife, filling the traditional gender role as the nurturer, has limited command of English and feels insecure about conversing with neighbors. The husband is usually at work for long hours and has little free time except to spend with the family.

Joining social organizations is a strong American orientation, as noted by Tocqueville and many others. Possessing neither time nor yet fully acculturated, few Asian Americans get involved in such typical suburban activities as parent-teacher organizations, team sports coaching, or scouting leadership. In time, this situation will probably change, but the present noninvolvement maintains Asian social distance from other Americans in their local communities. In response, suburbanites often view Asians as not giving to, but only taking from, the community. This reaction is especially acute when Asian American children, reflecting the high motivation and goal achievement instilled in them by their parents, appear overrepresented in garnering awards and recognition in scholarships and music.

If multiculturalism means maintenance of an alien culture and lessening community cohesiveness, then many Americans oppose multiculturalism.

The "Racial Thorns"

Except for extremist groups like the Ku Klux Klan, the National Association for the Advancement of White People, and neo-Nazis, few talk openly of race in their opposition to multiculturalism. Nevertheless, race is an important component of the multiculturalism debate.

The United States may be a less racist country than in earlier years if civil rights legislation, public opinion polls, and the social indicators of education, occupation, income, and elected officials serve as a barometer. Yet racism still exists, perhaps less intensely in some areas than others, but it remains nonetheless, and flares up occasionally as in the 2007 case of the Jena 6.[20] It also can be found in numerous conversations, avoidance responses, subtle acts of discrimination, and myriad interaction patterns.

Institutional racism—the established laws, customs, and practices that systematically reflect and produce racial inequities in society—is a more significant factor than individuals committing overt racist actions, however. Biases remain built into the social structure, causing many individuals unknowingly to act without deliberate intent to hinder the advancement of non-Whites.

Although the Commission on Civil Rights (1981) identified areas where affirmative action could take aim at institutional racism (job seniority rules, nepotism-based recruitment or union membership, bank credit practices, culturally biased job performance tests), more than a quarter century later, some of these remain problem areas. De facto housing segregation and disparities in school funding for urban and suburban schools are other examples of the multigenerational continuation of a subtle, structural racist practice. The pervasiveness of institutional racism remains both an obstacle in the path of upward mobility to many racial minority group members and a basic impediment to better interracial relations.

As successful as the United States has been in assimilating national minorities, it has been far less successful in assimilating racial minorities. African and Native Americans are still not fully integrated as mainstream Americans. Because we have never fully resolved our centuries-old twin problems of race relations and racial integration, the growing presence of people of color from developing-world countries exacerbates the matter.

Racial tensions have heightened in some areas because of the influx of racially distinct, "clannish" strangers into neighborhoods unaccustomed to their presence. When this influx has occurred in previously homogeneous middle-class suburbs, the reactions may be more subtle, but the resentment is real and finds expression in avoidance responses, zoning regulations, and verbal complaints within one's circle of family, friends, and neighbors.

If multiculturalism means an increased racial presence and/or increased racial power that puts their own racial group to any disadvantage, then many Americans oppose multiculturalism.

THE "ROSES" OF MULTICULTURALISM

Roses bud, bloom, and fade away. Rosebuds give us the promise of new beauty about to arrive, and when the flowers are in full bloom, their beauty in our lives must be experienced to be appreciated fully. Gradually, however, the roses fade and their petals gracefully fall to the ground, covering the dark earth with their pastel colors. With modest pruning, the gardener can coax other roses to appear and repeat the process again and again.

Multiculturalism, however, is not a rose that will fade away in the United States, which has always been a land of diversity and a destination for millions of immigrants. However, some "blooms" of ethnicity do fade away as, for example, has been "the twilight of ethnicity" among European Americans.[21] Moreover, what appear to some people as thorns may actually be roses instead. Let us extend our metaphor of roses from the four types of thorns just discussed.

The "Immigrant Roses"

If a nation's strength lies in its people, then the strength of the United States clearly lies in the diversity of its people. Immigrants from all over the world have come here, and in one way or another, each group has played some role in the nation's evolution into its present superpower status.

Past immigrants built our cities, transportation systems, and labor unions and enabled us to come of age both agriculturally and industrially. Many of today's immigrants have revitalized our cities; helped our high-tech industries remain competitive; and pumped billions of dollars annually into the national economy through their businesses, occupations, and consumerism.

Combating negative stereotyping, societal ostracism, and fear about their growing size, each immigrant group then and now has worked hard to survive and put down roots. Viewed as a threat, each has proved to be an asset.

Although the immigrant roses bloom, others do not often appreciate their beauty. It is the exceptional individual who admires immigrants when they are immigrants. Only after the immigrant rose fades and its falling petals mingle with the soil that contains all our roots do we look back and cherish the bloom that is part of our heritage.

The "Language Roses"

Unlike the people of most nations who are at least bilingual, most Americans are monolingual. This limitation encourages ethnocentrism and provincialism and places the business community at a disadvantage in the global marketplace. Mastery of a second language enhances one's mental mobility while enriching cultural insights and perspectives.

If Americans were to become proficient in a second language, encouraged to do so by the Asian and Latino population cohorts now living here, the result could easily be a society reaching greater maturity and tolerance in its intergroup relations. Most Europeans have long been at least bilingual, and their cultures and societal cohesion have not suffered. Bilingual advocates argue that bilingualism would not undermine U.S. culture either, only enrich it.

For those who do not buy into bilingualism for all citizens, the consistent findings of public opinion polls and scientific studies about English language acquisition offer comforting news. A 2009 Public Agenda study funded by the Carnegie Foundation revealed that 7 in 10 of those who came here knowing very little or no English at all took classes to improve their English, a jump from 23 percent in 2002. Notably, 74 percent of immigrants say it is more important for schools to teach immigrant children English as quickly as possible than it is to teach them other subjects in their native language.[22]

Today, first- and second-generation Americans become fluent in English at a faster pace than did past immigrants. In one of the largest-ever longitudinal studies of second-generation Americans (5,200 immigrant children in Miami and San Diego), researchers found that 99 percent spoke fluent English and less than one-third maintained fluency in their parents' tongues by age 17.[23] Another study of 5,700 Asians and Hispanics living in Los Angeles and San Diego found that native language usage drops significantly, even in the home, with each succeeding generation. By the third generation, 96 percent of these immigrants—Chinese, Filipino, Guatemalan, Korean, Mexican, Salvadoran, and Vietnamese—preferred to speak only English at home.[24]

Despite all fears of Asian and Hispanic immigrants posing a threat to the English language, assimilation is still, as Nathan Glazer (1993) asserted, "the most powerful force affecting the ethnic and racial elements of the United States."[25] As the American Jewish Committee once stated, "The use of additional languages to meet the needs of language minorities does not pose a threat to America's true common heritage and common bond—the quest for freedom and opportunity."[26]

To allay further the anxieties of those who fear that the large Hispanic American presence is an unprecedented threat simply because of its size, we have a comparable example in our past, with the almost 4.9 million Germans who entered the United States between 1841 and 1900. Keep in mind that the U.S. population was much smaller then (23.1 million in 1850 and 62.9 million in 1890, compared with

313 million in 2012). Also, today's films, TV, music, and Internet are ever-present English-learning aids that were unknown at the time of this large German presence.

In the mid- to late 19th century, so many hundreds of thousands of Germans lived in the area among Cincinnati, Milwaukee, and St. Louis that it became known as the "great German triangle."[27] Because so many German children attended public schools in the German triangle, the states passed laws permitting all academic subjects to be taught in German whenever the demand was sufficient to warrant it. Ohio passed its statute in 1837, and the others followed in the 1840s.

Consider the enormity of this action. In major cities, as well as in rural regions, the states of Ohio, Missouri, and Wisconsin (other states, too) authorized German as an official language for all classroom instruction. Cultural diversity, including that of language, was not only tolerated, but also encouraged.

The use of German in the public schools served a purpose other than academic instruction. It was intended to preserve the whole range of German culture even more so after the unification of Germany in the 1870s. With an increased pride in their origins, German immigrants and their children developed a greater sense of their ethnicity than they possessed before their emigration. Because language enhanced their sense of being German, the German Americans continued to speak their language in their schools, homes, churches, and everyday business transactions.

As extensive German immigrant settlement in the region continued decade after decade, German-language instruction in all subjects continued in the public schools. Such was the case in the private schools as well. By 1910, more than 95 percent of German Catholic parishes had parochial schools taught in German, and more than 2,000 parishes conducted German-language services, much to the consternation of the Irish American church hierarchy. During World War I, however, patriotic hysteria to drive the "Hun" language out of the schools prompted states such as Ohio and Nebraska to pass laws prohibiting instruction in German in all schools, public and private. A legal challenge to this action reached the U.S. Supreme Court in *Robert Meyer v. Nebraska* (1923).

Although the Court upheld the states' right to determine public school instruction in English only, its ruling on private and parochial schools was an important one with regard to language rights. Ruling that all state laws prohibiting the teaching and use of German in private or parochial schools were in violation of the 14th Amendment and therefore unconstitutional, the Court declared that the rights of both parents and private/parochial schools to teach their children in a language other than English was within the liberty guaranteed by that amendment.

Despite (a) the institutionalization of academic instruction in German, (b) the steady influx of large numbers of German immigrants, and (c) more than 60 years of German language maintenance, German language usage declined. That process had already begun by 1885, as indicated by the complaints then of German American leaders that the younger generation was losing the German tongue and that parents no longer insisted on their children studying German in the schools.

As with other ethnic groups, English gradually replaced the homeland language, even among the millions of Germans so heavily concentrated in regions such as the German triangle. The German language rose once bloomed mightily in the United States, but it has faded, its petals drifting downward and blending with others that fell earlier. Perhaps the Spanish language is another such rose.

The "Cultural Roses"

The United States contains many persistent subcultures, people who steadfastly adhere to their own way of life as much as possible, resisting absorption into the dominant culture. These are usually religious groups—such as the Amish, Hutterites, Mennonites, and Hasidim—or groups whose ancestors predate the United States, such as the Native Americans and Spanish Americans in the Southwest. One also could argue that a persistent subculture exists among one-fourth of the Black Americans mired in poverty for multiple generations. Until society finds an effective means to end their deprivation, these hard-core Black poor will continue to subsist within a subculture necessary for their survival.

Most racial and ethnic groups, however, are part of a convergent subculture gradually disappearing as its members become integrated into the dominant culture. For some their "cultural roses" bloom longer than others, but at some point the roses do fade. Besides the Germans just discussed, we have dozens of other examples of once-vibrant ethnic subcultures, ones that contemporary native-born Americans considered both persistent and a threat to the dominant culture, but that eventually converged into the mainstream.

Ethnic subcultures do not undermine the dominant culture. The United States has always had them, and at the time of their growing strength and vitality, they often contained separatist advocates. It is not uncommon for outsiders to become anxious about subgroup loyalties posing a danger to the larger society. Theodore Roosevelt's famous remark that "there is no room in this country for hyphenated Americanism" spoke to the same fears of subversion of American culture that Schlesinger addressed as the "disuniting of America."[28]

When immigrants come to the United States, they come to join us. In forsaking their ancestral lands, they pay us the highest compliment: They want to spend the rest of their lives with us in a country where they hope to realize their dreams of a better life. They come to be a part of us, an "us" they have imagined after exposure to thousands of pictures, films, TV shows, stories, letters, and rumors. They come to join us, not to keep separate from us. It may take some time, longer than some Americans' patience, but for most, that integration into the dominant culture occurs.

The falling petals of fading cultural roses also mingle with the soil containing all our roots. U.S. society, reflecting its multicultural past and present, continually becomes even more enriched with architecture, art, creative works, cuisine, music, and other cultural contributions from the diversity of its people.

The "Racial Roses"

Here we have a rare species of rose because its bloom in a multiracial setting in the United States is difficult to produce. Filling too much of our past and present has been racial animosity, exploitation, and violence. As I said earlier, we have never fully resolved the twin problems of race relations and racial integration in our society.

Part of our problem has been our cultural mind-set. With a simplistic White and non-White racial classification system, we have insidiously enmeshed race within our social structure. We have created and consistently reinforced the us-and-them mentality that manifests itself in social distance, differential treatment, deprivation, and suffering. Furthermore, our monoracial categories ignore the multiracial backgrounds of millions of African Americans, Filipinos, Latinos, Native Americans, and Whites. We have taken a step forward in the deconstruction of race with the multiple racial census choices and in the growing recognition of the millions of biracial Americans.

As changing demographics make an increased multiracial society more evident to Americans, perhaps we shall see the removal of the weeds of racism (particularly the rooting out of institutional discrimination) and the blooming of the racial roses. Such a change will not be easy. But as the non-White segment of the U.S. population increases, so may the multiracial component of the American identity. If no longer relegated to the periphery, racial groups will be more at the center, and at the center one finds both power and integration.

Increased racial tensions remain a distinct possibility, however, and we certainly find examples of that today. However, with the greater sharing of power that must come, that very same sharing of power could also cause greater racial acceptance.

At the risk of being accused of wearing rose-colored glasses in depicting the racial roses, I would suggest that if we can get the racial roses to bloom in this land—get to that point where each of the races displays its full beauty—then we can look past that point to the next horizon. When the racial rose petals fall and mingle with the soil common to us all, we will have moved past race as a divisive aspect of our society. This was Martin Luther King's dream, that one day his children would be judged by the content of their character instead of the color of their skin.[29]

IS MULTICULTURALISM THE ENEMY?

On the battlefield of multiculturalism, pluralists and assimilationists wage war, but neither side will vanquish the other. As always, both forces will remain an integral part of U.S. society. The United States will remain a beacon of hope to immigrants everywhere, keeping the rich tradition of pluralism alive and well. Assimilationist forces, as consistently demonstrated for centuries, will remain strong, particularly on immigrant children and their descendants. Multiculturalism will no more weaken that process than the many past manifestations of ethnic ingroup solidarity have.

Social observers of different eras—Alexis de Tocqueville, Gunnar Myrdal, and Andrew Hacker, among others—have commented on the separate racial worlds within the United States. These separate worlds are not the result of multiculturalist teachings. Only when we break down the remaining racial barriers, eliminate institutional discrimination, and open up paths free of obstacles to a good education and job opportunities for everyone will racial integration improve. Afrocentrist schools do not undermine a cohesive society any more than Catholic schools, yeshivas, or other religious schools do. Multiculturalism is not the enemy; systemic racism is.

NOTES

1. Martin E. Spencer, "Multiculturalism, 'Political Correctness,' and the Politics of Identity," ed. Vincent N. Parrillo, "Multiculturalism and Diversity," *Sociological Forum*, 9 (December 1994): 547–67.

2. Diane Ravitch, "Multiculturalism: E Pluribus Plures," *American Scholar*, 59 (1990): 337–54.

3. See Molefi K. Asante, *The Afrocentric Idea*, rev. ed. (Philadelphia: Temple University Press, 1998).

4. Arthur M. Schlesinger, Jr., *The Disuniting of America: Reflections on a Multicultural Society*, rev. ed. (New York: W. W. Norton, 1998).

5. See Linda Chavez, "Hispanics vs. Their Leaders," *Commentary* (October 1991): 47–9.

6. Horace Kallen, "Democracy versus the Melting Pot," *Nation* (February 18, 1915): 220.

7. Harry C. Triandis, "The Future of Pluralism," *Journal of Social Issues*, 32 (1976): 179–208.

8. Gerald Graff, *Beyond the Culture Wars: How Teaching the Conflicts Can Revitalize American Education* (New York: W. W. Norton, 1993).

9. Ronald Takaki, "Multiculturalism: Battleground or Meeting Ground?" *The Annals of the American Academy of Political and Social Science*, 530 (1993): 109–21.

10. Michelle Lee, "Constructing National Identity through Policy: Discourses of Multiculturalism and Reconciliation in Australia," *Dissertation Abstracts*, October 2006.

11. Scott Poynting and Victoria Mason, "The New Integrationism, the State, and Islamophobia: Retreat from Multiculturalism in Australia," *International Journal of Law, Crime and Justice*, 36 (2008): 230–46.

12. See Irene Bloemraad, *Becoming a Citizen* (Berkeley: University of California Press, 2006), pp. 235–6.

13. David Cameron, "PM's Speech at Munich Security Conference," (February 5, 2011). Available at http://www.number10.gov.uk/news/pms -speech-at-munich-security-conference/. (Accessed January 13, 2012.)

14. Quoted in Lauren Collins, "England, Their England," *New Yorker*, 87 (July 4, 2011): 38–34. .

15. Human Rights Watch, *Everyday Intolerance: Racist and Xenophobic Action in Italy* (March 20, 2011). Available at http://www.hrw.org/node/97231 /section/1. (Accessed January 13, 2012.)

16. See Rita J. Simon, "Old Minorities, New Immigrants: Aspirations, Hopes, and Fears," *The Annals of the American Academy of Political and Social Science*, 530 (1993): 62–3.

17. Federation for American Immigration Reform, "The Fiscal Burden of Illegal Immigration on United States Taxpayers." Available at www.fairus.org. (Accessed January 13, 2012.)

18. Vincent N. Parrillo, *Strangers to These Shores*, 10th ed. (Boston: Allyn and Bacon, 2011), pp. 98, 108.

19. U.S. Census Bureau, *2010 American Community Survey*, Table B06007.

20. See "The Case of Louisiana's 'Jena Six,'" NPR. Available at www.npr
.org/series/14533821/the-case-of-louisiana-s-jena-six. (Accessed January 14,
2012.)

21. Richard D. Alba, *Italian Americans: Into the Twilight of Ethnicity*
(Englewood Cliffs, NJ: Prentice Hall, 1985).

22. Public Agenda, *A Place to Call Home: What Immigrants Say about Life
in America*. Available at www.publicagenda.ord/files/pdf/Immigration.pdf.
(Accessed January 14, 2012.)

23. Rubén G. Rumbaut and Alejandro Portés, *Ethnicities: Children of
Immigrants in America* (Berkeley: University of California Press, 2001).

24. Rubén G. Rumbaut, Douglas Massey, and Frank D. Bean, "Linguistic
Life Expectancies: Immigrant Language Retention in Southern California,"
Population and Development Review, 32 (2006): 447–60.

25. Nathan Glazer, "Is Assimilation Dead?" *The Annals of the American
Academy of Political and Social Science*, 530 (1993): 123.

26. "English as the Official Language" (New York: American Jewish
Committee, 1987).

27. Carl Wittke, *We Who Built America*, rev. ed. (Cleveland: Case Western
Reserve University Press, 1967), pp. 196–9.

28. Roosevelt's remarks come from a speech delivered in 1917 and preserved
in Ralph Stout, ed., *Roosevelt in the Kansas City Star* (Boston: Houghton Mifflin,
1921), p. 137.

29. King's famous "I Have a Dream" speech was delivered on August 28,
1963, during the March on Washington for Jobs and Freedom. His actual words
were, "I have a dream that my four little children will one day live in a nation
where they will not be judged by the color of their skin but by the content of
their character."

11

The Next Horizon

We cannot always build the future for our youth, but we can build our youth for the future.

—*President Franklin D. Roosevelt*

What kind of nation we will be, what kind of world we will live in, whether we shape the future in the image of our hopes, is ours to determine by our actions and our choices.

—*President Richard M. Nixon*

Against a backdrop of the blackness of space and Earth's surface, the orbiting International Space Station moves toward the continually changing horizon in its ongoing mission to observe and study what lies beyond its current vista.

N ativists' reactions against increased U.S. diversity were often not just a response to what they perceived as a clear and present danger to the United States as they understood it. Besides their concern about the growing presence of those undesirable strangers in their midst, they also worried about their impact on the future of U.S. society.

A limerick from the early 20th century captured that concern in lines not found amusing by WASPs, who were feeling threatened by the influx of so many unlike others:

In nineteen hundred and seventy-five,
Folks gathered round like bees in a hive,
To see in a tent
An American gent,
The very last Yankee alive.[1]

Numerically, WASPs have been a minority group for some time now, but they are hardly an endangered species. Still their reduced presence and projections about their further shrinkage, along with all non-Hispanic Whites, have rekindled fears about the loss of dominance implied in the previous limerick.

One final word about the limerick: *Yankee* is an interesting word that helps us understand the expanding mainstream category discussed in Chapter 9. It once meant a New Englander, but by the time of the Civil War, its connotation had changed to indicate a Northerner. Ever since World War I, *Yankee* has meant any American, although baseball fans apply the word more narrowly to a New York team. At the time of this limerick, however, its usage was understood to be a reference to its earlier connotation of an Anglo-American, much like Mark Twain's popular work, *A Connecticut Yankee in King Arthur's Court* (1889). Words change in their meaning, just as perceptions do about immigrants, people of color, and diversity.

THE 21ST CENTURY

We are now in the second decade of the 21st century. Passage into this century marked a major calendar change, not only of the passing of 100 years, but also of 1,000 years. This combination of a new century and millennium had the futurists busy prognosticating about life in the future. These predictions, as usual, ranged from the ridiculous to the sublime. Some may be accurate and others not. No one really knows what the future holds. We can only make educated guesses.

Those alive when the United States entered the 19th century could not have foretold with precision new immigration patterns, or that the nation's size would triple, or such technological advances as electric generators and lights, steam locomotives and ships, the telegraph and telephone, the reaping machine, vulcanized rubber, dynamite, radio, and moving pictures would revolutionize the way we live.

Similarly, those who were witness to the beginning of the 20th century could not accurately envision atomic energy, jet engines, radar, transistors, test-tube babies, or the changing waves of immigration. How civilization will change in the remainder of the 21st century and what world events will affect migration are really unknown, but that does not stop many from suggesting the possibilities.

Sometimes the predictions seem uncanny. In 1898, Secretary of State John Hay remarked, "The Mediterranean is the ocean of the past, the Atlantic the ocean of the present, and the Pacific the ocean of the future."[2] Given California's population, birth rates, and China's rise to a world economic power alongside Japan and Korea, Hay's prophecy seems quite accurate.

One consideration as we look to the future of multiculturalism is the continuing economic integration occurring through free trade agreements, in 1993 involving Canada and Mexico, and in 2011 involving separate pacts with Colombia, Panama, and South Korea, and how these will affect other aspects of intergroup relations. Furthermore, the fast-paced globalization of the world economy and its effect on living conditions in other countries will most likely influence future migration patterns. Outside social forces, as always, will play a major role in shaping the U.S. multicultural experience.

THE LARGER CONTEXT

The Population Reference Bureau (2011) reported that, although fertility rates are dropping worldwide, world population growth may grow from 7 billion in 2011 to more than 8 billion by 2025 depending on fertility and mortality rates. As Europe grows by 6 million, Africa will increase by more than 393 million, Asia by 564 million, and Latin America and the Caribbean by 80 million. Less-developed countries (excluding China) will account for a greater share of the world population by 2025, representing about 67 percent of the total. If we include China, the figure is 84 percent.[3]

The significance of these patterns lies in their impact on immigration to the United States and this country's subsequent change in population composition. The inability of a country to support its large population has been an important push factor in its people emigrating elsewhere. The decline in natural population growth in more-developed countries often requires them to seek foreign workers to maintain their economy and "feed" the pension system for retired workers. Consequently, as population pressures mount in less-developed countries in the oncoming years, so will immigration pressures in more-developed countries.

Not surprisingly, the major immigrant-receiving nations— Australia, Canada, United Kingdom, and United States—now receive the bulk of their newcomers from less-developed countries. Similarly, many European countries are becoming far more racially and culturally diverse than ever before, and—lacking a history of large-scale immigration and therefore a cultural orientation toward the integration of foreigners—they often view the still-increasing diversity in their midst with alarm.

Such an us-and-them mentality fosters discontent on both sides throughout Europe. The riots in France, mentioned in Chapter 9, offer some of the more dramatic recent examples of minority discontent. Involving mostly alienated youth living in ethnic ghettos on the city outskirts, that violence was an expression of anger against ongoing racial and job discrimination, high unemployment, and police harassment. The French media and public use of the expression "second generation of immigrants" to describe the rioters, even for those born in France, revealed a cultural mind-set about who was "really" French.

Although the violence may be more isolated and less intense in other European countries, hostility elsewhere toward recent arrivals who feel that sense of rejection is nonetheless a matter of concern. It is a social problem that will not go away soon. The combination of high migration and low birth rates will result in most European countries becoming less homogeneous and more multicultural with each succeeding year.

Current projections show continued high birth rates in most African, Asian, and Latin American countries, outpacing their ability to provide a decent quality of life. In many of these nations, the fertility rate may be dropping, but the population continues to rise startlingly because of the high proportion of their populations under the age of 16. With so big a segment entering the childbearing years, a built-in factor exists for further population expansion because none of these countries is anywhere near zero population growth, where two adults have only two children. As a closer-to-home example, Mexico quadrupled its population between 1950 and 2011, going from 27 million to 115 million. It might be 131 million by 2025. As our next-door neighbor and largest sending country, Mexico thus seems destined to send us millions more immigrants in the next few decades.

U.S. POPULATION PREDICTIONS

The U.S. Census Bureau offers projections about the future of American diversity in its portrait of U.S. society in 2050. The government demographers base their forecast on the current population (Figure 11.1) and the continuance of current trends. They assume that the current birth rate will remain constant and life expectancy will increase slightly, whereas immigration will remain similar to the annual average now from the same sending countries.

These assumptions may be reasonable, but they are by no means certain. We can no more anticipate the actualities and ramifications of social change several decades from now than could past Americans witnessing the advent of the 19th and 20th centuries. Actually, high-, middle-, and low-range projections exist to give us a continuum of future possibilities. Even so, these projections rest on assumptions that may not hold true. What follows are the midrange projections from the U.S. Census Bureau.[4]

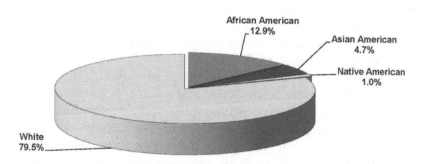

FIGURE 11.1 U.S. Population by Race in 2010
Source: U.S. Census Bureau.

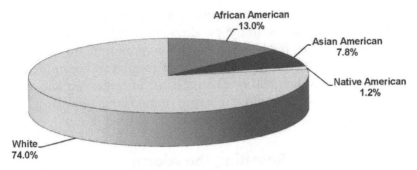

FIGURE 11.2 Projected U.S. Population in 2050
Source: U.S. Census Bureau.

Hispanic Americans could increase their share of the population from 16 percent in 2010 to 30.3 percent in 2050. In the racial categories, African Americans would remain fairly constant,
12.86 percent in 2010 and 12.97 percent in 2050, as would Native
Americans (1.0 percent in 2010 and 1.2 percent in 2050). Asian
and Pacific Islanders would increase from 4.7 to 7.8 percent, while
non-Hispanic Whites would decrease from 64.7 to 46.3 percent.
However, ignoring ethnicity, Whites would drop from 79.5 to 74.0
percent (see Figure 11.2).

The Alarm Bells Ring

These projections have triggered alarm bells not just among nativists,
who have consistently opposed liberal immigration policies, but also
among some pluralists, who believe in the value of diversity. De-
mographer Leon F. Bouvier is one such example. He worried about
projections showing the United States growing at a faster rate than
other industrial nations. With about half this growth anticipated to
be from immigration, Bouvier suggested the need for immigration
restrictions to strengthen America's economic stability, cultural cohesion, and quality of life.[5]

To achieve these goals, Bouvier argued for a reduction of immigration to 450,000 annually to reduce the intensity of the racial
shift. A lower ceiling, he maintained, also would enhance cultural
adaptation and not cultural separatism by cutting back the source of
ethnic vitality. Without the sizable continued inflow of low-level
workers holding us back, he believed that American industry would
be forced to improve technologically to compete internationally.

Since the 1990s, other immigration opponents and organizations, such as those mentioned in the previous chapter, have continued to use these arguments and U.S. Census Bureau projections to campaign for dramatically lowering the number of immigrants permitted to enter. They insist that, although large-scale immigration may have been beneficial to the nation at one time, it is no longer the case given the size and complexity of today's society.

Resetting the Alarm

Alarms keep us from oversleeping. Sometimes, however, we set them too early or, forgetting to turn them off, they awaken us on the wrong day, causing us to lose sleep needlessly. We need to be careful that we set our alarms properly so that we do not fall victim to a false alarm.

Today's decisions affect tomorrow's outcomes, so it is important to be vigilant about the consequences of our actions as we attempt to define what kind of society we wish to become. The problem is that too many actions often have unintended consequences. Just look at how immigration changed far differently than the sponsors of the 1965 immigration act expected. Trying to ascertain the future of immigration or population composition is no easy task.

As previously stated, a source of this nation's strength has always been in its people, including the positive contributions to our society and culture from tens of millions of immigrants. Millions more from around the world would like to move to the United States if they could. Yet although immigrants are a valuable addition, this country could not possibly absorb all who want to come. Some limits are necessary, and a key part of the current debate is what those limits should be. Only a few subscribe to the radical position of open borders without any restrictions whatsoever.

Because some anti-immigration arguments are predicated on U.S. Census Bureau projections, several points need to be made that might possibly aid us in determining whether the alarm has been set incorrectly. The crux of the matter rests on the accuracy of the predictions. Because we cannot know until the time arrives whether the predictions were indeed accurate, the only viable approach at this time is to identify what variables could affect even the most conservative scenario of U.S. population projections. In this way, we can understand the matter more fully and have additional insights for the formulation of public policy.

Certainly, more restrictive immigration laws would affect the projections. Anti-immigration lobbying groups, economic unrest, and public sentiment are influential variables that could influence legislation to reduce immigration totals and thereby alter the population composition.

Homeland conditions in the sending countries are a key factor in determining their emigration rates. Unless Mexico and the other less-developed countries boldly expand their economies and reduce their birth rates, mounting population pressures will encourage a high exodus to more-developed countries such as the United States. However, the world is a rapidly changing place in birth rates, technology, cultural diffusion, and global interdependence. Perhaps the social changes sweeping the world will alter circumstances in less-developed countries significantly enough to affect their emigration rates.

Multinational conglomerates operate not out of compassion, but for profit. Less-developed nations offer them major opportunities for expansion and increased profits, so it is reasonable to expect them to open even more new factories and offices in these countries to expand their labor and consumer markets. As they do, hopefully the expanding economies will improve life opportunities in those countries.

Perhaps the next 40 years also will bring such an infusion of aid from more-developed countries to less-developed ones that their quality of life will reach satisfactory levels for their citizenry. However, why should the more-developed nations do this? Although humanitarian reasons might be a partial motivation, in actuality, the developed nations could find such aid in their own self-interests in that improved conditions in these countries would likely reduce the influx of immigrants from those countries.

If these nations develop sufficiently, the demographic transition already evident may accelerate, lowering the fertility rates sufficiently to stabilize population growth in the mid-21st century. Such a scenario would mean the lessening of the causes for migration and consequently a change in the immigration patterns currently experienced by the United States.

THE DILLINGHAM FLAW IN REVERSE

In earlier discussions of the Dillingham Flaw, we spoke of using oversimplified categorizations and imposing present-day sensibilities on the past when such perceptions did not exist in those times. We also can apply the Dillingham Flaw when the same errors are committed by anyone looking into the future.

How can we be certain that today's group categories will still be valid by 2050? Right now many White Americans bear witness to mixed European ancestry, but two generations ago those Americans of southern, central, and eastern European backgrounds were far more likely to be of a single national lineage and religion. Group identity then was not the same as group identities today because large-scale intermarriage has generated such a blending of people that the terms *Whites* and *Euro-Americans* became synonymous.

In the 20th century, Italian, Polish, and Slavic Americans were once members of distinctive ethnic groups lacking economic, political, and social power. They displayed all the characteristics of a minority group in their ascribed status, endogamy, unequal treatment, and visibility. Today, most are part of the societal mainstream, displaying the traits of civic, marital, and structural assimilation. As a result, *Euro-American* serves as a generic term for heritage, not for everyday ethnicity, subcultural participation, or minority status.

European immigrants still arrive, and they begin the accultura- tion process anew, as earlier European arrivals once did. Most Euro- Americans, however, are two or more generations removed from the ethnic experience. They are, for the most part, homogenized into a mainstream American identity, with ethnicity simply an appreciation for their roots, occasionally marked by symbolic celebrations. Just as yesterday's categories for European ethnic Americans no longer fit today's Americans of mixed European ancestry, today's racial cat- egories already fail to cover some of today's Americans, as we soon discuss. How, then, can we know with any certainty what are the right categories for tomorrow's Americans?

Using today's categories for Americans living in 2050 can easily be an unwitting application of the Dillingham Flaw in reverse. Project- ing our perceptions and the existing social distance between groups onto a distant future carries a presumption that they will remain the same. Yet the only constant in life is change, and so our categories may be inadequate or irrelevant to our descendants.

FACTORS INFLUENCING CHANGE

Other demographic patterns exist to help us anticipate the future besides the fertility, mortality, and migration rates used by the U.S. Census Bureau. Some of these, particularly those dealing with mar- riages and children, give cause for being cautious in predicting group composition in 2050. We can detect some growing patterns that suggest different group categories in the future.

Interethnic Marriages and Children of Mixed Ancestry

Just as European nationality groups have blended together extensively through intermarriage in a multigenerational progression toward assimilation, so, too, may we expect Hispanic Americans to do the same. This process has been underway for decades and increasing steadily through the years.

Hispanics, who can be of any race, are increasingly marrying other Latinos of different national origins. About 6.2 million married Hispanic couples now fit this category, compared with 1.9 million in 1980. Even more revealing is the outmarriage pattern. One sign of closing social distance and the final stage of assimilation is the widespread intermarriage of minority group members with those of the mainstream group. In 2010, about 2.3 million Hispanic Americans were married to a spouse of non-Hispanic origin.[6] Although that is a small percentage of all Hispanic married couples, it reflects a continuing upward trend.

Given the past history of other groups assimilating and the current assimilationist patterns of so many second-generation Hispanic Americans, we may reasonably expect two things. First, a greater increase in Hispanic outmarriages is inevitable. Second, Hispanic achievement of social, economic, and political power—together with widespread intermarriage—will enlarge the mainstream American category once more to include them. One might even speculate that these two trends could become so universal that, one day, Hispanic American will be no more a separate ethnic category than Italian, Polish, or Slavic American is now.

Interracial Marriages and Biracial Children

Elimination of the racial barrier in the United States by 2050 may or may not occur, but a present-day trend suggests that the present-day simplistic racial categories are already obsolete. In recognition of this reality, the U.S. Census now allows multiple answers in the racial category. More than 9 million people did so, claiming biracial status, and this number keeps climbing as a result of an increasing interracial marriage rate. This self-reporting of mixed racial heritage is another example of the social constructionist aspects of race and ethnic relations, and it may well have a long-range effect of deconstructing the rigidity of race and therefore on how we see ourselves in the future.

Since 1980, the total number of interracially married couples has more than tripled, going from 651,000 to more than 2.4 million in 2010. The Black/White married couple category more than tripled, increasing from 167,000 to 558,000. Interracial couples of Whites married to a spouse other than Black (mostly Asian) grew from 450,000 to 1.7 million, whereas interracial couples of Blacks married to a spouse other than Whites increased from 34,000 to 132,000.[7] Although the number of Black/White intermarriages is only about one-third that of other White-racial combinations, 558,000 is still a significant number. Such continued increases and their biracial offspring should generate pressure for the deconstruction of race as we know it and its subsequent reconstruction into more than the simplistic White/non-White classifications.

Many other Americans also have a multiracial ancestry, such as virtually all Latinos and Filipinos, and many Native Americans and Native Hawaiians. Among Black Americans with a multigenerational history in the United States, experts estimate that somewhere between 30 and 70 percent are multiracial, and so, too, are a sizable proportion of those classified as Whites.

Race always has been primarily a social construct, not one simply rooted in biological features.[8] It is defined differently in different societies, with racial boundaries blurred or distinct depending on geographical, cultural, and political factors. In the United States, arbitrary or single-race classifications no longer apply to an increasing number of Americans. In fact, in the 2010 Census, more than 18 million Latinos checked the "other" box rather than select more than one race, which was their option. It appears that for many Latinos, racial identity is more about culture than color because they are too racially mixed to associate themselves with the standard U.S. demographic groups.[9]

Perhaps the day is not too far distant when the American people and their government will either broaden racial categories to include gradations between Black and White, as Brazil does, or create new official census categories like Eurasian, Afroindian, and Amerlatino. Or, perhaps biracial Americans may create their own categories as did golf champion Tiger Woods—who is one-fourth Chinese, one-fourth Thai, one-fourth African American, one-eighth Native American, and one-eighth Dutch—by calling himself a Cablinasian, a word fusion that he created of Caucasian, Black, American Indian, and Asian.

THE CHALLENGE OF RACIAL DIVERSITY

Despite questions about categories or the accuracy of the demographic projections, the United States is clearly becoming a more multiracial society than ever before.[10] What does this mean for race relations? U.S. society may be less racist than in the past, but racism still saturates the land. Discrimination and violence sometimes raise concerns that race relations are deteriorating rather than improving.

Racial tensions, confrontations, and violent acts continue to occur in many geographic locales. Even though the total number of bias incidents has been dropping in recent years (6,001 in 2010, 9,006 in 2008), racial prejudice still motivates the majority of all ethnoviolent incidents in the United States.[11] In 2010, racial bias was the motivation behind 49 percent of all hate crimes. Sexual orientation bias accounted for another 25 percent, followed by anti-Hispanic (10 percent), anti-Jewish (6 percent), anti-ethnic (5 percent), and anti-Islamic (2 percent).[12]

Increased racial diversity poses a crisis for U.S. society (in the Chinese and Greek meaning of the word *crisis*). In those languages, *crisis* means both danger and opportunity. The danger lies in race relations worsening. Will African Americans accept the presence and competition of Asians and Latinos? Will Asians and Latinos accept each other when they often share urban territories? Will Whites peacefully accept the growing presence of Asians in their suburban neighborhoods? Will Whites calmly accept their diminishing status as non-White groups steadily grow in numbers and strength?

The opportunity lies in a heightened awareness about the pluralist reality of U.S. society. The predominance of an Anglo-American assimilationist model worked to the disadvantage of those considered different or unassimilable. Understanding the American tradition of racial diversity could lead to an appreciation of its existence and ultimately to greater societal cohesion. Such a possibility would make the United States as powerful a world model for intergroup harmony as its political system has served as a government model for more than 220 years.

Among the range of race relations possibilities, then, lies increased tensions and violence at one end of the continuum and interracial harmony at the other. Obviously, we should strive to attain the latter and avoid the former. America's real future may fall short of the ideal, but that is not reason enough to stop trying to fulfill the dream of Martin Luther King, Jr.

INCREASED RELIGIOUS DIVERSITY

Earlier immigrant waves changed the United States from an almost exclusively Protestant nation into a country of three major faiths: Protestant, Catholic, and Jewish. Because religion is so closely intertwined with ethnicity, current migration patterns offer clues about the religious preference of future Americans, if present trends continue.

Protestants currently account for 51.3 percent of the total population in 2012. Furthermore, within that category, evangelical Protestant church membership (26 percent) exceeds mainline Protestant church membership (18 percent), with historically Black churches including an additional 7 percent. Catholics comprise 23.9 percent, Jews 1.7 percent, Mormons 1.7 percent, Buddhists 0.7 percent, Muslims 0.6 percent, and Hindus 0.4 percent. Sixteen percent of Americans express no religious preference (see Figure 11.3).[13]

Because Latin America and Asia are the major sending regions for nearly 80 percent of all immigrants to the United States, we can identify the prevailing religions in those countries and project them onto those entering the country. Realizing also that immigrants tend to have a higher birth rate than native-born Americans, and that some religions are more zealous in seeking religious converts, demographers can factor in those variables as well, when projecting the future of religious affiliations.

Latin America and the Philippines are mostly Catholic, and as major sources of new immigrants accounting for more than half the total, they will help Roman Catholics increase dramatically in

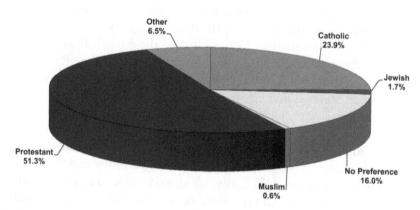

FIGURE 11.3 U.S. Religious Membership in 2010
Source: Pew Center on Religion and Public Life, *U.S. Religious Landscape Survey.*

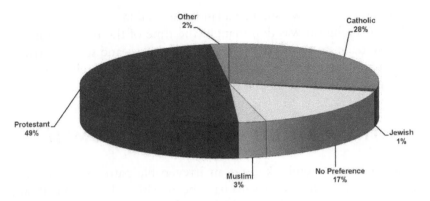

FIGURE 11.4 Projected U.S. Religious Membership in 2050

Source: Extrapolated data from U.S. Census Bureau, Pew Center on Religion and Public Life, and unpublished data.

size, perhaps to 28 percent by 2050. They also might constitute the majority of residents in such heavily populated states as California, Florida, Texas, and New York.

Another rapidly growing religious group is Muslims. Appealing to many African, Middle Eastern, and Asian Americans, Islam is becoming a more noticeable presence as mosques now pepper the American landscape. Perhaps within a generation Muslims may surpass Jews to become the third-largest religious denomination in the United States. By the middle of this century, Muslims may account for 3 percent of the U.S. population, whereas Jews may decrease to about a 1 percent share of the population (see Figure 11.4).

Other Eastern religions—particularly Buddhists, Hindus, and Sikhs—should continue to grow substantially in the United States. By 2050, they may comprise 2 percent of U.S. society. In contrast, Protestants will likely drop below 50 percent.

One should not assume that cultural homogeneity will prevail among the two rapidly growing Catholic and Muslim faiths. Both will be composed of many unassimilated minorities. Catholics will be found among multigenerational Americans of European and African ancestry and among such newer groups as Haitians, Filipinos, Indochinese, Latinos, and others. Muslims will include native-born African, Arab, and Asian Americans, as well as immigrants from those regions.

Religious diversity is becoming ever more pronounced throughout the land. If the projections hold true and American Protestants fall below 50 percent, then no major religious faith will be dominant in the United States. We shall be a land where all faiths are minorities. When no religion was dominant at the time of the nation's founding, we benefited from the separation of church and state doctrine. Perhaps a future with all religions in the minority foretells a time of even greater ecumenism and tolerance.

THE MAINSTREAMING OF WOMEN

U.S. society has embarked on an irreversible path toward gender equality. Great strides forward have been achieved since the 1960s, but much remains to be accomplished before parity with men is a reality. Only when women achieve social, economic, and political power equal to men, will they then be fully integrated into the society or mainstreamed.

All the indicators point toward further progress. By 2020, the U.S. Department of Education projects that the number of women enrolled in undergraduate degree programs will increase to 11.4 million (59 percent of the total), up from 10 million (57 percent) in 2010.[14] An increasing number of women continue to choose college majors and careers that were mostly male domains previously. More women are (1) becoming CEOs, lawyers, and judges; (2) seeking elected political office; and (3) moving into positions of power and influence. Although the U.S. Department of Labor projects the female civilian labor force participation rate to remain fairly constant at 57 percent for the foreseeable future, it remains to be seen if their salary ratio to men improves or if it remains constant as well.[15]

As these trends continue and as women's higher expectations go onward, we may anticipate the experiences of women to be as different from now in 2050 as today's women find their opportunities in contrast to those in 1950. Furthermore, the glass ceiling of limited upward mobility that women experienced in 20th-century work settings may well disappear if present-day trends and challenges continue.

THE EVER-CHANGING MOSAIC

The metaphor of a mosaic to describe U.S. society is helpful in many ways. When we examine a mosaic up close, it is easy to see the individual tiles with their different colors. It also is easy to see the flaws—those individual tiles that are chipped, cracked, or spotted. We cannot help but notice the mortar between the tiles that separates (joins?) them.

Up close, we see everything and we see nothing. It is another version of failing to see the forest for the trees. We are able to focus on the individual differences of the tiles, but until we step back, we are unable to grasp the beauty of the big picture that the tiles collectively present to us. When we do step back, the borders between the tiles fade as they blend into one another. The flaws about which we were so critical now are meaningless in appreciating the beauty of colors and design that the artist has provided for our enrichment and enjoyment. The whole is greater than the sum of its parts, to coin a phrase.

In a real sense, the United States is a mosaic of men and women of different colors, religions, and national origins. We are a microcosm of the world. We have become what Ben Wattenberg calls the "first universal nation."[16] Yet one aspect of the mosaic metaphor does not fit us at all. A mosaic is something fixed, static, and unchanging, and we have never been that. Tens of millions of people from all around the world have come to this country, made it their home, and invigorated it with their energy and determination. From its colonial diversity to its present-day diversity, each year the United States has experienced new arrivals and new changes to its population mix.

If we are a mosaic, then we are an ever-changing one. Some might prefer to call us a kaleidoscope to allow for continually changing patterns, but I prefer the idea of an ever-changing mosaic. Looking into a kaleidoscope is an individual experience, but gazing at a mosaic can be a shared one, and shared experiences are what the metaphor is partly about. Moreover, the mosaic metaphor extends the analogy further, enabling us to use its close-up flaws as comparable to the criticisms often directed against non-mainstream groups.

Whether one uses the metaphor of an ever-changing mosaic or a kaleidoscope to describe its people, the United States continues to manifest a dynamic cultural pluralism that has always marked its existence, even in colonial times. Although it has a greater mix of races and nationalities today, we have examined in this book how, in some ways, the United States is actually less multicultural than in its past. What we are experiencing today in large-scale immigration and minority group (including female) challenges to the status quo is part of the continuing dynamics of a nation evolving to make its reality resemble more its ideals.

Despite fears about divisiveness, the mainstream group is larger than ever before. Despite male apprehension about the feminist movement, women are becoming a more integral part of the mainstream and dispelling many myths as they do. Despite concerns about language retention, today's immigrants want to learn English and do so no slower than past immigrants and perhaps even more quickly.

Despite some people's fears about the fabric of U.S. society unraveling, more immigrants than ever before choose to be woven into that fabric through citizenship. In the last decade, 6.6 million foreign born became U.S. citizens.[17] Despite nativist anxieties about non-Westerners not blending in, Asians are demonstrating their desire to integrate by having higher naturalization rates than any other part of the world.

Multiculturalism is neither new nor a threat to the stabilization and integration of U.S. society. Extremists come and go, but the core culture remains strong, the American Dream prevails, and men and women seek to be part of it, bringing with them the diversity that is America. Multiculturalism, then, is an old, continuing presence that strengthens not weakens, enriches not diminishes, and nourishes not drains—a civilization whose character and temperament have long reflected the diversity of its people.

NOTES

1. J. M. Flagg, *Life* (January 12, 1922).

2. Quoted in Leo Melamed, *For Crying Out Loud: From Open Outcry to the Electronic Screen* (New York: Wiley, 2009), p. 137.

3. *2011 World Population Data Sheet* (Washington, DC: Population Reference Bureau, 2011).

4. U.S. Census Bureau, "National Population Projections, 2008," Table 6. Available at www.census.gov/population/www/projections /summarytables.html. (Accessed January 12, 2012.)

5. Leon Bouvier, *How Many Americans?* (New York: Random House, 1995).

6. U.S. Census Bureau, *Statistical Abstract of the United States: 2012* (Washington, DC: U.S. Government Printing Office, 2012), Table 60.

7. Ibid.

8. See Joan Ferrante and Prince Brown, *Social Construction of Race and Ethnicity in the United States,* 2nd ed. (Upper Saddle River, NJ: Prentice Hall, 2000).

9. Mireya Navarro, "For Many Latinos, Racial Identity Is More Culture Than Color," *New York Times* (January 14, 2012), p. A11.

10. See, for example, Huffington Post, "Multiracial Americans Become Fastest-Growing US Group" (May 29, 2009). Available at www.huffingtonpost .com/2009/04/29/multiracial-americans-bec_n_208989.html. (Accessed May 13, 2012.)

11. The Prejudice Institute, "What Is the Extent of Ethnoviolence in the United States?" Available at www.prejudiceinstitute.org/ethnoviolenceFS.html. (Accessed January 16, 2012.)

12. Federal Bureau of Investigation, *Hate Crime Statistics 2010,* Table 1. Available at www.fbi.gov. (Accessed May 13, 2012.)

13. Pew Center on Religion and Public Life, *U.S. Religious Landscape Survey.* Available at http://religions.pewforum.org/pdf/report-religious-landscape -study-full.pdf. (Accessed May 13, 2012.)

14. National Center for Education Statistics, *The Condition of Education 2011* (Washington, DC: U.S. Government Printing Office, 2011), Table A-8-1.

15. U.S. Bureau of Labor Statistics, "Labor Force (Demographic) Data." Available at www.bls.gov/emp/ep_data_labor_force.htm. (Accessed May 13, 2012.)

16. Ben Wattenberg, *First Universal Nation* (New York: Free Press, 1992).

17. U.S. Department of Homeland Security, *2010 Yearbook of Immigration Statistics* (Washington, DC: U.S. Government Printing Office, 2011), Table 20, p. 52.

Index

aboriginal America, diversity in, 22–40
Adams, John, 78, 143, 190
Addams, Jane, 7
additive multiculturalism, 184
affirmative action, 126–127, 193
Afghanistan, 146
Afghanistan refugees, 131
Africa, 126
African Americans
  in 19th century, 95–97
  in colonial times, 59
  culture of, 52, 110
  disenfranchisement of, 109
  diversity among, 131–133
  in early national period, 71
  economic condition of, 110, 132–133
  families, 96, 132
  Hispanics and, 136
  hostility toward, 2
  in industrial age, 108–110
  in information age, 131–133
  intermarriage and, 14
  melting pot concept and, 11
  middle class, 110, 177
  Northern, 97, 110
  as percent of population, 169, 170, 207
  poverty among, 197
  religious groups, 69
  in Revolutionary War, 59
  slavery reparations and, 3
  violence against, 109–110
African immigrants, 133
African Methodist Episcopalian (A.M.E.)
  Church, 69

African Methodist Episcopal Zion
  Church, 69
African music, 96
Africans, 48, 49, 51
Afrocentrists, 183, 184
agrarian reform, 108–109
agribusiness, 112–113
agricultural labor, 112
agriculture, 89
Alabama, 95
Alba, Richard, 14
alcoholism, among Native Americans, 114
Alexander II (czar), 106
Alien Act (1798), 78, 143, 146
Alien Nation (Brimelow), 3
American culture, 76–78
American Dream, 2, 125, 160, 218
American English, 65
  See also English language
American Federation of Labor (AFL), 112
American frontier, 12, 67, 77
American Immigration Control Founda-
  tion (AICF), 189
American Party, 99–100
"American Progress" (Gast), 82
American Protective Association (APA),
  118–119
American Revolution, 59–60, 63
anarchists, 143
Anglicans, 55, 66
Anglo-Americans, 12, 50, 57, 71–72,
  112, 203
Anthony, Susan B., 79
antiforeign sentiment, 77–78